HIST
OF
Smoking

Fig. 1. Picture of a Smoker lighting his Pipe with Difficulty

A HISTORY OF Smoking

COUNT CORTI

TRANSLATED BY
PAUL ENGLAND

BRACKEN BOOKS
LONDON

A History of Smoking

First published in 1931 by George G. Harrap & Co. Ltd, London

This edition published in 1996 by Bracken Books, an imprint
of Random House UK Ltd, Random House,
20 Vauxhall Bridge Road, London SW1V 2SA

Copyright © Count Corti & Paul England 1931

ISBN 1 85170 543 0

Printed and bound in Guernsey by The Guernsey Press Co. Ltd

TO

MY DEAR WIFE

Sublime tobacco ! which from east to west
Cheers the tar's labour or the Turkman's rest ;
Which on the Moslem's ottoman divides
His hours, and rivals opium and his brides ;
Magnificent in Stamboul, but less grand,
Though not less loved, in Wapping or the Strand ;
Divine in hookas, glorious in a pipe,
When tipp'd with amber, mellow, rich, and ripe ;
Like other charmers, wooing the caress,
More dazzlingly when daring in full dress ;
Yet thy true lovers more admire by far
Thy naked beauties—Give me a cigar !

LORD BYRON, *The Island*

PREFACE

THE following work owes its origin to a casual conversation which took place ten years ago. In the course of a talk on history some one who was smoking a cigarette said to me, " Tell us, who actually invented the cigarette, and where did the habit of smoking come from ? "

Now, though I had heard people talk vaguely about America and Columbus in this connexion, I could give no clear account of the matter, and so promised to look into it when the opportunity occurred. As chance would have it, I had on my table at the time the letters of August Ludwig von Schlözer, the eighteenth-century historian and publicist, and the following passage reminded me forcibly of the conversation referred to :

> A history of tobacco would be of at least as universal interest as the history of Tamerlane the Great, or of the ancient Assyrian Empire; admitting, of course, that a subject must be connected, as cause and effect, with the great changes that the world has seen, before it can make any such claim. This view is certainly not yet generally accepted, but it is to be hoped that it will in time become so, in spite of the opposition of our tedious chroniclers.
>
> The historian of tobacco must consider his subject from seven different aspects—religious, therapeutic, medicinal, sociological, this last accounting also for the remaining three—viz., economic, commercial, and financial.
>
> The theme has been handled by writers of all descriptions— travellers and theologians, physicians and merchants, agriculturists,

manufacturers, statesmen and poets—but never by an historian. Hence the innumerable mis-statements which have been universally disseminated since the year 1600, and are repeated even now, in one book after another. . . . Perhaps a time will come when one may be allowed to mention the word tobacco without being thought affected or new-fangled.

It is certain, however, thinks Schlözer, that "the first man who has the courage to make the attempt will find himself at loggerheads with the historian of the Jena school"—by which he means the whole professional brotherhood—

who will rate an *Origines Tabaci* far below an *Origines Thuringicæ*, and will not be able to see that the one demands at least as much scholarship, honest hard work, and nervous energy as the other. These reflections, however, should not scare our historian from his task.

The field for investigation is of vast extent, and the fact that the material is to be found in the daily life of the majority of men and women entitles it to a thorough examination of the historical documents. The daring fellows of whom Schlözer prophesied have certainly appeared, though, in spite of much diligent and painstaking work, they have found but little recognition.

Among the most important we may mention in the first place Friedrich Tiedemann, who in 1854 wrote an exhaustive work on tobacco; next, a man of far greater authority, the Neapolitan Professor O. Comes, with his *Histoire, géographie, statistique du tabac* (1900); and finally G. L. Apperson, whose *Social History of Smoking* is concerned exclusively with England. More recently men like Pilz, Hartwich, Kolumbus, and others have rendered valuable service in handling the subject under various specific aspects.

My object has been rather to survey the matter as a whole—to give a general view of the development of smoking, the manner of its diffusion, and the attitude of mankind toward it from the earliest times, so far as this is possible, down to the present day, a thing which none of the writers above mentioned, in spite of their many excellent qualities, has accomplished. This work, in short, is an attempt to present, on broad lines, a true panorama of the course of events, and is offered as a contribution to the history of something which plays an important part in the daily life of the great majority of people.

As for my own personal attitude, it would afford me the liveliest pleasure should the reader, after finishing my book, find himself unable to decide whether I am a smoker or not!

In conclusion, I desire to offer my warmest thanks to all who have so kindly helped me in the preparation of this work.

E. C.

CONTENTS

[11]

CONTENTS

ILLUSTRATIONS

ILLUSTRATIONS

"Other patients will lie on their bellies and inhale the smoke from tobacco sprinkled on live coals; this, taken in through the mouth and nostrils, and so diffused throughout the entire body, produces vomiting, and removes the cause of suffering.

"They have also a plant, the original name of which is lost, but the Brazilians call it *petum*, and the Spaniards *tabak*; when the leaves have been carefully dried they pack the stuff into the broad end of a tube, light it, put the narrow end to their mouths, and draw in the smoke so vigorously that it comes out again through the lips and nostrils, thus producing an abundance of moisture. These clouds of smoke are a specific against venereal disease, so that nature would seem to have provided them with her own remedy, close at hand."

ILLUSTRATIONS

ILLUSTRATIONS

A HISTORY OF SMOKING

CHAPTER I

RELIGIOUS ORIGINS : THE MAYAS AND THE AZTECS

THE latest researches into the manners and customs of primeval man teach us that in the very earliest times, before the dawn of history, one of the oldest cults of all was the worship of the sun and stars, and that this was really the beginning, so to speak, of what to-day we call religion. Anything that primitive man was unable to explain was held to be of divine origin; consequently many of the most natural phenomena which met his gaze came to be regarded as holy and worthy of reverence. Fire, for instance, which was probably first revealed to man in the lightning's stroke, became a sacred mystery; so soon as he found out how to kindle it and use it for his own purposes he at once set up a cult for the worship of fire in the abstract. As he watched the curling tongues of flame and the dense clouds of smoke soar upward primitive man conceived the idea of worshipping the sun with offerings of holy fire and holy smoke. As time went on the priests, whose lives were spent in the service of the altar, found the smoke from the sacrifice injurious to their breathing, and in consequence endeavoured to mitigate the harmful effects of the acrid fumes by burning sweet herbs and odoriferous gums; this led to the discovery of incense, which was to play so important a part in the religious ceremonies of the earlier dwellers in Mesopotamia as well as of the oldest Egyptian dynasties on the banks of the Nile (see Fig. 2). Even to-day in the tombs of the Pharaohs— for instance, the newly discovered tomb of Tutankhamen —may be found little pellets of some resinous substance, greyish brown in colour, which were burned in splendid vases of translucent alabaster, and sent up their perfumed smoke as an offering to the gods. From inscriptions in the Pyramids sacrificial offerings of perfumes such as myrrh and various kinds of incense can be traced back as far as 3000 B.C. To the worshippers it seemed as if the skyward-soaring smoke ascended to the thrones of the gods in heaven.

From Egypt the use of incense gradually spread to every nation of the ancient world. In Jerusalem before the curtain that hid the Holy of Holies there stood a special altar of incense, on which, both morning and evening, the costliest spices were offered. We find mention of a similar custom in both the Old and New Testaments ; every one, for instance, will call to mind how the Magi, the Three Holy Kings, brought to the infant Jesus their offerings of gold, frankincense, and myrrh, according to the pagan custom.

From the cult of earlier religions the Greeks and Romans also borrowed, with much else, the practice of burning incense to the gods. In Greece the custom was introduced in the seventh or sixth century B.C. At Delphi the Pythian prophetess who was employed by the priests to deliver their own dark oracles was accustomed, in order to make her utterances the more impressive, to inhale the fumes from burning laurel and barley-meal, which caused her to pass into a state of trance, in which her pupils would dilate, while the soaring clouds of smoke by which she was surrounded served to deepen the mystical impression.[1]

The Romans were rather later in importing the use of incense, which they employed especially in connexion with the libations which they offered to their gods. In the chronicles of the pre-Roman period there is not the slightest evidence of opiates and perfumes having been burnt in order to produce a pleasurable stupor. On the other hand, among both Greeks and Romans we get the first indications that smoke was employed not only in religious ritual, but also for other, and especially medicinal, purposes. The famous Greek physician Hippocrates, who lived at the time of the Peloponnesian War, advised the use of smoke, by inhalation and injection, in the case of certain diseases of women. Among the Romans, too, we find the inhaling of smoke recommended in the case of an obstinate cough. Pliny, the greatest writer of antiquity on natural history, who lived in the reigns of Nero and Vespasian, and perished in the eruption of Vesuvius in A.D. 79, in his great work on natural history in seventy-three books, twelve of which are devoted to medicines derived from plants, recommends the inhaling of coltsfoot for the same complaint. In Pliny, too, we find, in the passage where he says that the smoke should be drawn in through a reed (*arundo*), the first hint of anything resembling a pipe.

[1] For further information on incense and burnt-offerings see Dr Hans von Fritze, *Die Rauchopfer bei den Griechen* (Berlin, 1894), and Max Löhr, *Das Räucheropfer im Alten Testament* (Berlin, 1927).

Although neither in Greek nor in Roman literature is there any reference to smoking in the modern sense of the term, the Greeks were aware that some barbarian tribes in the region of the Lower Danube, as well as in Eastern countries, were in the habit of inhaling certain narcotic plants for pleasure, even to the point of stupefaction. Herodotus, the oldest Greek historian, whose writings are evidently the work of a keen and versatile observer, and display a remarkably critical spirit, reports that about 450 B.C. the Scythians, who occupied the districts which correspond to the Bulgaria and Northern Greece of to-day, were in the habit of scattering hemp-seed on red-hot stones, which gave out a smoke " superior, in their estimation, to any Grecian vapour-bath." This, according to Herodotus, took the place, with them, of the ordinary water bath, and he adds that as the fumes arose the Scythians would shout for joy. The Babylonians also, he tells us, had a similar custom.

Later authors, such as Tyrius, Pomponius Mela, and his contemporary Plutarch, inform us further that this burning of hemp-seed generally took place after meals. Pomponius Mela says that the inhaling of the rising vapour induced a certain hilarity resembling intoxication, while Plutarch, in the treatise on rivers which is usually ascribed to him, remarks that the Scythians dwelling on the banks of the Hebrus (now the Maritza) who indulged in this habit would gradually become torpid and sink into a deep slumber.

We do not know whether these two authors ever visited the countries they describe, or merely copied and embellished the account given by Herodotus, from whom they were not slow to borrow on other occasions. In any case, we must not make too much of the fact that some form of smoking was practised by the Scythians, Thracians, and some other races; their knowledge was confined to the narcotic effects of burning hemp, just as the Orientals at that time used opium for a similar purpose, but these occasional instances are very far removed from the universal practice of to-day.

Moreover, in all legendary history, either Greek, Roman, or German, there is not a single reliable allusion to smoking as we understand it. Nevertheless there have been, and still are, certain fanatics who maintain that pipe-smoking was known in Roman times, as well as throughout Europe in the Middle Ages. Lothar Becker and a Swiss lecturer named Reber have endeavoured to prove their case on the ground that certain objects resembling pipes, belonging to Roman and Celtic tribes, have been brought to light in the course of modern excavations; but the so-called proofs adduced by them in support of their theories have since turned out to be either entirely fallacious or else in some way connected with the use of smoke for medicinal or ceremonial purposes, to which we have already referred.

With these reservations, then, it can be said that the habit of smoking as a means of social enjoyment was totally unknown to the civilized nations dwelling on the Mediterranean littoral during the classical and medieval periods.

The use of smoke in worship, as a medicine, and here and there as a means of producing stupor may have predisposed the nations of the Old World—who were unacquainted with the tobacco plant before the discovery of America—to accept the later developments, but they had actually no connexion with smoking as we understand it.

In all probability the practice had its rise in the countries where the tobacco plant originally flourished. This theory is further supported by certain facts of history, the investigation of which brings us at once to some important ethnological problems connected with America before the so-called 'discovery' by Columbus.

Tobacco is originally a sub-tropical plant, which flourishes best in the ideal climate of the Antilles and the more westerly regions of Central and sub-tropical America. Here, too, as in the Old World, the wonders of nature, common to both, moved a primitive people to sun-worship, the adoration of fire as a holy thing, and the offering of incense. Here, too, the priests (called *caciques*) established a powerful tyranny over the people by claiming close kinship with the gods—the performance of the ceremonial rites was an honourable office which exalted them above all their fellows. In feeding the sacred fire they used dry twigs and leaves of aromatic plants, as in the Old World, but especially those of the tobacco plant, which in its wild state often attained a remarkable luxuriance of growth. While thus engaged, the priests would naturally blow on the red-hot embers, inhale the smoke, and so come to realize the pleasing narcotic effects, especially of tobacco, which possessed far more valuable properties than any herb employed in similar ceremonies in the Old World. Hence we may conclude that in some remote period of antiquity the practice of smoking for one's personal satisfaction took its rise from the religious ceremonies of the priests in the region of the Antilles and the neighbouring coastal districts of Central America and the country which to-day we call Mexico.

The probability of this theory is supported by the records in stone, which are still to be found in this region, of its oldest civilization, that of the Mayas who inhabited Central America and Yucatan (see Fig. 3). The latest authorities [1] place, at a cautious computation, the beginnings of this civilization in at least the first century before Christ. The central stronghold of their culture was the district now occupied by the Mexican provinces of Tabasco and Chiapas. Here, utterly abandoned, deeply hidden in the jungle of the primeval forest, but still eloquent of a high degree of civilization, lie the ruined cities of Palenque, Ococingo, etc.

The Mayas were an Indian people, dwelling on the eastern slope of the Cordilleras, in cities adorned with magnificent buildings and temples, at once the focus of their political power and the centre of their religious activities. All our information goes to prove that the Mayas were under the dominion of a powerful priestly caste. The central feature of their religion was sun-worship; they erected their temples and other buildings on either a natural hill or, where this was not practicable, on a series of artificially constructed terraces of earth; on top of the building stood a sort of altar adorned with stone slabs, finely carved in relief, representing human figures in three-quarter length. The artistic value of the carvings is in no way inferior to the statues of ancient Egypt.

[1] See Paul Radin, *The Story of the American Indian* (London, 1929).

The religious ceremonies of the Mayas included the use of incense made from the leaves of the local tobacco ; this they blew, out of some object resembling a pipe, in the direction of the sun and the four points of the compass. Fig. 3 contains a relief from the so-called Cross Temple at Palenque, representing a priest engaged in a ceremony of this kind ; he has a headdress in the form of an eagle, a serpent between his feet, and a leopard-skin on his back ; in his hand he holds something in the form of a tube from which smoke is emitted.

As time went on smoking ceased to be a privilege of the priestly caste and became a universal habit. Throughout the whole region of the Antilles, as well as in Central America, men began to roll palm-leaves into a sort of tube into which they put dried and powdered tobacco, as well as leaves of other aromatic plants : thus arose the earliest form of pipe. In some cases reeds and bamboo were used for the same purpose.

The narcotic effects of tobacco smoke, which, when obtained from leaves in the raw state and inhaled in any great quantity, led to a sort of intoxication, were employed by the priests to persuade primitive communities into the belief that their condition was the result of divine possession, a state in which they were able to utter their various prophecies, concerned, for the most part, with the good or evil fortunes of the campaigns in which they were engaged.

The smoking of tobacco and other similar herbs for pleasure gradually spread through Central America, the native tribes of Mexico, and the Antilles. The priests, who, as the term 'medicine-man' shows, were in most

Fig. 2. King Sethos I burning Incense before Osiris and Horus

Fig. 3. Maya Temple in the Ruined City of Palenque

cases physicians also, credited the plant with specific powers of healing; they laid the fresh leaves of it on open wounds, caused it to be inhaled in cases of pulmonary diseases, and prescribed its juice and smell for headaches and similar complaints.

The Maya civilization reached its highest point between A.D. 470 and 620. Then, according to Radin, a fearful catastrophe seems suddenly to have overtaken their flourishing cities, which were all abandoned by their inhabitants, some of whom wandered northward, some to the peninsula of Yucatan, where their original culture entered upon a second period of great magnificence, which lasted for several centuries.

Meanwhile the habit of smoking not merely for ceremonial purposes had spread among the Nahua tribes who had settled in the other part of what we call Mexico, and notably among the Aztecs, the youngest and most highly civilized of that race. In the few examples of the venerable and precious hieroglyphic writings which survived the fury of the fanatical Bishop Zumarraga—who, after the Spanish Conquest, had them all collected and burned, as being abominable proofs of "heathen morals and godless living"—are to be found presentments of priests and soldiers engaged in smoking. The pictures resemble those of the Mayas in form and character; but, besides palm-leaves, the smokers also employ reeds, which in some instances are shaped like a primitive pipe.

In more northerly countries, where reed and bamboo were not known, the inhabitants at the introduction of smoking were compelled to fashion artificial substitutes for the natural tube out of such bones, wood, or clay as were suitable for their purpose; countless examples of these are found in the famous ' mounds '—a sort of earthen structure serving both for dwelling-place and sepulchre—which are scattered over the whole of the Mississippi basin, and are supposed to be the work of the aboriginal Indians of North America. These curious erections occur most frequently, and in their most perfect form, in the Ohio valley, as far as the shores of the Great Lakes, and most of these contain fragments of pipes beautifully moulded and of fantastic design.

The latest researches have revealed many points of similarity between the Maya civilization and that of the Aztecs as exemplified in these mounds, which leads us to conclude that an intimate connexion must have existed between the two. Arguing from the close affinity between the mounds and the conventional mound-like foundations of the Maya temples, Radin holds that, instead of any migration from north to south of the Mississippi valley, part of the scattered Mayan population migrated from their original home in Central America northward by way of the coast as far as the mouth of the Mississippi river, and then fought their way along the river to the lake region, erecting these mounds in the course of their journey. Should Radin's view be correct, then nothing is more probable than that the Mayas took with them the knowledge of tobacco and the habit of pipe-smoking on their journey northward and introduced them to the aboriginal Indians with whom they came in contact. This theory is confirmed by the fact that many of the pipes found in the more northern districts—Ohio, for instance—were ornamented with carvings or mouldings of birds, reptiles, and other creatures which occur only in the tropical countries of Central America and the Antilles.

Among these wandering Mayas the use of smoke was always found in conjunction with worship, whether of sun, fire, or other deities, and this practice spread to the various Indian tribes, who soon began to offer tobacco to their god Manitou, and to feed the holy fires with it, and who finally came to believe that the spirit of their all-powerful god lay concealed in the rising clouds of smoke. From this belief sprang the whole system of religious and political rites and usages of the North-American Indians, which found their highest expression in the pipe of peace and war, the sacred calumet, made of red clay and adorned with feathers.

Little by little the practice of smoking spread over the whole of North America, but it is naturally in the most important centres of civilization that we find the most extensive traces of its existence, whether for purposes of worship or enjoyment. In the period preceding the invasion of America by the Spaniards the country of the Aztecs was pre-eminent for its culture, which rose to its greatest height, politically and socially, in the reign of Montezuma, and to which the city of Mexico, with its 300,000 inhabitants, its splendid palaces, and its giant pyramidal temples, bore witness. The Emperor ruled his land with a despotic sway which knew no limits; for the rest, the power was in the hands of the priests and chieftains, who, in order to get closer to the sun, chose the highest platforms of their soaring temples on which to offer not only incense made from tobacco-leaf, but also human sacrifices to their gods. It was the custom of Montezuma and his chieftains to smoke after meals, as well as at the ceremonies. Thus we read of the youth who, according to Aztec custom, was elected each year as the incarnation of one of their deities, and who lived for twelve months in a blaze of splendour, with the fairest maidens in the land for his companions, only to be sacrificed to the gods at the expiration of the term, when, amid dances, flute-playing, and the eloquence of orators, his last duty was to smoke a pipe of tobacco to the glory of the gods and the happiness of mankind.

The Aztecs extended their conquest over the neighbouring tribes until the whole of Central America became familiar with the use of tobacco, while in the Antilles, where the plant attained to its finest growth, it found favour with a people of a far higher type, descendants of the Indian tribe of Arawaks, who, at some indefinite period of antiquity, had colonized the archipelago from the north-east of South America and the region of the Amazon.

Shortly before the coming of the Spaniards there had been a fierce conflict between the inhabitants of the Antilles and the warlike and predatory Caribs, who, sailing from the mouth of the Amazon, attacked and pillaged the peace-loving islanders. As a result of similar migrations and conflicts the custom of smoking seems to have spread to the coast of the country that is now called Venezuela, Guiana, and Brazil. To the rest of South America it was apparently unknown until the arrival of the Spanish at a later date. Nevertheless the habit had already conquered almost the whole of North and Central America, and we

Fig. 4. Maya Priest smoking: Carving from the
Temple at Palenque

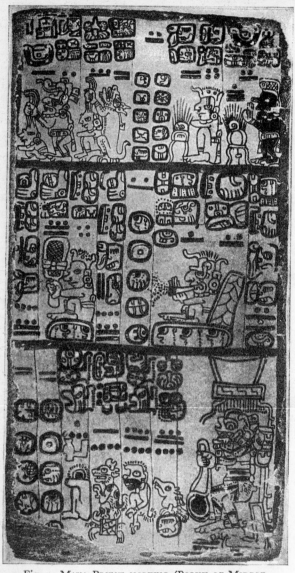

Fig. 5. Maya Priest smoking (Right of Middle
Division)

may now contemplate the striking contrast between the New World, which had smoked for centuries, and the Old, which knew as little of tobacco as it did of the newly discovered continent. It was in the natural order of things that the Old World which had conquered the ocean should discover the New, and, as chance would have it, Columbus, the earliest adventurer, happened on his first voyage to strike the Antilles, the very centre of the region where the finest tobacco grew, and where, in consequence, its uses had been most extensively developed.

CHAPTER II

COLUMBUS DISCOVERS AMERICA

TOWARD the end of the fifteenth century the Old World was obsessed by a passion for discovery. The coming of the Turks and the conquest of Constantinople had barred the way in the East and forced the nations of Western Europe to turn their attention to West Africa and the ocean as new fields for the extension of their commercial and political ascendancy. It was not, however, the international situation which urged the Portuguese Bartholomew Diaz in 1486 to undertake that perilous voyage which resulted in the discovery of the Cape of Good Hope. The success of this expedition, together with the tales and rumours of districts still unexplored which were said to contain untold riches of every kind, especially the much-coveted gold, filled lovers of adventure with a passionate desire for discovery. The lure of gold and gain, mingled with a certain national and personal envy of the success of others, was the chief incentive to these lovers of adventure. Thus, Christopher Columbus came of a race of money-getters; his father was a weaver of Genoa, who afterward took to selling wine and cheese. It was the writings of Marco Polo, so widely disseminated, thanks to the recent discovery of printing, that fanned the flame of adventure in the Genoese stripling, already seasoned by many a sea-voyage. The idea of a round earth, which already had the support of many learned men, suggested to him that by sailing westward he might reach the wealthy Indies, and even Zipangu (Japan), that fabulous land of gold in the Far East. Columbus is said to have consulted the venerable scholar, mathematician, and physician Messer Paolo del Pozza Toscanelli, of Florence, who appears to have shared his views and to have encouraged him in his venture. A map drawn by Messer Paolo representing the earth as a sphere came into Columbus's possession, though by what channels is uncertain.

In Lisbon, that El Dorado of seafarers, Columbus failed to find support. The detailed chart he had prepared of his proposed voyage was submitted to John, King of Portugal, and by him to a bishop and two of the Court physicians, who decided that the success of the scheme was much too uncertain to justify the necessary risk of money and life. He next applied to Spain, in the hope of finding some sympathy, if only on account of that country's jealousy of Portugal's successes on the sea. His proposals were favourably received by Ferdinand of Aragon and Isabella of Castile, Spain's joint rulers, who realized the danger of the acquisition of unlimited sea-power by Portugal. But first the plan had to be submitted to the theologians and scholars for their judgment. That of the pundits of the University of Salamanca was as follows: if, they said, the earth was actually a sphere the voyagers must come eventually to a slope, off which they would naturally fall into the watery abyss; if, on the other hand, by some miracle, they should escape such a fate, how would it be possible for them to climb the upward curve on the other side?

[35]

However, Columbus succeeded in overcoming all such misconceptions, and Spain's rulers declared themselves willing to take the risk and to supply ships and all things necessary for the expedition. On August 3, 1492, the three insignificant wooden vessels, with their crews of about a hundred and twenty men, set sail for the far regions of the vast unknown.

Their voyage seemed as if it would never end; by September they had left behind them the last of the islands in which men were known to dwell; for weeks they were alone upon the broad waste of waters. Again and again were they deceived, by the appearance of birds and objects floating on the waves, into thinking that land was near, and still no land was to be seen. The men grew sullen, and even threatened mutiny, when, in the second week of October, certain unmistakable signs assured them that here was land at last. When the night of October 12, 1492, was drawing to a close Columbus descried a light on the distant horizon, and with the break of day the hardy seamen saw before them in the glorious sunlight an island resplendent with all the marvels of sub-tropical vegetation. They decided to land before noon. Columbus, with the captains of the other ships, put off from the admiral's vessel, and, with the royal standard borne before him, set foot in all the radiant joy of victory on the New World. First, falling on their knees, they gave thanks to God; then, unfurling the flag of Castile, they solemnly took possession of the country in the name of Spain.

While they were thus occupied groups of naked dusty savages had gathered not far away, making gestures of

Fig. 6. First Landing of Columbus

36

Fig. 7. NORTH AMERICAN 'MOUND,'
AND DETAILS

Above: External view.   *Middle:* Uncovered mound, with cairns
and skeletons.   *Below:* Pipe with figure of man's head, found
in a mound

measureless astonishment as they watched these strange new arrivals and their mysterious actions. Meanwhile a number of sailors had landed, and others were rowing to the spot in their long boats, hollowed from the stems of trees, to see these incredible white-skinned beings clad in garments made of hair, who had plainly come from heaven down to earth.

At first there were no signs of hostility; with gifts of beads, little bells, looking-glasses, and the like Columbus managed to allay the fears of the natives, who in turn hastened to respond with offerings of such things as they prized most highly. Believing that these white-skinned wonders had come straight from the skies, they gave them of their best; strange fruits, wooden javelins, balls of cotton, were among the choicest gifts, as well as the dried leaves of some plant which had a remarkable odour. Columbus smiled when he saw these primitive offerings, but, not to hurt the givers' feelings—for he saw how highly they prized these things—gave orders for them to be taken aboard. Truth to tell, the Spaniards, while finding the fruit acceptable enough, flung away the dried leaves as worthless. These were, of course, the leaves of the tobacco plant; they had been brought by the Arawak Indians, an aboriginal tribe whose islands had not yet been conquered by the Caribs.

To the little island on which he landed Columbus gave the name of San Salvador, in gratitude to the Redeemer for the happy issue of his undertaking; he then turned his attention to the further exploration of the archipelago which we now know as the Greater and Lesser Antilles.

A few days later, while cruising among the islands,

they encountered an Indian canoe with only one man in it, and as they needed a pilot they took him on board. They then found that, besides some bread and a gourd full of water, he had with him a quantity of the dried leaves which had been offered to Columbus on first landing, and which were evidently held in high honour by all the natives. This man made a similar offering, and with such ceremonious gestures that the admiral noted the fact in his diary, with the remark that these leaves were evidently something very precious.

As Columbus had seen but little gold in the islands among which he had landed he determined to explore farther, in the hope of finding those rich deposits of which he was always dreaming. At the beginning of November 1492 he came to the huge island which the natives called Cuba. On landing, the dense tropical vegetation prevented him from forming any idea of the interior, so he decided to send two men of an adventurous spirit to explore further and, more particularly, to search for gold. The men of his choice were Rodrigo de Jerez and a Spanish Jew, Luis de Torres; the latter could speak Hebrew, Chaldæan, and Arabic, and it was thought that with one of these he might be able to make himself intelligible to the natives. They were accompanied by two Indians from other islands, who were to seek out the king of the island and, after presenting him with a necklace of beads, question him as to the position of the goldfields of his country.

The expedition returned at the end of a fortnight deeply impressed with all the wonders they had seen. They had found a number of villages, each consisting of fifty or more houses, and with a total population of about a thousand, so far as they could estimate. These people also had accepted them as heavenly visitants, and received them with all possible respect, while the most important members of the community had reverently escorted them to the first hut in the village, where the natives had kissed the feet of the strangers and passed their hands over them to discover if they were actually flesh and blood. The two Spaniards watched their actions with amazement; they noticed that the men carried in their hands certain dried leaves which they kindled at the glowing coals, and with which they apparently perfumed themselves. In order to keep the leaves alight they repeatedly held them to their mouths, alternately blowing on them and inhaling the smoke, to the complete mystification of the Spaniards.

After an absence of seven months Columbus returned to Spain in triumph on March 15, 1493, after a narrow escape from destruction in a terrific storm only a short distance from his native shores.

We do not hear that any mention was made of the natives' use of smoke, nor do the sailors appear to have brought the habit of smoking with them on their return from this first voyage, though Rodrigo de Jerez is said to have tried or even permanently adopted it. The first report of the custom appeared in Romano Pane's work, *De insularium ritibus* (*Concerning the Customs of the Islanders*), 1497. This Pane was one of the monks who, by command of Pope Alexander VI, the Borgia who condemned Savonarola to be burned, accompanied Columbus on his second voyage in 1493 in order to convert the Indians to Christianity. Columbus commissioned him to write a book upon the religious rites and customs of the people of the Antilles, especially the Caribs who inhabited San Domingo (Haiti). His conception of the practice of smoking, which he calls "making Cohobba," is extraordinarily naïve. The natives, he tells us, frequently employ smoke as a purgative, or sniff it up through a hollow piece of wood, fork-shaped, so as to fit into both nostrils. He goes on to describe how the priests (caciques) and medicine-men had a double purpose in their use of tobacco : firstly, to honour the gods ; and, secondly, to persuade the faithful, who thirsted for oracles, that they, the priests, drank in divinity with the smoke and, thus inspired, were able to prophesy and give advice about coming events. In the latter case the cacique would inhale so much tobacco that he became intoxicated, or as one beside himself, and in this condition would utter his frenzied prophecy of victory or defeat, of a year of plenty or a ruined harvest. Pane adds that a sort of cake made of tobacco was given to the sick to eat in order to make them vomit, and so get rid of the evil humours of the body. He does not make it quite clear that he is talking of actual tobacco smoke, but later authors distinctly state that this was the plant employed, and that the caciques, in their daily sacrifice to their sun-god, would often inhale the smoke in such quantities that they fell senseless to the ground.

Columbus, for his part, was far too preoccupied by his lust for gold to take much interest in the manners and customs of the strange people among whom he found himself. However, the great explorer, when at the Court

Fig. 8. FORKED PIPE-STEM AND HAMMOCK

of Granada, had recognized an old acquaintance in Gonzalo Fernandez de Oviedo y Valdes, who was formerly page to the Infante Don Juan, the only son of Ferdinand, and who developed later into an historian. He had shared Columbus's triumph, and in 1514 had gone to the West Indies as superintendent of the gold-smelters, and for thirty-four years had devoted himself to the study of the manners and customs of the natives. In the work he published in 1526 he discusses Romano Pane's account of their way of using tobacco, vague as it is, and dealing only with the priests or caciques. "Among other evil practices," writes Oviedo, in his *Historia general y natural de las Indias*,

> the Indians have one that is especially harmful, the inhaling of a certain kind of smoke which they call tobacco, in order to produce a state of stupor. . . . The caciques employed a tube, shaped like a **Y**, inserting the forked extremities in their nostrils and the tube itself in the lighted weed; in this way they would inhale the smoke until they became unconscious and lay sprawling on the earth like men in a drunken slumber. Those who could not procure the right sort of wood took their smoke through a hollow reed (*cañuela*); it is this that the Indians call *tabacco*, and not the weed nor its effects, as some have supposed. They prize this herb very highly, and plant it in their orchards or on their farms for the purpose mentioned above.
>
> I cannot imagine what pleasure they derive from this practice, unless it be the drinking which invariably precedes the smoking. I am aware that some Christians have already adopted the habit, especially those who have contracted syphilis,[1] for they say that in the state of ecstasy caused by the smoke they no longer feel their pain. In my opinion the man who acts thus merely passes while still alive into a deathly stupor. It seems to me that it would be

[1] This disease was not known in Europe before the discovery of America; it was first introduced by sailors, who had caught it from the native women.

better to suffer the pain, which they make their excuse, for it is certain that smoking will never cure the disease. Lately too many of the negroes who live in this town, and indeed in all parts of the island,[1] have acquired the habit. They grow the plant on their owners' farms and inhale its smoke, for they say that if they take tobacco when their day's work is over they forget their fatigue. It seems to me that here we have a bad and pernicious custom.

Oviedo adds that, after they have been stupefied by the smoke, the Indians lie down to sleep in "a strange sort of bed which they hang up between the trees"; he refers, of course, to the hammock (Fig. 10), which was quite unknown in Europe at that date.

It was not long before another form of smoking, which most nearly resembles the cigar of our own day, attracted the attention of Bishop Bartolomé de las Casas, who accompanied the Spanish to America as a missionary, and devoted himself wholeheartedly, though without success, to the task of protecting the natives from the cruelty of their conquerors. In a general history of the Indies (still in manuscript) he reports the description of smoking given by the Spaniards engaged in the exploration of Cuba, though his account is evidently coloured by later experiences. "The herb which the Indians inhale," wrote the bishop in 1527,

> is rolled up like a sort of bundle in a dried leaf. . . . They then light one end of it and draw in the smoke at the other; the effect is a certain drowsiness of the whole body accompanied by a species of intoxication, in which state they declare that they no longer feel any sense of fatigue. These *mousquetons*, or *tabaccos*, as they call them, have been adopted also by the settlers in this region;

---

[1] The Spaniards had recently brought slaves from Africa for employment on the newly acquired territory.

I have seen many Spaniards in the island of Hispaniola who used them and who, when reproached for such a disgusting habit, replied that they found it impossible to give it up. I cannot understand what enjoyment or advantage they derive from it.

The bishop speaks also of a kind of cigar-case made of bast in which the Indians carried their tobacco-leaves already rolled and filled. Not only were the Spaniards incorrigible smokers themselves, but they also taught the habit to their companions, who eagerly followed their example; so that it spread rapidly, especially among the sailors, who, in the course of a long voyage in fine weather, found plenty of leisure to indulge in it.

Moreover, owing to the frequent intercourse between Spain and the newly discovered regions of America— Columbus had as many as seventeen ships under his command—the number of those who were familiar with the use of tobacco was constantly increasing. The ships that plied between America and Spain, and, later, Portugal, brought over the tobacco plant for cultivation, and thus enabled the European nations to become acquainted with its properties and to acquire the habit of smoking.

The explorers had fixed their headquarters in Cuba, whence they began to extend their investigations westward. By 1517 their coasting expeditions had taken them as far as the peninsula of Yucatan, but their lack of provisions soon obliged them to turn back. However, the tales they told in Cuba of the wonderful houses and temples of stone they had seen in those parts induced the Governor to send his nephew, Juan de Grijalva, to make further investigations. Striking northward, Grijalva found himself in the ancient country of the Mayas, and gazed astounded upon the stupendous ruins of their age-old civilization. On taking leave of that country the Spaniards exchanged gifts with the natives, who presented them with, among other things, hollow reeds of about a span long filled with dried herbs and sweet-smelling liquid amber which, when lighted in the way shown by the natives, diffused an agreeable odour.

Grijalva's adventure led to the fitting out of an expedition on a large scale which, thanks to the ability, energy, and courage of its commander, Ferdinand Cortez, achieved well-nigh fabulous results.

Almost at the moment of starting certain differences of opinion arose between Cortez and his superior, the Governor of Cuba, who decided to relieve him of his command. Cortez, however, relying on the ships and men committed to his charge, sailed away with the entire fleet of five hundred men and seventeen horses, determined to penetrate to the heart of this legendary land of gold. As soon as he set foot on shore he burned his boats behind him, so that he might not be tempted to turn back.

His first landing-place was Tabasco, a province of the Mexico of to-day, where tobacco had been in use since the time of the Mayas, both in religious ceremonies and for personal enjoyment. The Spaniards found that so long as friendly relations were maintained between the two parties the natives offered them tobacco as a pledge of peace and good will, and that they also burned it as incense in their temples. They saw with astonishment that their pipes were artistically painted with figures of animals, men, and even flowers.

Fig. 9. Indian Tomahawk-pipe

Fig. 10. FROM THE AZTEC PICTURE-WRITINGS

The Aztec name for tobacco was *picietl* or *yetl*; the word tobacco is said to have been introduced into Mexico by the Spaniards, it being the name for pipes among the natives of the Antilles. The origin of the word tobacco is a question which perhaps will never be settled; it is very probable, however, that it is connected in some way with Tabasco, in Mexico, where tobacco has flourished from time immemorial, as it does to-day; while in the largest island of the Antilles, which for ages past had had commercial relations with the mainland of Mexico and Yucatan, the pipe may well have got its name after the introduction of smoking. Finally, the Spaniards, who found a fresh name for the plant, as well as the habit, in every newly discovered country,[1] extended the name given to the smoking tube in the island of Cuba to the plant itself, and introduced it wherever they went. This theory is supported by the fact that Cortez's men found tobacco in cultivation both in the province of Tabasco and also in the Aztec kingdom, whereas in the Antilles only the wild growth was to be had; they themselves were the first to introduce the cultivation of the plant into Cuba and the other islands at a later date.

Cortez found that the Mexicans were also acquainted with the use of tobacco in the form of snuff—*i.e.*, as a powder to be applied to the nose in order to induce sneezing. This custom seems originally to have had a medical purpose, its object being to dislodge the deposit of mucus in the nose and thus afford relief in cases of

---

[1] In Cuba it was called *tabacco*; in Haiti *kohaba*; in Mexico *yetl*; in Brazil *petum*.

catarrh. Another use was the application of warmed fresh tobacco-leaves to swellings and open wounds.

Cortez and his men could only wonder at the strange world they saw around them. Montezuma, the all-powerful ruler of the country, on the first news of these strange beings who had come from the skies, dispatched messengers to collect information and, if possible, to dissuade them from advancing farther. Among the messengers was one who, the better to illustrate his report, made rapid and notably clever sketches of the Spaniards, their fire-arms, and their horses, "swift as the wind," which were a special object of interest to the natives, to whom they were quite unknown.

But Cortez could not be turned from his purpose : he ruthlessly destroyed all who crossed his path, and, with the help of certain tribes, at that time subject to the Aztecs and impatient of their rule, he undertook his adventurous expedition against Montezuma's capital, Tenochtitlan. That he succeeded in carrying out his ambitious scheme was due to three factors : first, the superstition of the natives, who saw in this stranger a benevolent deity who, according to the legend, had been driven from among them, and whose return had long been expected ; secondly, the audacious coup by which Cortez contrived to possess himself of the person of the Emperor, who had come out in all his glory to welcome him as a friend ; and, lastly, the effect produced by the strange fire-arms and horses, unlike anything the Aztecs had ever seen.

Tenochtitlan, the Mexico of to-day, was, for that time, a city of enormous dimensions. Bernal Diaz, who accompanied Cortez, describes it as resembling Venice, a regal city of 300,000 inhabitants, built on the shores of a lake, with towering palaces and gigantic temples, pyramidal in form. In the market-place the most splendid wares were exposed for sale, ranging from the finest examples of the goldsmith's art to delicate silken tissues, from fans displaying the brilliant plumage of the humming-bird to swords with golden hilt and blade of hard obsidian. There, too, one might buy the 'smoking tubes' already described, made, in every variety of form, of painted reeds and woods, or even of silver; or tobacco-leaves could be had for little money, ready dried and bound together; amber, too, or 'liquid amber,' as it was called, an aromatic gum, and essence of roses, ingredients to be mixed with tobacco for smoking.

Before Cortez had Montezuma removed as a prisoner to the Spanish camp he and his companions had opportunities of observing the great monarch in all his glory in his palace with its thirty gates, where he lived surrounded by a brilliant Court, in luxury almost without a parallel. At every meal two hundred dishes would be served of the choicest delicacies for the Emperor to choose from. The banquet ended, a bevy of the fairest maidens of the land would appear with water in silver bowls for the cleansing of mouth and hands. Retiring, they would reappear with beautifully painted 'smoking tubes,' filled with tobacco and liquid amber. The tobacco was ground in a rosewood mill, which added its peculiar fragrance to the odour of the herb. Then the Emperor, leaning back in his leather chair, would smoke his pipe while he watched the group of graceful dancers and the amusing tricks of the jugglers and Court fools.

This idyllic state of affairs was rudely shattered by Cortez, who compelled Montezuma to move into the Spanish quarters; this meant the forcible confinement of one who had hitherto ruled with a despotism almost unparalleled over a population of millions.

The conquest of Mexico and the further development of Cortez's enterprise attracted to the new colony a constant stream of Spaniards, who gradually yielded to the narcotic charm of tobacco, and spread the novel habit among all with whom they came in contact.

Meanwhile new tracts of America had been discovered and opened up by explorers from Europe.

The Portuguese Cabral, who, in 1500, endeavoured to reach the East Indies by rounding the Cape of Good Hope, was driven by stress of weather far out of his course, and finally wrecked on the coast of Brazil, a hitherto unknown country.

Here also, as Cabral found, the natives were acquainted with the practice of smoking : their wizards or medicine-men made a curious sort of pipe by inserting the hollow shaft of an arrow into a gourd cut to the shape of a human head ; in this they burned the leaves of a certain plant, the smoke of which, when inhaled, induced intoxication ; in this state they would stagger about, roll their eyes, gnash their teeth, and foam at the mouth, finally breaking into a frenzied dance, which the onlookers took to be the effect of divine inspiration. These violent results, we may assume, were produced by various narcotic plants, not merely tobacco.

Cabral's account proves that the habit of smoking already existed in the land which the French at a later period named Brazil—from the highly prized dye-wood introduced from the real West Indies. On the other hand, in the rest of South America, which was only gradually explored, no trace of any such habit was found, and the tobacco plant was unknown.

Pizarro, attracted by reports of a powerful empire rich in gold in the far south of America, succeeded in what looked like a desperate adventure when, with a hundred and sixty Spaniards and no confederate aid, he overthrew the mighty kingdom of the Incas. He followed the example of Cortez in seizing, by means of a trick, the person of the Inca who offered him a friendly welcome; the effect of this proceeding was to throw the entire population into such confusion that both soldiers and civilians were scattered in every direction. In spite of the highly developed state of their civilization, no trace of smoking was to be found among the Incas, and it was left to the Spaniards gradually to introduce the habit into both Peru and Chile.

It was not long before parts of North America also began to attract the attention of explorers. The French mariner Jacques Cartier [1] was the first to penetrate by way of the St Lawrence river to the highlands of Montreal, the chief seat of the Indians in those regions. Wherever he went he found the natives smoking their pipes, and he speaks of the great stores of tobacco they accumulated, and how they carried a certain quantity in little bags

[1] Michelin and Ramé, *Relation originale du voyage de Jacques Cartier au Canada en 1534* (1867).

hung round the neck. Furthermore, Cartier gives a clear description of what we call a pipe, explaining how they drew in the smoke through the mouth and expelled it through the nose—" like smoke from a chimney," as he says. "We tried to imitate them," he continues, "but the smoke burnt our mouths as if it had been pepper." The Frenchman, however, took no further interest in his discovery, and was not instrumental in introducing the tobacco plant into Europe.

In the meantime, not only the report of the smoking habit, but also the materials for practising it, in the form of dried tobacco-leaves, had been brought to the Old World by Spanish sailors and missionaries home from their voyages, and the rapidly increasing intercourse between the two countries naturally led to a wide diffusion of the custom. Rodrigo de Jerez, known as the first man to set foot on Cuban soil, was also the first to smoke tobacco in Europe on returning to his native town of Ayamonte. His people, on seeing a cloud of smoke suddenly issue from his mouth and nose, were horribly alarmed and, concluding that the Devil had got hold of him, hurried off to the priest, who referred the matter to the Inquisition. The result was that Jerez found himself in prison, and was only released after some years to find that numbers of his countrymen had taken to the very practice for which he had had to pay so dearly.

On his return from America in 1519 Oviedo and some of his men had brought dried tobacco-leaves with them, just at the time when the reports of it were being widely disseminated by the many published descriptions of the newly discovered countries. Peter Martyr of Anghiera, a follower of Columbus, had published his account of the New World at Seville as early as 1511, in which he had made use of Romano Pane's *Observations*.[1]

About the middle of the sixteenth century the seed of the tobacco plant was introduced also into Spain, Portugal, and France at about the same time, but through different channels. The very general assertion that Cortez himself brought it to Spain is not proven.

In 1543 we find tobacco first recommended for its healing properties by a certain professor at the University of Salamanca. In 1559 Philip II had sent his own physician, Francisco Hernandez de Toledo, to Mexico, to study the plants, animals, and minerals of that country; he collected and described no fewer than 1200 species of the flora of America, and among the many varieties of seeds he brought back with him we know that those of the tobacco plant were included.

Hernandez, however, seems to have been struck rather by the beauty of the plant than by its practical uses, and it is from this date that we begin to trace, first in the coastal towns and later in the interior of both Spain and Portugal, the cultivation of tobacco, especially in pleasure-gardens, as an ornamental plant with medicinal properties.

Somewhat earlier—perhaps in 1556—tobacco seeds from Brazil found their way to France. As a result of the religious troubles in that country some French Protestants, among them André Thevet, an ex-Carmelite monk, and Nicolas Barré, an ardent Calvinist, had founded a colony where Rio de Janeiro now stands. In a report

---

[1] I have a German edition of this work, printed at Basle (1582), as part of *Der Newen Welt und Indianischen Widergängischen Königreichs*.

which Barré sent to Paris (1557) on the uses of tobacco, or *petum*, as the Brazilians called it, he asserted that the natives could subsist on it for eight or nine days, without any other kind of food. Thevet[1] followed, in 1558, with further details; he describes a roll of palm-leaves about the size of a candle filled with dried tobacco, which the natives light at one end and inhale through mouth and nostrils. "They say," he adds, "that this is very good for loosening and carrying off the superfluous humours of the brain."

According to Thevet, smoking was already the custom in Brazil, and was practised to the point of dizziness and intoxication; only the women abstained from it. "Christians living in Brazil," he writes, "have been known to become passionately attached to the scent of this plant." Although he hints that its use is not without its dangers, often leading, in his own experience, to fainting-fits, he makes a specific claim to have introduced tobacco to France, and called it *angoulême*, after his native place. However this may be—and a contemporary declared that Thevet was not only a cosmographist, but also a colossal liar—it was not Thevet who first made the French nation acquainted with the use of tobacco; that was reserved for a perfectly unknown man who, though he had never seen the plant in its original habitat, was destined to popularize it in his own country, and to give it a name which it has kept ever since.

[1] André Thevet, *France antarctique* (Antwerp, 1558).

CHAPTER III

FROM THE OLD WORLD TO THE NEW

IN the second half of the fifteenth century Portugal was a rich and haughty nation, and a first-class European Power. Henry the Navigator and John III had done their best to further the new spirit of maritime adventure, and, thanks to them, the resources of the motherland had been enormously increased by the importation of precious metals, spices, dyes, etc., from the newly acquired territories in Africa, India, and South America. Portugal possessed something like a monopoly of the trade with India, and at the same time very wisely maintained with Austria, the dominant European Power, friendly relations, which were further cemented by the marriage of King John to the younger sister of the Emperor Charles V.

Lisbon, the chief city, renowned for its superb harbour, was an important centre of commerce : when King John died, in 1557, and was succeeded by his grandson Sebastian, a child of thirteen, Portugal's capital was attracting the attention of the whole world. Everywhere people were dreaming of discoveries, conquests, and the fabulous wealth that could be had almost for the asking in lands beyond the sea—of strange fruits and plants, of endless novelties for use and ornament. The gold fever seized hold of Portugal at a time when she was mistress of the seas, and was attracting vast numbers of adventurous souls to her colonies in Asia, Africa, and Brazil. Since the beginning of the sixteenth century the growing wealth of the country showed itself in the increased magnificence of the Court and the rapid expansion of the capital, which in 1559 contained 100,000 inhabitants, not counting the suburbs; while, among other claims to distinction, Lisbon had become known as a centre for the most highly finished productions of the goldsmith's art. The fame of Portugal soon spread far and wide; ships of all nations came to Lisbon in search of the products of other countries—particularly spices—and their crews listened with keen interest to the tales the Spanish and Portuguese sailors had to tell of the manners and customs of distant countries; wondered at the curious fruits and vegetables they showed them; and were delighted with the reports of all the strange things to be found in the New World. At the same time the habit of smoking, already common among the Spanish and Portuguese sailors in the various ports, was adopted by those of other nations in ever-increasing numbers, and the way was thus paved for its universal diffusion.

Lisbon being the place above all others where the latest importations from overseas were to be found, merchants and physicians flocked thither in the hope of getting useful knowledge, but none were keener in the pursuit than the ambassadors from foreign Powers accredited to the Portuguese Court. In 1559 a certain Jean Nicot of Nîmes was sent from France in this capacity. Although merely the son of a humble notary, he had managed to obtain employment in the service of the Keeper of the Great Seal of France, and finally to attract the attention of the King, who made him his private

Fig. 11. Jean Nicot

54

Nicotiana inserta infundibulo ex quo hauriunt fumũ Indi & nauācleri.

Fig. 12. THE EARLIEST REPRESENTATION OF A TOBACCO PLANT AND THE OPERATION OF SMOKING

secretary, an appointment which naturally brought him into contact with the royal family, as well as with the other members of a Court which was thronged with persons of wealth and reputation. He was only twenty-nine when he set out for Lisbon in order to negotiate a marriage between the fifteen-year-old King Sebastian and the sixteen-year-old Marguerite de Valois, daughter of Henry II. While engaged on this business—which came to nothing—Nicot took an extraordinary interest in the colonial progress of the Portuguese, and made it his business to inform his countrymen of every novelty that came to Lisbon from abroad : for instance, he sent specimens of indigo to the King, recommending it as a vegetable dye of such excellence as to put all those hitherto employed in the shade. Tobacco too had arrived, not only in the dried leaf, but also in the form of seeds, to be planted in the pleasure-garden or grown for medicinal purposes. Nicot was an intimate friend of the celebrated Damião de Goes, scholar, musician, palæographer, and keen botanist, who was able to give him much valuable information, especially with reference to the flora of the newly explored regions. Once, when Nicot was dining with his friend, the latter showed him the tobacco plant growing in his own garden, and told him of the marvellous healing properties ascribed to it. Nicot at once begged for some cuttings, which he had planted in the garden of the French Embassy, well pleased at having found yet another novelty with which to earn the gratitude of his sovereign. He had heard from Damião de Goes and others that the application of this plant to a cancerous tumour (*noli-me-tangere*, as it was called), as well as to all sorts of 'eating sores,' had been known to work wonders. Consequently, when a friend of one of his attendants desired to try the effects on a wound in his face Nicot took charge of the young man, and gave him a ten days' treatment, with the result that the wound was completely healed. Other similar successes with wounds and ulcers which had been pronounced incurable came under Nicot's observation, and numbers of people came to him to beg the help of the plant that could do such wonders.[1] Nicot, always on the look-out for such discoveries, was now fully convinced of the healing properties of the plant; he found, moreover, that when applied to the nose or forehead its cooling fragrance relieved his headache in a wonderful manner.

He had lately heard from some friends in Paris that the wife of a nobleman living at the Court, Montigny by name, had just died of cancer of the breast, and how a Russian countess had sent for all the leading physicians of the kingdom to cure her of a tumour in the face, but to no purpose : it occurred to him that his new discovery might be of incalculable benefit to his native country. He determined, therefore, to send specimens of the plant, with directions for use, to some important personages in the French Court whom, or whose relatives, he knew to be suffering from a similar disease. Accordingly he wrote to Cardinal Francis of Lorraine to say that he had in his garden a wonderful Indian plant that had worked miraculous and well-attested cures in cases of cancer and other diseases pronounced incurable by the doctors.

[1] See Charles-Étienne and Jean Liebault, *L'Agriculture et la maison rustique* (Paris, 1570).

Nicot promised the Cardinal some seeds as soon as they were ripe, as well as a specimen plant in a large pot, with directions how to set and rear it.

On only one previous occasion had any rumour of the curative properties of tobacco reached the French Court. In 1523 Giovanni de Verazzano, in a letter to the French King, Francis I, had referred to the custom among the Indians of using the smoke as well as the leaves of certain plants for curative purposes, but with the death of the King the matter was forgotten. Nicot's praise of tobacco was based solely on its healing properties, no word being said of smoking or sniffing, though later, on his return to the French Court, he seems to have recommended its administration through the nose in the form of either smoke or powder as a *clysterium nasi*, in the professional jargon of the later Italian apothecaries.

A few months after Nicot's letter to the Cardinal of Lorraine, the latter's brother, the Grand Prior, one of the highest ecclesiastical dignitaries and a very perfect cavalier, who, after the death of Francis II, had accompanied his widow, Mary Stuart, to England, arrived in Lisbon with a fleet of galleons. His mission was to cement the friendship between the two kingdoms of France and Portugal, and wipe out the bad impression made by the fiasco of the proposed matrimonial alliance. The Prince of the Church naturally called upon the French ambassador in Portugal, who invited him to be his guest, and showed him his garden, where the tobacco plants which had been sown in the spring had already grown to a stately height and, after blooming freely, were now laden with ripe seed-vessels. Nicot informed his Eminence of the plant's wonderful healing properties, which report had by this time enormously exaggerated, and gave him both seeds and seedlings for winter cultivation. On the return of the Grand Prior to Paris he entrusted him with similar gifts for the Queen Mother, Catharine de' Medici, a lady who, as we know, was peculiarly open to the influence of magicians, alchemists, and astrologers, and who was a prey to every kind of superstitious practice. She probably suspected some supernatural power in the wonder-working plant, and interested herself in it accordingly, while the Grand Prior did so much to popularize it throughout the country that it finally became known as *l'herbe du Grand Prieur*.

The number of complaints which the plant was said to cure was fabulous. Nicolò Monardes, a celebrated physician of the University of Seville, who was employed at the time in investigating the various products which kept arriving from the West Indies with reference to their usefulness in medicine, gives a long account [1] of the wonderful virtues of tobacco as reported to him by the Spanish sailors. After a casual mention of the ' smoke tubes ' of the Mexicans he devotes the bulk of his work to its medicinal properties : coughs, asthma, headache, cramp in the stomach, gout, and diseases of women were some of the ills which, according to Monardes, were unable to resist the effect of tobacco ; the mere application of the fresh leaves to the belly would at once expel any intestinal worms that might be present, while a salve prepared from the same substance would rapidly heal all open wounds and malignant tumours.

[1] *Historia medicinal de las cosas que sirven al uso de Medicina* (Seville, 1565).

The professor's treatise made a profound impression throughout the whole of Europe, which was suffering at the time from the incompetence and the frequent fraudulent imposition of its physicians, many of whom pretended to cure disease by exorcism and other superstitious practices. The genuine desire for better medicines and methods of healing resulted in Monardes' book being translated into Latin, French, English, and Italian. The Latin translator, Charles Clusius, adds an account of how the physician of the Emperor Charles V, Stephanus by name, had convinced himself of the efficacy of a cataplasm of fresh tobacco-leaves as a remedy for goitre, and concludes with the assertion that *petum*—the Brazilian name for tobacco—is a sort of panacea, a cure for every kind of sickness.

Gohory, the French translator, who brought out a new edition of the book in 1572,[1] was anxious to obtain a wide popularity for the work in France. He knew that Catharine de' Medici, who acted as regent during Charles IX's minority, was interested in the plant and believed in its curative power; accordingly, to ensure a favourable reception at the Court, he described the tobacco plant as *Herbe Médicée* on the title-page of his book, a copy of which was duly presented to the Queen Mother through the mediation of a friendly physician. As a result, the name *Herbe Médicée* persisted for some time in France, and gave rise to the legend, among others, that the Queen was the original inventress of snuff, which, however, was actually introduced into France at a much

---

[1] *Instructions sur l'herbe petum, dite en France l'herbe de la Reine Médicée* (first Part); *et sur la racine de Mechoacan* (translated from the Spanish of Monardes).

later date. Indeed, there is no proof that Catharine either smoked or took snuff; like the rest, she seems to have known the plant merely as a medicine, and to have used it either on herself or one of her two sons, Francis II or Charles IX, to cure headaches.

The translator also added some observations, made in his own country, in which he says that M. de la Brosse Chapelin, the King's chief physician and mathematician, had reared some tobacco plants in his garden, seven feet high. In surgery, he added, tobacco had proved so beneficial that Race, the King's surgeon, had planted large quantities of it in a garden adjoining the Temple.

Meanwhile Nicot had returned to France. Still smarting under the failure of his diplomatic mission, he resolved to give up politics and devote himself to learned pursuits and, among other things, to the compilation of a French dictionary. The absence throughout this work of any equivalent to the word 'to smoke' points to the fact that, though he foresaw the great possibilities of the plant, he regarded it merely from the medicinal aspect; nevertheless, his well-known enthusiasm on its behalf caused his name to be for ever associated with its introduction into France.

The brothers Liebault, in their *L'Agriculture et la maison rustique* (1570), were the first to call the tobacco plant by its accepted botanical name of *Nicotiana*, "after the original discoverer," while the poisonous principle in it, first discovered in the nineteenth century, was given the name of nicotine, both terms thus preserving the memory of the French ambassador, Jean Nicot.

Meanwhile, drawings of the plant appeared in various herbals of the time,[1] and the culture of tobacco spread through Europe from the south-west to the north and east. It was grown at first merely for its ornamental appearance and medicinal properties, the practice of smoking being known only in the seaports where sailors congregated, especially in England and Holland. In the latter country it was widely cultivated as early as 1560, partly owing to the presence there of refugees from the religious persecutions in France. In the next few years a number of descriptions and illustrations of the plant came from the Press, especially in Antwerp, till at last a second Monardes appeared in the person of the Dutch physician Everard, who agreed with the Spaniard in praising tobacco as a wonder-working panacea for every ill.[2]

It would be no easy task to trace the various channels by which the plant passed through the hands of one botanist after another—from France and Holland to Germany, Switzerland, and Italy; but there are certain names which may be recorded in this connexion. The Town Physician of Augsburg at that time was a certain Adolf Occo, who was familiar with the use of many medicinal herbs and had compiled an *Apothecaries' Guide* which was highly esteemed by his contemporaries. In 1565 a friend of his, a certain French doctor, sent him some botanical specimens, including some dried tobacco-leaves, without further explanation, whereupon Occo consulted Johann Funk, a doctor of Memmingen, who

---

[1] *E.g.*, in Dodonäus Lambert, *Cruydebock* (Antwerp, 1563).
[2] À Everartus, *De herba panacea* (Antwerp, 1587).

replied that the plant was new to him. He then decided
to send it to the most famous botanist of the time, Conrad
von Gesner [1] of Zürich, who confessed that he, too, knew
nothing of it. However, he even went so far as to taste
it—contrary to his custom, as he was fearful of injuring
his health; as a result of the experiment he spat out
most of it and then fell into a faint. He then inserted
some of the herb in a piece of meat and gave it to his
dog, who shortly afterward vomited. To settle the question 'the German Pliny,' as Gesner was called, applied
to the learned Professor Aretius in Berne, the only
naturalist, he used to say, who could teach him anything.
Aretius replied by sending him a drawing of a tobacco
plant from his own garden, which enabled Gesner to
declare Occo's gift to be the plant known in France as
Nicotiana. On November 5 Gesner communicated the
intelligence to Funk and Occo, and on November 24 to
Aretius, begging him to send him some seeds on the next
opportunity; unfortunately he did not live to receive an
answer, as he died of the plague on December 13.[2]

We see, then, that tobacco was to be found in Switzerland in certain botanical gardens in the fifteen-seventies,
but, as we gather from the reports of the town clerk of
Lucerne, the plant was known and esteemed only for its
healing virtues.

For our knowledge of its introduction into Italy the
accounts given by the Milanese Girolamo Benzoni are
largely responsible. Under the spell of the prevailing
craze for foreign adventure he spent no less than fourteen

---

[1] See Conrad von Gesner's letter to Adolf Occo of November 5, 1565.

[2] *Epistolarum medicinalium C. Gesneri* . . ., Book III, ff. 79b, 96b, and 113b
(Zürich, 1577).

years in exploring the newly discovered countries in the West Indies. In his account of the New World Benzoni describes how the natives used to gather certain leaves, rather larger than those of the walnut, tie them in bundles, and dry them by exposure to the air.

They then take the stalk of a certain plant and wrap one of the dried leaves round it, and thus make something resembling a pipe, one end of which they hold over the fire while they apply the other end to their lips, and inhale the smoke or vapour. Thus they fill mouth, gullet, and the whole head with the powerful fumes until at last their monstrous lust is sated, when they fall about as beasts that have no reason, and lie senseless on the ground like dead men. Some there are who inhale so greedily that they collapse suddenly, as if attacked by the falling sickness, and will often lie for a night and a day deaf and blind to all that goes on around them. Others are satisfied with feeling a certain dizziness in the head, after which they cease to inhale. It is hardly possible for one who has not experienced it to realize how injurious, how poisonous is this hellish practice; many a time when travelling through Guatemala, if I chanced to enter the dwelling of an Indian who was in the habit of using the herb—*tabacco* the Mexicans call it—I was compelled to fly as soon as the diabolical stench reached my nostrils.[1]

Benzoni tells us further how the native priests and doctors employed tobacco in their so-called magical healing of the sick. His book, published at Venice in 1565, was followed by the translation of Monardes' work into Italian at about the time when the plant itself was introduced into Italy.

The first specimen came from Lisbon, where the Papal Nuncio, Monsignore Prospero Santa Croce, had made its acquaintance at the same time as Nicot, and

[1] Girolamo Benzoni, *Storia del Nuovo Mundo* (Venice, 1565).

probably through his introduction. All Lisbon, at the time, was talking about the wonderful herb, and it is not surprising that the Nuncio, on his return in 1561 from his diplomatic mission to the Portuguese Court, brought with him some seeds for the acceptance of his sovereign the Pope, together with Nicot's fallacious report of its valuable healing properties. His Holiness in turn passed on the seeds to his monks, with orders to plant them in the Vatican garden, where the plant was known as *Herba di Santa Croce*, in memory of the donor.

About this time, too, the sailors, Spanish and Portuguese, and those Italians who had followed in Columbus's footsteps, were introducing the tobacco plant as well as the habit of smoking to the ports of Genoa, Naples, and, a little later, Venice, whence it found its way to the Brenta valley, where the first experiments in systematic cultivation were made.

Next came the turn of Rome and that of Florence, at that time under the rule of Cosimo the Great, the first Grand Duke of Tuscany. Cosimo was one of the most learned men of his time; chemistry was his principal study, but he also made excursions into the realm of botany, and sent emissaries to all parts of the world to keep him in touch with the latest events and developments, not only in politics, but also in the various branches of science. It was natural, therefore, that Nicolo Tornabuoni, who was Cosimo's agent in Paris from 1560 to 1565, should lose no time in reporting to the Grand Duke on the new medicinal herb which Nicot had introduced to that city. Some seeds were forwarded from Paris to Florence, where Nicolo's brother Alphonso,

Bishop of Saluzzo, took charge of them and had them planted in his garden; he also sent specimens to Cesalpinus, a famous botanist of the time, living at Pisa, who named the plant *Herba Tornabuoni*, after the sender.

From the Italian ports the knowledge of tobacco spread to Eastern Europe. Thanks to the relations between the Austrian and Spanish branches of the house of Habsburg the plant was brought to Austria and Hungary, where it was cultivated as early as 1568, though chiefly in the gardens of the nobility, either for its beauty or its healing qualities, there being still no mention of its being used for the purpose of smoking.[1] Its popularity naturally grew more rapidly among the ports and coastal towns than in the interior regions of countries such as Russia and Turkey; but here, too, the Spanish and Portuguese sailors assisted in its distribution. It was the Portuguese who, by the discovery of the Cape of Good Hope route to the East, gave tobacco to the Asiatic Indians; while about the same time Ferdinand Magellan, the famous Portuguese who discovered the straits at the southern extremity of South America, introduced it to the Philippines, whence, as well as from India, it reached Eastern Asia, Japan, and China.

The Portuguese sailors, as we have seen, were the chief agents in spreading the knowledge of the precious plant throughout the world as it was then known, Lisbon being at that time the centre from which all lines of communication radiated, though England, a little later,

---

[1] See Dr Franz Wieser, *Über die Produktion, den Konsum und die Besteuerung des Tabaks im Kronlande Salzburg von 1657 bis zur Einführung des Tabakgefälles im Jahre 1817*, in *Fachliche Mitteilungen der österreichischen Tabakregie*, 8th year, Part I, March 1906.

was to carry on the work begun by Portugal. What Britain had to offer to the rest of the world, however, was no mere supposititious panacea, but the actual habit of smoking, which had already brought all classes of the islanders under its sway.

CHAPTER IV

THE RISE OF SMOKING IN ENGLAND

NO sooner had Columbus in the sixteenth century shown the way to the new lands far overseas than a host of explorers began to follow in his train; from every nation they came in haste, eager to imitate the example of the Spaniards, and acquire, each for his own country, as many El Dorados as they might discover. The whole world was drawn as if by magic to that wondrous land in the West known as America, after the Florentine explorer, Amerigo Vespucci, whose name, although Columbus had preceded him by seven years, came to be associated with the New World merely from the fact that he had written and published such a glowing account of his travels as could not fail to appeal to the popular imagination.

It was only natural that this universal rush for new discoveries should give rise to bitter rivalry and even open hostilities among the various nations concerned. Of these the first place must be given to England for her attempt to outbid both Spain and Portugal, although her navy was no match for the combined fleets of the Peninsula. So long as Mary of England, the wife of Philip II of Spain, was a party to the persecution which sought to bring back the Catholic religion to Protestant England it was possible to keep the rival interests of the opposing countries in the background; but on her death early in

1558 the peace was broken and open war ensued, in which the English did not hesitate to attack any Spanish vessel that crossed their path. Men like Admiral Hawkins, Drake, and Raleigh were little better than pirates in their dealings with the Spaniards, pillaging and destroying without scruple. As these encounters took place off the coast of Central and Southern America the English sailors were brought into contact with the natives of these parts, and were thus enabled to make their first acquaintance with the use of tobacco in the very land of its origin. Hawkins, describing his second voyage (1564–65), notes the existence of smoking among the natives of Florida, but he, like others, completely misunderstood their object, his theory being that they smoked in order to appease their hunger, since they were thus able to go for four or five days without eating or drinking.

It was about this time that a few specimens of the tobacco plant, together with the seed, found their way to England by way of Portugal and France. There has been much dispute as to who can claim the honour of having first introduced the plant into that country; there seems to be no certainty about the matter, nor is it of special importance; we only know that it was brought from America by the sea-captains, who were the first to smoke publicly in the streets of London, to the great amazement of the people, who collected in crowds to see so strange and incomprehensible a sight.[1] In England, as opposed to the Continent, tobacco seems to have been regarded from the first less as a medicinal herb than as the means by which the pleasant habit of smoking might

[1] See G. L. Apperson, *The Social History of Smoking*, p. 12 (London, 1914).

Fig. 14. SIR WALTER RALEIGH (1552–1618)

be enjoyed. At first, however, the number of smokers was few, and they were looked upon as a curiosity, the custom becoming general only after the discovery of Virginia, when the British colonists returned home after a prolonged sojourn in that country. To Sir Walter Raleigh, the famous 'general on land' and 'admiral on the seas,' Queen Elizabeth, who succeeded her sister Mary on the throne of England, assigned the royal privilege of exploring unknown lands and planting colonies in North America. Starting from Florida, Raleigh followed the coast northward and gradually arrived at what we now call the state of Virginia, where he founded the colony which took its name from 'the Virgin Queen.' He returned to England soon after this achievement, and was followed in September of the same year by his fellow-captains Amadas and Barlow, who brought three 'Indians' from Virginia home with them. These men, unable to give up their habit of smoking, brought supplies of tobacco with them, and Raleigh was thus enabled to acquaint himself with their method of using it.

In the spring of 1585 Raleigh, who had been loaded by a grateful sovereign with honours of every kind, sent his cousin, Sir Richard Grenville, to Virginia to complete the occupation and establish order. On returning to England after the successful conclusion of his task Grenville left behind him 107 men under the command of Captain Lane, with instructions to make a thorough study of the country and its inhabitants, with a view to its further development. Among the party was Thomas Hariot, a mathematician by profession, Raleigh's intimate friend and right hand, to whom, in conjunction with

Grenville, the admiral assigned the tasks of observing and reporting the progress of events in the colony, and also that of investigating anything new or worthy of note in the field of natural science. Hariot was particularly struck by the universal prevalence of pipe-smoking among the Indians, and on his return made a lengthy report to Raleigh on the subject. In this document, which was afterward printed, he describes the process, and remarks that smoke expels the superfluous moisture from the body and opens all the pores, with the result that the Indians enjoy better health than the civilized English settlers. Such was the reverence in which the herb was held by the Indians that they believed the gods themselves used tobacco; consequently, they offered it up as a sacrifice, and when a storm was raging they would throw tobacco-leaves into the angry waves to propitiate the offended deities. "We ourselves," wrote Hariot,

> tried their way of inhaling the smoke, both during our stay in Virginia and after our return, and have had many rare and wonderful proofs of the beneficial effects of this plant, which to relate in detail would require a whole volume to itself.[1]

He adds that the natives looked upon tobacco as a gift from the Great Spirit, bestowed upon them for their personal enjoyment.

The first attempt to found a colony in Virginia was, however, a complete failure. When Drake, in 1586, immediately after his return from his piratical adventures in the West Indies, went to the assistance of Virginia he

[1] See Thomas Hariot, *A Brief and True Report of the New Found Land of Virginia: Sir Walter Raleigh's Colony of MDLXXXV*, p. 31 (London, privately printed, 1900; first printed 1588).

found the colony in a lamentable condition. Governor Lane had not been able to come to a good understanding with the Indians, with whom his men soon found themselves in a state of constant war. Moreover, the colonists had to fight against disease, aggravated by improper feeding, with the result that those who still survived implored Drake to take them home in his ship; accordingly all the colonists, including Lane and Hariot, returned to England in 1586. In the year and a half they had spent in constant touch with the natives they had contracted the habit of smoking, and become so attached to it that they continued the practice after their return to England. Great was the astonishment of their countrymen at the sight of these pipe-smokers. Camden, the Court historian of Elizabeth's reign, describes tobacco as an evil-smelling vapour, and relates with amazement how the ex-colonists inhaled the smoke and expelled it through mouth and nostrils with insatiable avidity and apparent enjoyment, declaring that the practice kept them in good health.

Raleigh, thanks to his intimacy with Hariot, had been initiated more deeply than most into the mysteries of smoking and the wonderful properties of tobacco; not only was he a heavy smoker who thoroughly enjoyed his pipe, but he was also quick to recognize in tobacco an article of commercial value from which incalculable profit might be derived. Sir Walter's London house was by the river-banks, on ground now occupied by Adelphi Terrace, and it is here that Shakespeare is said to have visited him, though the story of their smoking together is probably untrue; there is no mention of smoking in any of the plays, as there surely would have been had the poet been a devotee of this novel and epoch-making fashion. Raleigh, on the other hand, loved his pipe and smoked persistently, to the amazement of those to whom the thing was merely strange and incomprehensible, and whose attitude is summed up in the following well-known anecdote, told not only of Raleigh, but also of other celebrities of the day. Raleigh, so goes the story, was sitting in his room one day enjoying a quiet smoke when one of his gardeners entered to ask for orders; as soon as he caught sight of Sir Walter enveloped in a cloud of smoke that issued from his mouth and nostrils he ran in terror from the room, to return immediately with a bucket of water, which he emptied over his unfortunate master, whom he supposed to be in danger of burning to death.

Raleigh, who was a great personage at Court, made many converts there, and even the Queen, on hearing of the new custom, is said to have given it a trial. In later times those who have endeavoured to explain her coarse manners and eccentric way of life by asserting that she was really a man have adduced her smoking habits as an additional proof of their theory. All the evidence, however, tends to show that her first attempt was the last; Elizabeth was not herself a smoker, although, unlike her successor, James I, who was the most bitter opponent of the habit, she had no objection to smoking by others.

In an incredibly short time smoking spread from one end of England to the other—this 'barbarous habit' had become the mode in London. The pipes used were of various materials—from the costly article of silver down to the makeshift consisting of a walnut-shell with a straw for stem. In those early times pipes were rare and precious possessions; in the so-called *tabagies*—meeting-places resembling the ordinary taverns—they were passed from hand to hand, so that the same pipe served many people in the course of a sitting.

Although tobacco and the potato were brought to England about the same time, the former at once attained to widespread popularity, whereas the cultivation of the potato had at first to be made compulsory, and a hundred years passed before it became general. Alexander von Humboldt has the following commentary on the contrast:

> As an ignorant child, if offered the choice between a piece of bread and a glowing coal, stretches out his hand first to the latter, even so did the people of Europe choose between potatoes and tobacco.

By the end of Elizabeth's reign smoking was general among all classes of society; it was especially the mark of the young man of fashion, and Robert Burton, in his satirical enumeration of the accomplishments necessary to the perfect gentleman, ranks smoking with dancing, riding, hunting, and card-playing.

On the Continent the use of tobacco for smoking was hardly known; when Paul Hentzner, the German professor, visited England with a pupil in 1598 he could scarcely believe his eyes when he saw everybody smoking, even in the theatres.

Such was the state of affairs at the time of the death of Elizabeth, that shrewd and crafty queen under whose rule England, in spite of constant domestic troubles, religious and political, had triumphed over the mightiest monarch in Europe. Elizabeth was succeeded (1603) by

James I, the son of Mary Stuart—long since reconciled with the murderers of his ill-fated mother, so as not to imperil his succession to the throne. The personality of James is a matter on which there is an extraordinary difference of opinion : some historians describe him as one not to be relied on, devoid even of personal courage, a hidebound pedant of the schoolmaster type; others, Disraeli among them, regard him as a man far in advance of his time, the victim of misrepresentation on the part of those who failed to take into account the spirit of the age, which valued authority above personal judgment. To form a proper estimate we must travel back through the centuries to the time when women were burned as witches, when wizards had great power, when the Devil himself was held to be the direct agent in all manifestations of evil—a time when anyone who dared to denounce the current traditions of magic and diabolism as mere folly went in danger of his life, while his writings were condemned to the flames.[1] James was blamed for trying to establish an absolute despotism, and the charge still holds good, in spite of Disraeli's denial; in the eyes of the world James I must always be reckoned among the bad Kings of England.

He was a man of some literary activity, and those of his writings which deal with the popular superstitions of the day show clearly that he himself, in common with the most enlightened men of his day, had come under their influence. Nowhere in his collected works do we find the slightest evidence of independent thought, or any real grasp of the important problems of the day;

[1] Reginald Scot, *Discoverie of Witchcraft* (1584).

yet this was the monarch who, by reason of his birth, and through the force of circumstances, was called upon to end the age-long feud between Scotland and England for which the greatest of the Plantagenet and Tudor kings had shed their blood, and to weld them together into a kingdom united at least so far as their foreign policy was concerned. A striking exception to the general run of his work is to be found in his book on *Demonology, or Doctrines of Evil Spirits*, in which, according to the fashion of the time, he investigates the Devil's usual methods of procedure, and discusses, among other things, his apparently senseless preference for witches—*i.e.*, old women, instead of young girls, as his victims. Other of his writings bear witness to some hard thinking and a general recognition of the grave errors of his time, though here, too, the prevailing note is that of personal conviction, the wisdom or folly of which is of course open to question.

In the closing years of Elizabeth's reign the enormous increase in the habit of smoking had filled the King with astonishment and dismay; so far had it gone that many a man could boast of having "drunk tobacco," as the expression went, with the highest nobles of the Court. To acquire the art of smoking was the duty of every man of fashion, and it was considered a disgrace not to be able to inhale smoke through the nose; there were even professors of smoking who initiated beginners into the mysteries, and were not satisfied until their pupils had acquired the art of blowing smoke-rings in the air.

The price of tobacco at that time was extravagantly high: when first introduced into England it was literally worth its weight in silver—*i.e.*, a pound of tobacco was sold for an equal weight of silver coins—so that the sums spent on this latest craze were a serious item in the budget of any man of fashion. King James, however, was absolutely opposed to the habit; he saw in it a barbarous and pernicious custom, borrowed from a wild, uncivilized people, and he was quite incapable of comprehending its fascination; to him it was merely the ' stink,' as he called it, which the smokers diffused around them, and with which, in the days of the late Queen, the young gentlemen-in-waiting had poisoned the atmosphere of the very Court itself. It annoyed him to see a man of the highest rank, like Sir Walter Raleigh, given over to the pernicious habit. However, so long as the Queen lived he was forced to look on in silence, but in his heart he swore that on the day that he ascended the throne he would make an end of " this disgusting business."

That day had arrived. James was King of England, and the whole nation was soon aware that the ship of State was in the hands of an autocrat with very decided likes and dislikes; and he had not been many months on the throne when he published a bitter and violent protest against the habit of smoking.[1]

In it he shows how the golden age of England had been brought about by the bravery of her sons in war and their obedience to the monarchy in time of peace, but, as is always the case, an excess of power and wealth had resulted in a certain state of moral decline: the clergy had grown lax, the nobles sunk in idleness and luxury, extravagance and greed threatened the *moral* of rulers and people alike, to the serious detriment of the

---

[1] James I, *Misocapnus sive de abusu Tobacci lusus regius* (London, 1603).

Fig. 15. Smoke as a Cure for Illness

Fig. 16. INTERIOR OF A SMOKING TAVERN (TABAGIE) IN
LONDON IN THE TIME OF THE STUARTS

internal welfare of the State. In such circumstances it was the monarch's duty to oppose the spread of these evils, to compel the citizens to exercise a decent restraint in their pleasures, and, in general, to bring all men back to the paths of contentment and hard work.

" And surely in my opinion," wrote the King,[1]

> there cannot be a more base, and yet hurtfull, corruption in a Countrey, then is the vile use (or rather abuse) of taking *Tobacco* in this Kingdome, which hath moued me, shortly to discover the abuses thereof in this following little Pamphlet.
>
> . . . My onely care is, that you, my deare Countrey-men, may rightly conceive even by this smallest trifle, of the sinceritie of my meaning in greater matters, never to spare any paine, that may tend to the procuring of your weale and prosperitie.

Smoking, he suggests, belongs to

> that sort of customes, which having their originall from base corruption and barbarity, doe in like sort, make their first entry into a Countrey, by an inconsiderate and childish affectation of Noveltie. . . . For *Tobacco* . . . was first found out by some of the barbarous *Indians*, to be a Preservative, or Antidot against the Pockes, a filthy disease, whereunto these barbarous people are (as all men know) very much subject, . . . so that as from them was first brought into Christendome, that most detestable disease, so from them likewise was brought this use of *Tobacco*, as a stinking and unsavourie Antidot, for so corrupted and execrable a Maladie, the stinking Suf-fumigation whereof they yet use against that disease, making so one canker or venime to eat out another. . . . Shall we . . . that have bene so long civill and wealthy in Peace, famous and invincible in Warre, fortunate in both, . . . shall we, I say, without blushing, abase ourselves so farre, as to imitate these beastly *Indians* ? . . . Why doe we not as well imitate them in walking naked as they doe ? . . . yea why do we not denie God and adore the Devill as they doe ?

[1] The passages quoted are from *A Counterblaste to Tobacco* (London, 1604).

The smoking habit, the King goes on, had been brought into England by some two or three savages.

> But the pitie is, the poore wilde barbarous men died, but that vile barbarous custom is yet alive, yea in fresh vigor: so as it seemes a miracle to me, how a custome springing from so vile a ground . . . should be welcomed upon so slender a warrant.

They must clearly understand that all the fabulous properties ascribed to tobacco were entirely non-existent. The claim, for instance, that smoke, because it is warm and dry, is actually beneficial to the cold and moist element in the human body, was sheer nonsense. But, supposing it to be a medicine, no healthy man ought to take it—to employ medicine when one was not ill was not only impious, but actually injurious. Tobacco, in short, "hath a certaine venemous facultie joyned with the heat thereof." The smell of it alone was sufficient to create an antipathy against it; should anyone be so peculiarly constituted as not to object to the hateful odour, that man's sense of smell must be either untrustworthy or corrupt. As for the argument that the multitude would never have sung the praises of tobacco with such persistence had they not found by experience that no better remedy could be found for mortal ills, James declared bluntly that the ridiculous habit had its rise in the universal readiness to adopt anything in the way of a novelty, and the infatuation of the many who follow the example of others without troubling to think for themselves. The explanation of its supposed healing properties could be explained quite simply,

> because peradventure when a sicke man hath had his disease at the height, hee hath at that instant taken *Tobacco*, and afterward

his disease taking the naturale course of declining, and the patient consequently recovering his health, O then the *Tobacco*, forsooth, was the worker of that miracle.

Moreover, a new race of physicians was springing up day by day—cunning peasants, crazy old women, simple-minded girls, who persuaded the sufferers to try the 'holy' antidote which they had found so beneficial in their own case, or that of their friends—credulity and blind confidence did the rest, and the sick man recovered! It was easy to see how such 'physicians' profited by people's ignorance of the truth. In this way many who owe their recovery to the simple processes of nature have attributed it to the use of tobacco. But when anyone died from the ill-effects of smoking (a thing by no means uncommon) no one thought of making tobacco responsible for his death.

Similarly those drunkards who, in spite of their intemperate habits, have managed to attain to a sickly old age persuade themselves that life can be prolonged by tippling, and quite forget how many have made shipwreck of their lives in the ocean of debauchery and died before their time.

And what greater absurditie can there bee, then to say that one cure shall serve for divers, nay, contrarious sortes of diseases? It is an undoubted ground among all Phisicians, that there is almost no sort either of nourishment or medicine, that hath not some thing in it disagreeable to some part of mans bodie . . . whearby the contrarie in this case, such is the miraculous omnipotencie of our strong tasted *Tobacco*, as it cures all sorts of diseases. . . . It cures the Gowt in the feet, and (which is miraculous) in that very instant when the smoke thereof, as light, flies up into the head, the vertue thereof, as heavie, runs downe to the little toe.

It helpes all sorts of Agues. It makes a man sober that was drunke. It refreshes a weary man, and yet makes a man hungry. Being taken when they goe to bed, it makes one sleepe soundly, and yet being taken when a man is sleepie and drowsie, it will, as they say, awake his braine, and quicken his understanding.

Furthermore, tobacco is said to cure the scabby American vagabonds of their Pockes (syphilis):

. . . many in this kingdome have had such a continuall use of taking this unsavorie smoke, as now they are not able to forbeare the same, no more then an olde drunkard can abide to be long sober, without falling into an uncurable weaknesse and evill constitution: for their continuall custome hath made to them, *habitum*, *alteram naturam*: so to those that from their birth have been continually nourished upon poison and things venemous, wholesome meates are onely poisonable.

Such arguments as these King James imagined were sufficient to refute and overthrow any possible apology for the "stinking weed"; it only remained for him to explain in detail the loathsome and scandalous results of this mania for smoking.

Drunkenness, he asserted, was the root of all the vices, and among its evil consequences was an unquenchable desire for tobacco. Now just as hardly anyone succumbs to the vice of drinking on his first visit to the tavern— *nemo repente fuit turpissimus*—but yields gradually to the lure of intemperance, till, after a long course of bestial indulgence, he comes to rejoice in his servitude, so the smoker at first hesitates between his liking for the reek of tobacco and his natural shrinking from so unnatural a habit, but soon becomes so obstinately addicted to it that he would sacrifice every pleasure in life rather than give it up—and this species of lunacy they attribute to " the magic power of tobacco " !

" Thirdly," says the King,

is it not the greatest sinne of all, that you the people of all sortes of this Kingdome, who are created and ordeined by God to be-stowe both your persons and goods for the maintenance both of the honour and safetie of your King and Commonwealth, should disable yourselves in both ? In your persons having by this con-tinuall vile custome brought your selves to this shameful imbecilitie, that you are not able to ride or walke the journey of a Jewes Sabboth, but you must have a reekie cole brought you from the next poore house to kindle your *Tobacco* with ? whereas he cannot be thought able for any service in the warres, that cannot endure oftentimes the want of meate, drinke and sleepe, much more then must hee endure the want of *Tobacco*. In the times of the many glorious and victorious battailes fought by this Nation, there was no word of *Tobacco*. But now if it were time of warres, and that you were to make some sudden *Cavalcado* upon your enemies, if any of you should seeke leisure to stay behinde his fellowe for taking of *Tobacco*, for my part I should never bee sorie for any evill chance that might befall him. To take a custome in any thing that cannot bee left againe, is most harmefull to the people of any land. *Mollicies* and delicacie were the wracke and overthrow, first of the Persian and next of the Romane Empire. And this very custome of taking *Tobacco* (whereof our present purpose is) is even at this day accounted so effeminate among the Indians themselves, as in the market they will offer no price for a slave to be sold, whome they finde to be a great *Tobacco* taker.

Now how you are by this custome disabled in your goods, let the Gentry of this land beare witnesse, some of them bestowing three, some foure hundred pounds a yeere upon this precious stinke, which I am sure might be bestowed upon many farre better uses. I read indeede of a knavish Courtier, who for abusing the favour of the Emperor *Alexander Severus* his Master by taking bribes to intercede, for sundry persons in his Master's Care (for

[81]

whom he never once opened his mouth) was justly choked with smoke, with this doome, *Fumo pereat, qui fumum vendidit* (he who sells smoke, by smoke let him perish); but of so many smoke-buyers, as are at this present in this kingdome, I never read nor heard.

And for the vanities committed in this filthie custome, is it not both great vanitie and uncleanenesse, that at the table, a place of respect, of cleanlinesse, of modestie, men should not be ashamed, to sit tossing of *Tobacco pipes*, and puffing of the smoke of *Tobacco* one to another, making the filthy smoke and stinke thereof, to exhale athwart the dishes, and infect the aire, when very often, men that abhorre it are at their repast. Surely Smoke becomes a kitchin far better then a Dining chamber . . . The publike use whereof, at all times, and in all places, hath now so farre prevailed, as divers men very sound both in judgment, and complexion, have bene at last forced to take it also without desire, partly because they were ashamed to seeme singular . . . and partly, to be as one that was content to eate Garlicke (which hee did not love) that he might not be troubled with the smell of it, in the breath of his fellowes. And is it not a great vanitie, that a man cannot heartily welcome his friend now, but straight they must bee in hand with *Tobacco*? No it is become in place of a cure, a point of good fellowship, and he that will refuse to take a pipe of *Tobacco* among his fellowes (though by his own election he would rather feele the savour of a Sinke) is accounted peevish and no good company. . . . Yea the Mistresse cannot in a more manerly kinde, entertaine her servant, then by giving him out of her faire hand a pipe of *Tobacco*. But herein is not onely a great vanitie, but a great contempt of Gods good giftes, that the sweetenesse of mans breath, being a good gift of God, should be willfully corrupted by this stinking smoke. . . .

Moreover, which is a great iniquitie, and against all humanitie, the husband shall not bee ashamed, to reduce thereby his delicate, wholesome, and cleane complexioned wife, to that extremitie, that either shee must also corrupt her sweete breath therewith, or else resolve to live in a perpetuall stinking torment.

In conclusion the King demands of his dear countrymen,

> Have you not reason then to bee ashamed, and to forbeare this filthie noveltie, so basely grounded, so foolishly received and so grossely mistaken in the right use thereof? In your abuse thereof sinning against God, harming your selves both in persons and goods . . . by the custome thereof making your selves to be wondered at by all forraine civil Nations, and by all strangers that come among you, to be scorned and contemned. A custome lothsome to the eye, hatefull to the nose, harmefull to the braine, dangerous to the Lungs, and in the black stinking fume thereof, neerest resembling the horrible Stigian smoke of the pit that is bottomelesse.

This denunciation from the throne made an enormous impression throughout the kingdom, but its results were not at all what the monarch had looked for. The practice had already taken too strong a hold on the people, and the devotees of smoking were prepared to risk the royal displeasure rather than give up their newly acquired luxury; besides, it was possible to indulge in the habit without making a parade of it. Every one read the pamphlet; flatterers and parasites praised it, though here and there a feeble protest was made; but things went on just as before, and the consumption of tobacco from Virginia soared to undreamed-of heights. Angry that his subjects should pay so little heed to his well-meant admonition, the King resolved to compel their obedience by an inroad on their purses; accordingly he commanded that the duty on tobacco should be raised, but, owing to the opposition in Parliament, the measure was never enforced.

James's personal antipathy to tobacco was not the only

motive for his action—there were also serious political considerations. As late as 1604 England was still at war with Spain, which at that time had possession of all the countries which were known to produce tobacco; and so great had grown the demand that each shipload of it represented a considerable sum of money. In consequence, the Spanish tobacco ships became the favourite prey of English sailors, while the Spanish viewed with strong disapproval the spread of the tobacco plantations in Virginia; this led to a state of constant hostilities, in spite of James's desire for peace and an alliance between the two countries. On the other hand, Gondomar, the Spanish ambassador at the Court of King James, never ceased to intrigue against the British colonists in Virginia.

As a result of the King's attitude less tobacco was imported, while the cultivation of the plant in England increased enormously; tobacco had in truth become so indispensable to the people that every repressive measure on the part of the King was met by them with a counter-manœuvre which generally succeeded in making the latest order of no effect. However, James persisted in his campaign, and lost no opportunity of publicly proclaiming his hatred of tobacco.

In August 1605 he called upon the Vice-Chancellor of Oxford University and expressed a desire to attend some of the debates on medicine and philosophy, and to take part himself in the ensuing discussion. As it was well known that his Majesty prided himself on his scholarship, as well as on an experimental knowledge of philosophy and science, the authorities decided to choose a subject upon which he was certain to be well informed, and in view of his recent pamphlet the choice naturally fell upon tobacco. It chanced that the physicians Henry Ashworth and John Cheynell (father of Francis Cheynell, the Nonconformist of later fame) had received their doctor's diploma on August 3, 1603, and these two were appointed to conduct a discussion on the tobacco plant and its abuse on the occasion of the royal visit. On August 27 the King, accompanied by the Queen and the Prince of Wales, arrived in Oxford. After two days spent on philosophy the turn of medicine came on the twenty-ninth, when the subject of debate was whether the use of tobacco was beneficial or not to a healthy man.

It required a brave man, and a learned doctor into the bargain, to stand up against the attack of the King and the most distinguished physicians of his Court, all of whom were naturally sworn foes of tobacco. Doctors and professors alike disputed hotly, for the King's benefit, about the nature and properties of the plant; the Court physicians joined in, while his Majesty listened with the liveliest interest to the discourse of the doctors, Ailworth, Gifford, Ashworth, and Gwyn. Ashworth made a telling speech in which he exposed the injurious nature of tobacco, and agreed with James in casting grave doubts on its healing powers. Many doctors supported him in this view, while others advanced arguments to the contrary.

After the King had heard the opinions of both sides he rose and delivered his own views. He declared that the stench of nicotine, or whatever was the right name for the plant and its use, should be excluded from the habits of sober men and from the schools of wise physicians. In all sciences there were fundamental axioms, and in medicine especially there were irrefragable doctrines, laid down by Hippocrates and Galen, not to be overturned by frivolous 'cures' contrary to the wise teachings of those great men. The brain must needs be oppressed and infected by the horrible and poisonous smoke of tobacco —certainly not, as some said, cleansed and freed from superfluous moisture. The King repeated in the main what he had said in his *Counterblaste to Tobacco*, and was especially severe on the notion that tobacco was a panacea. Where, he asked, had anyone ever seen a single remedy prove effective against all diseases? The climax of the King's speech was the remark that tobacco was first used by savages, and it was not fit for civilized men to borrow their customs from such tribes.

It was now Dr Cheynell's turn to speak. He ascended the tribune with a lighted pipe in his hand, and proved his courage and his true English independence by flatly contradicting the views of previous speakers, including the King, and glorifying the uses and virtues of the magic plant, both in medicine and for smoking. This daring speech, especially in that age, might have had serious consequences for the doctor ; but at any rate it vindicated the independence of the university in the field of science, though the majority of the professors thought it wiser to adopt the King's views.

Dr Cheynell declared that English physicians ought to learn the right use of tobacco smoke from those Indians among whom the plant first grew and was first valued. In the Indians' country it was laid down that the physician must intoxicate himself with smoke before he visits his patient. The doctor's speech for the opposition

JACOBUS. I.
Magna Britannia
REX.

Fig. 17. JAMES I, KING OF ENGLAND (1603–25)

Fig. 18. English Interior in the Time of the Stuarts

was so incisive and witty that the King and the rest of the audience laughed heartily; but of course the royal views prevailed in the end. James opposed Cheynell's proposal to use tobacco as a remedy, saying that this was the practice of Indian barbarians, who had as much idea of medicine as of civilized customs—that is, none at all. If tobacco smoke gave pleasure to many, that showed that they had sunk to the level of the savages, and if there were doctors who smoked themselves, and believed in the healing virtues of tobacco, they ought to be banished to the Indian country, where they could drug themselves freely among the smoke-sodden native doctors, and study the savage healing art without being a nuisance to England.

The debate, which lasted a whole morning, was closed with a courtly speech by the King's physician, Dr Warner. "Although the use of the smoking apparatus," he said,

that funnel, or (as it is generally called) pipe, has developed into a regular custom among our better classes, just as once it was fashionable in Athens to play on the double flute, yet as Alcibiades and Pallas Athene rejected the double pipe, so our heroes and heroines ought to despise, break, and cast away these foul, ugly, and stinking tobacco-pipes. But why should I cite Alcibiades or Pallas, when here we have King James, far mightier, wiser and more learned than Alcibiades, and his lady, the Queen, as wise as Pallas Athene, both of whom not only mislike but even hate such stench and dirt.

The physician ended with the hope that his sovereign, who had honoured the science of medicine so highly by his presence, his speeches, and his gracious attention, might seldom or never need the help of medicine himself;

and with this he prayed for every blessing on the King.[1]

When the King, later on, visited Cambridge the Vice-Chancellor issued an order that no member of the University, graduate or undergraduate, and no college servant should enter any smoking-house, inn, or tobacco-shop during the King's stay at Cambridge. No one, under penalty of being ' sent down,' was to take snuff in Great St Mary's Church or in the hall of Trinity College. As soon as the King left Cambridge these prohibitions were withdrawn.

The King's views and his polemic against tobacco gave rise to a host of books in England. These were mostly in accord with the King's opinions, and hostile to smoking. Even before James's accession tobacco had been denounced in print. Joseph Hall, Bishop of Norwich, in his *Satyres*, attacked the ' abject ' custom of smoking. In 1602 Dr Bushell, a Londoner, published a work with the title, *A Work for Chimney-sweepers ; or, A Warning to Tobacconists*. His denunciation ended with the remark, " It were better to be choked with an English hempen cord than poisoned with Indian tobacco." Most of the learned men who discussed the question after King James's declaration admitted the healing virtues of the new plant, but followed the King in sternly condemning the widespread custom of smoking. Among these writers was Edmund Gardiner of London, whose *Triall of Tobacco* appeared in 1610. He began by elaborately extolling the curative properties of the plant, and gave a long list of

[1] Sir Isaac Wake, *Rex Platonicus sive de potentissimi principis Jacobi Britanniarum regis ad illustrissimam Academiam Oxoniensem adventu, Aug. 27, 1605* (Oxford, 1615).

prescriptions for its use; but when he came to discuss smoking nothing was too bad to say about this. He satirized the waste of money on tobacco.

> Many a young nobleman's estate is altogether spent and scattered to nothing in smoke. This befalls after a shameful and beastly fashion, in that a man's estate runs out through his nose, and he wastes whole days, even years, in drinking of tobacco; men smoke even in bed.
> You see that tobacco is a phantastick tempter . . . and is taken by many, since they have naught else to do, more from wantonness than from necessity.

Sir William Vaughan, a physician at Queen Elizabeth's Court, and author of *Natural and Artificial Directions for Health*, praised tobacco in the first edition of his work, issued in 1602, but in the fourth edition, published in 1613, he went over to the King's side and attacked smoking.

In spite of the King's efforts and the high import duties the consumption of tobacco steadily increased, and smoking was still a topic of general discussion. The outbreak of the plague in London, in 1614, helped to popularize smoking; doctors declared that they had noticed that steady smokers were less subject to infection than others, and recommended tobacco as a disinfectant, with the result that smoking increased enormously, in spite of the King's antipathy. We can see the views of the time in William Barclay's book, *Nepenthes; or, The Vertues of Tobacco*, which appeared in the plague year, 1614. "When temperately used," he writes, "there is not in all the world a medicine comparable to tobacco. All of tobacco is wholesome." But when he touches on smoking the panegyrist is more sceptical, and ridicules the abuse of the plant by those of his contemporaries who turn their heads into chimneys.

An author named Deacon, in 1616, was far more severe. He declared that tobacco smoke was as dangerous to the life and health of the individual as it was ruinous to the commonwealth. Deacon's book is a dialogue between a merchant who sells tobacco and a clergyman. After nearly two hundred pages of denunciation the merchant is convinced, and vows to send his two hundredweight of ' beastly tobacco ' swimming down the Thames.

The prize for violent abuse, however, fell, as might be expected, to Joshua Sylvester, James I's Court poet, whose book *Tobacco Battered and the Pipes Shattered* appeared in 1615. He calls tobacco a hell-dust, England's shame, the Indian tyrant of the British kingdom, a madness, and a frenzy, that by the Devil's agency has been brought from the savages to England. His words agree remarkably with his royal master's views.

More than once tobacco was personified as a character in a satirical comedy, and was, of course, very roughly handled on the stage. An instance of this is Richard Brathwait's *The Smoking Age; or, The Man in the Mist*, a satirical play in which an evildoer, to escape Jupiter's wrath, is changed by Pluto, the god of the underworld, into tobacco, which, under the disguise of a gift, will bring men misfortune. In his farewell to the personified plant Pluto promises to help it to be well received by all men, so as to have occasion to ruin men's souls, especially in England.

It was at this time that Sir Walter Raleigh, the first

Fig. 19. Illustrated Title of Richard Brathwait's
"The Smoking Age" (London, 1617)

The young Heir newly come to his Eſtate.

Who very kindly doth invite you all,   To feaſt upon his Fathers funerall,
A new Medly of ſix Ayres.

Fig. 20. THE SMOKING PRODIGAL (LONDON, 1620)

of English smokers, forfeited his life. It was he who discovered and founded the colony of Virginia, later to be the home of tobacco. He had become an incessant smoker, and this was not likely to win James's favour. When James came to the throne Raleigh was suspected of conspiracy in favour of Lady Arabella Stuart, the heir-presumptive to the throne; he was condemned to death, and reprieved only on the scaffold. He was imprisoned in the Tower till 1616, and sorely missed his tobacco. After Arabella Stuart died, in 1617, he was released and given the command of a fleet to conquer the golden land of El Dorado. Raleigh resumed his pipe as soon as he was free; and on his voyage to Guiana and back he took in large stores of tobacco, to dispose of at home. He was strictly commanded by King James to avoid all encounters with the Spaniards; against Raleigh's will, however, a fight took place, in which his own son was killed. King James, untouched by pity, now gratified his old grudge against his enemy, and had the former death-warrant carried out. Shortly before Raleigh went to the block he smoked a pipe, which many men, and more women, thought the height of frivolity; but John Aubrey, who tells the story, says that the pipe was only to calm his natural agitation.[1]

The ever-growing demand for tobacco-leaf in England called for an increase in production and importation. This was a blessing to the new and struggling colony of Virginia. The colonists there, bitten with the gold fever, like all explorers of that age, had formed high hopes which soon vanished in thin air. They did their best,

[1] John Aubrey, *Letters Written by Eminent Persons* (1669).

but were worn out by toil and sickness; they had no white women among them, they suffered from the climate and their loneliness, and were on the point of giving up the struggle and returning home, when the sudden increase in the English demand for tobacco, which grew luxuriantly in Virginia, gave them hope again. All other crops were abandoned, and, with the help of the Governors, the whole of Virginia was turned into one tobacco plantation. It was soon clear that this crop was most lucrative; the importation of colonial tobacco into England grew enormously. Tobacco became so important in Virginia that it took the place of money: wages and the prices of goods were paid in bales of tobacco, and imports from England were bartered for the same commodity. When in 1620 the colony, most of whose inhabitants were young unmarried men, needed women, ninety girls were sent out from London, as a first instalment; the settlers had to pay only their travelling expenses—from 120 to 150 lb. of tobacco a head. King James objected to this growth of the tobacco industry in his colony, and had many disputes on the point with the energetic Governor, Sir Edwin Sandys, who went counter to James's Spanish proclivities by trying to exclude Spanish tobacco from England. In 1620 Virginia sent 40,000 lb. of tobacco-leaf to England, where a guild of pipe-makers was formed, which became so influential that it was admitted among the other guilds. On its shield it bore a tobacco plant in full bloom.

King James could hardly have thought it possible that his wishes should be disregarded, and that the custom he condemned should have spread so widely. However, he would not readily give way; at least he would try to stop the cultivation of tobacco in England, which was beginning to spread, and limit the trade as much as possible. Therefore, on September 30, 1619, he issued a proclamation with the purpose of prohibiting the cultivation of tobacco in England, and declaring the tobacco trade to be a royal monopoly. In this decree King James says that in spite of his aversion to the use of tobacco, which only results in the universal corruption of the body and mind of man, he is forced to choose between two evils; and he holds it a lesser evil that tobacco, like many other vain and superfluous things, should be imported from abroad rather than that it should be planted in the realm, thereby misusing and exhausting the fruitful soil. Therefore, from February 2, 1620, onward he forbids the sowing or planting of tobacco in his kingdom, as he is informed that unrestricted freedom of this use, or rather abuse, constitutes a danger and damage to the public weal. As this is a plant by no means necessary for use, he forbids any man to deal therein and keep tobacco in store, unless he be expressly authorized by royal patent.

This proclamation led to a debate in the Commons on April 16, 1621, in which the virtues and vices of tobacco were discussed. A loyal courtier, Sir William Stroud, proposed to banish tobacco from the realm, and forbid its importation from anywhere, or its use. One speaker said that if tobacco was not excluded from the kingdom it would soon be the ruin of hundreds of thousands in England, for it was so generally used that even the ploughman smoked his pipe as he followed the plough.

There were, however, so many smokers and tobacco lovers sitting in the Commons, and so much independence in the House, even in opposition to the King, that these drastic proposals found no acceptance—especially as they would have endangered the prosperity of Virginia.

We find many references to the new custom in the works of Francis Bacon. In his *Historia vitæ et mortis* he says :

> In our time the use of tobacco is growing greatly and conquers men with a certain secret pleasure, so that those who have once become accustomed thereto can later hardly be restrained therefrom.

When the royal enemy of tobacco died, in 1625, and his son Charles succeeded, matters changed but little. The new King, who had a Renaissance love for art and literature, was personally averse to smoking, though not so fanatical a tobaccophobe as his father. In his legislation he followed in James's footsteps, except that he paid more attention to the financial question, for his Court was one of the most brilliant and extravagant in Europe. His only resource was to evade Parliamentary control and introduce extensive monopolies ; he even took to speculating in pepper with the East India Company.

Charles I confirmed the latest decrees [1] of his " most dear father," and strengthened the royal monopoly of the tobacco trade ; but the proclamation he issued was little observed. A year later the King had to allow the importation of foreign, and especially Spanish, tobacco ; the import duties went into the King's pocket, and,

[1] Proclamation, *De herba nicotiana* (1625); another in 1626.

Fig. 21. Imaginary Smoking Scene, 1621

Fig. 22. CHARLES I, KING OF ENGLAND (1625–49)

together with the large sums paid by tobacco-dealers and importers for their monopoly, formed no inconsiderable part of the royal revenue.

In 1634 Charles issued a similar decree for Scotland. In this he professes his great care for the moral and physical health of his subjects, and ends by granting, for a suitable sum in cash, the monopoly of the tobacco trade to Sir James Leslie and Thomas Dalmahoy.

In England it was becoming clear that smoking would overcome all opposition, and the inevitable surrender of the Government was being made easier by the consequent rise in the revenue. In 1643 Parliament levied a moderate duty on colonial tobacco, and a heavy tax on home-grown tobacco—which shows that the former prohibition of tobacco-growing in England was not obeyed. On March 1, 1644, a further resolution was passed—that tobacco from the Spanish colonies should pay one shilling per pound duty, but Virginia tobacco, as formerly, only twopence per pound.

Gradually the change in public opinion was reflected in literature. James I was dead, and Charles I, though he disliked tobacco, was not so bitter an enemy to the new habit. In 1637 Dr Tobias Venner published a work on tobacco, *A Brief and Accurate Treatise concerning the Taking of the Fume of Tobacco*, in which he is more impartial, and condemns only the immoderate use of the plant. He admits the popularity of the habit of smoking, and allows it in moderation, though he personally finds that smoking leaves a nasty taste in the mouth. However, he draws a terrible picture of the consequences of the excessive consumption of tobacco. In 1640 appeared a poem called *The Tryumph of Tobacco over Sack and Ale*, celebrating the virtues of tobacco in the highest terms.

The only means of smoking at that time was the short clay pipe, much like that now in use in England, except that the stem was rather longer and not curved, as can be seen from Figs. 18–20.

Charles I had now more serious matters than tobacco to deal with. In the Civil War, that broke out in 1642, the two chief leaders, King Charles and Oliver Cromwell, were both non-smokers, but their armies, Cavaliers or Roundheads, agreed in enjoying their pipes. When Charles was a prisoner, and the Parliamentary army called for his death, his guards threw off all feelings of respect, and smoked freely before him, though they knew that the King disliked it—even their officers could hardly restrain them. In the account of Charles I's trial and execution left us by his physician we read that as the King walked calmly and solemnly to his place of trial the soldiers spat on him, puffed smoke in his face, and threw broken pipes in his path.[1]

Cromwell, as we have said, personally disliked smoking; but it was too late to stop the habit. All that subsequent sovereigns could do was to set up a barrier to the cultivation of tobacco in the home counties. This prohibition was often broken, but was finally embodied in a law which was strictly enforced and has held good until the present time, though many vicissitudes arose before this final settlement.

[1] See Apperson, *The Social History of Smoking*, p. 58.

CHAPTER V

THE SPREAD OF SMOKING THROUGHOUT CENTRAL EUROPE AND THE BEGINNING OF OPPOSITION

MEANWHILE the continent of Europe was passing through a time of unrest. With the dawn of the seventeenth century the Spanish and Catholic policy of the Habsburgs had suffered heavy reverses, and the struggle was extending to Central Europe; the discoveries and achievements in the New World had not gone far before the centre of interest was shifted from the far-off colonies to the heart of the old continent. Military operations, commerce, and general social intercourse had brought the people of Western Europe into closer touch with those of the centre, and now England, for all her isolation, was to make her entry into international politics. It was inevitable that all the various contacts, political and military, should facilitate a mutual exchange of the latest discoveries in the arts and sciences, as well as of manners and customs.

The bridge between England and the Continent was her near neighbour Holland, just then on the eve of extensive commercial developments by land and sea; as a natural result the practice of smoking, which, as we have seen, originated in England, was enthusiastically received in Holland, where it had been introduced by the sailors of both nations, and also by the English students who frequented the Dutch universities, especially that of Leyden.

Before 1590 it was exceptional to find a Dutchman who smoked, but now the custom spread rapidly throughout the country. It is probable that the charge of anachronism made on the first performance of Goethe's *Egmont* against the remark of the shopkeeper, "A soldier came in to buy tobacco," was justifiable; the action of the play passes in the year 1567, at which date tobacco was certainly not to be had from a Dutch shopkeeper, nor were soldiers likely to have a taste for it. But at the beginning of the seventeenth century the situation was very different: owing to the increasing demand, tobacco had become an important article of commerce, and was being imported from all the American colonies; Dutch vessels had even begun to ship African negroes to Virginia and the Antilles, where agricultural labourers were urgently needed, and to barter them for tobacco, which they brought back with them to Europe. A contemporary German witness, von Rusdorff, the Palatine ambassador at The Hague, writes:

> I cannot refrain from a few words of protest against the astounding fashion lately introduced from America—a sort of smoke-tippling, one might call it, which enslaves its victims more completely than any other form of intoxication, old or new. These madmen will swallow and inhale with incredible eagerness the smoke of a plant they call *Herba Nicotiana*, or tobacco.[1]

He goes on to describe in detail how they light the weed from a live coal or burning tinder, blow on it till it smoulders, drink in the smoke through a pipe of white clay, and breathe it out through mouth and nostrils till the whole atmosphere is poisoned by the pestilential stench.

[1] J. Joachim von Rusdorff, *Metamorphosis Europæ*, p. 145 (1627).

Fig. 23. Drinking and Smoking Bout in Amsterdam at the Beginning of the Seventeenth Century

Fig. 24. Interior of a Dutch Smoking Tavern

In Holland the spread of the habit was greatly helped by the prevailing opinion that smoke was a most valuable disinfectant as well as a prophylactic in cases of epidemics. The country had been stricken by the plague in 1636, and, as the medical science of the day had proved quite helpless in the face of the awful visitation, every one, naturally, clung like a drowning man to the slightest hope of a protection against it. A Dutch physician, Isbrand von Diemerbroek, who, when the plague was raging at Nimeguen, did all that was possible to keep up the spirits of the terrified people by his fearless example as well as by the unflinching discharge of his duties, gives a lively picture of the prevailing conditions.

" The people,"[1] he writes,

who always turn to their superiors for guidance, turned in plague time to the doctors for instructions how to avoid the danger of infection. It was my habit at that time to smoke daily after each meal, and, whenever the foul effluvia from my patients became more than I could bear, I stopped work for a time and had recourse to tobacco. As I have proved by long experience, tobacco is the most effective means of avoiding the plague—provided the leaf is in good condition. One day, when I was visiting one of the victims, the reek of the pestilence seemed to overpower me, and I felt all the symptoms of infection—dizziness, nausea, fear; I cut my visit short and hurried home—where I smoked six or seven pipes of tobacco. I was myself once more, and able to go out again the same day. I experienced many similar attacks so long as the plague lasted, but smoking always drove them away as quickly as on the first occasion. Only once, when I was visiting a married couple sick with the plague, I delayed too long in trying my usual antidote, and nearly lost my life in consequence; although I smoked

[1] Translated from the Dutch by W. Bendt (*Deutsche Tabakzeitung*, April 15, 1901).

several pipes I felt so ill that I lay down again and passed into a state of unconsciousness. When some hours later my servant woke me to say that a number of sick persons were waiting for me I got up, and it was only with my servant's help that I was able to reach the fire-place, where lay my pipe—but, after smoking it, I made an instantaneous recovery. I can testify that many other persons besides myself never failed to derive the greatest benefit from smoking when attacked by the plague.

By 1620 the tobacco habit had made its way across the Rhine and penetrated into Eastern Europe. Hitherto the plant had been confined to the private grounds of the nobility and a few botanical gardens where herbs were grown for medicinal purposes. Now that France and Holland had discovered the bliss to be derived from smoking the custom spread, with the culture of the plant, throughout the length and breadth of Germany, Switzerland, and Austria. The earliest account of the impression made by the new habit on the inhabitants of these countries comes from a Franciscan monk of Aix-la-Chapelle, who, in 1587, wrote to his Superior in Cologne as follows :

> There are many Spaniards here who have brought their bad habits with them; in particular they have a new sort of debauchery which they call smoking. . . . Their soldiers do swagger about puffing fire and smoke from their mouths, and the silly people look on and gape with astonishment.

In Germany the habit spread less rapidly; but war has always been the great encourager of smoking, and the tragic events of the years from 1618 to 1648 gave an enormous impulse to the movement. The Thirty Years War, in which nearly every European Power was involved, was the result partly of the religious antagonism between Catholics and Protestants, and partly of the struggle between the Imperial claim to absolute authority and the determination of the other countries to assert their independence. Germany was pre-eminently the theatre of war where the armies of the nations were assembled in bloody combat. Spanish soldiers occupied the banks of the Rhine; Lusatia and the Electorate of Saxony were full of the English mercenaries sent by James Stuart to the aid of his hard-pressed son-in-law, the "Winter-King" of Bohemia. Both armies had long been inveterate smokers, unable to dispense with the habit; in consequence, wherever they went the population gazed with astonishment at the strange new habit of 'tobacco-drinking,' and natural curiosity soon led them to try it on their own account. Dutch troops in Germany, too, helped to spread the habit, the whole of Swabia succumbing to it with surprising rapidity. According to a contemporary,

> If time hang heavy and he has nothing else to do, a man will drink tobacco. Is he moody, angry, or perplexed, he sticks his pipe between his teeth and takes a long pull at it. Should his wife begin to nag, the man will fill his mouth with smoke and puff it in her face.

All other principalities, temporal and ecclesiastical, and all the cities of Germany and Austria speedily followed suit. When the Swedes under Gustavus Adolphus entered the war in 1630 and marched through Pomerania and Mecklenburg toward Saxony and South Germany they too picked up the habit from their opponents. Though hitherto it had been confined to a few of the Scandinavian ports it is noteworthy that the Swedes, like all the Northern races, developed a quite extraordinary passion for both smoking and chewing.

Tilly's and Wallenstein's armies were not slow in acquiring the habit and transmitting it to Bohemia and Hungary, and about the same time it was brought by English sailors by way of the Baltic to Russia, and by Venetians through the Mediterranean to the Levant and Constantinople. Here also the plant had long been cultivated in the Sultan's gardens purely for its medicinal properties, and so highly was it esteemed that when in the fifteen-eighties Sultan Murad III wished to make a valuable present to Stephen Báthori, King of Poland, he included some dried leaves of the precious novelty. This was its first introduction into that country. In 1590 we find the Polish ambassador at Constantinople, Uchénski by name, sending some seeds of the plant, as a great rarity from overseas, to the widowed queen, Anna Jagiello, a great amateur of botany, who had the plants raised in her own garden, and was fond of showing them to her guests as a particularly precious novelty. From Poland tobacco naturally made its way into Russia, though by a different route from that by which the English sailors had already introduced it.

During the first half of the seventeenth century, when, thanks to the Thirty Years War, smoking became general throughout the whole of Central Europe, tobacco was credited with marvellous healing virtues which naturally engaged the special attention of physicians. From the first the plant had created a sensation among them; they believed in its healing powers, wrote wonderful reports of its efficacy, and could not sufficiently recommend

Fig. 25. PIPE-SMOKER OF THE TIME OF THE THIRTY YEARS WAR

102

Fig. 26. A SOLDIER SMOKING

it as a panacea for every ill. At first their attitude was generally accepted without questioning, but few people had any definite information, and no one had had any personal experience. All they knew was that a number of celebrated physicians, such as Ziegler, Vittich, Johannes Neander, and Franken, had written extravagant eulogies of its fabulous efficacy in every sort of illness. Dr Johannes Vittich, for example, writes:

> There can be no doubt that tobacco can cleanse all impurities and disperse every gross and viscous humour, as we find by daily experience. It cures cancer of the breast, open and eating sores, scabs and scratches, however poisonous and septic, goitre, broken limbs, erysipelas, and many other things. It will heal wounds in the arms, legs, and other members of the body, of however long standing. The place must first be bathed with white wine, or human urine, and wiped with a clean sponge or rag, one or two fresh tobacco-leaves must then be pounded together with the juice, and applied to the wound with a white napkin to protect it; the treatment to be continued until the cure is complete.

Here we have a mild example of the 'horse-doctoring' to which the unhappy victims of that age were compelled to submit. The plant attracted all the more attention from the fact that it was something new; although the doctors had never heard of it before, they at once began to discuss its pros and cons, and to prescribe for its employment as if it had been well known since the time of Galen and Hippocrates. Every doctor, of course, knew better than his colleagues, and it is amusing to note the difference in the methods of treatment they recommended. One was for administering it in its pure state, another would give it mixed with sweet herbs; in one case the patient must take it before, in another after, meals;

sometimes it must be applied as a poultice, sometimes swallowed like a syrup; one doctor made an oil from it, another a salve. Dropsy, worms, wasting, swelling, carbuncle, cancer, scabs—there was nothing tobacco could not cure. But universal remedies are never to be trusted —as a rule they are worthless. Even in the early years of the seventeenth century there were sceptics, like Scriverius of Haarlem and Francesco de Leyra y Aguilar of Cordova. Nevertheless, most of the medical books of the time spoke with enthusiasm of " the healing plant," and even the practice of smoking, which was now generally recognized, received the approval of the profession.

Perhaps its greatest apologist and panegyrist was Johannes Neander of Bremen, in whose book *Tabacologia* (Leyden, 1622) tobacco is lauded to the skies, and recommended as a remedy for all the ills to which the flesh is heir. His account of how tobacco was first brought to Europe is so prejudiced and one-sided that one can only laugh at it to-day; but at that time, when every one was eager to believe in 'cures,' and the novel enjoyment of smoking had turned people's heads, the book made an enormous impression all over the world, and was speedily translated into several languages. Not content with his own experiments Neander sent copies of his book to three of the most famous physicians of the time, with a request for their opinion on his theory of the nature and value of tobacco in its different uses.[1]

The first of them, Dr Wilhelm van der Meer, returned a rather evasive answer; he was not such an enthusiastic

---

[1] *De tabacco: Epistolæ et judicia clarissimorum aliquot medicorum* (Utrecht, 1644).

devotee of the plant as Neander, although he allowed that it possessed certain mysterious properties—for instance, a cold in the head could no more resist it than could iron the magnet. On the other hand, he positively denied that tobacco was a cure for syphilis—it was much better, he maintained, to abstain from visiting brothels. At the same time, he declared, they erred who condemned tobacco on the ground that it originated with a barbarous people, since in that case a thousand other plants, etc., such as the highly esteemed rhubarb, must be rejected with equal reason. Some people, he said, seemed to have a personal hatred of tobacco, going even so far as to declare that smoking made people drunk; but of this he had no proof—it was certainly not true of the habitual smoker; besides, such an argument would lead us to forbid the use of wine, which was certainly more likely to produce such a result.

The second physician whom Neander consulted gave a remarkably prudent answer: while he could not approve of the excessive use of tobacco, he was of opinion that a moderate indulgence in it was by no means harmful, especially in the case of those who suffered from catarrh, and were regular smokers.[1]

The verdict of Hadrianus Falckenburgius, the last of the three, was altogether unfavourable; he was convinced that tobacco was injurious to the brain. While it was true that many were able to use it apparently without any ill results, he advanced a thousand reasons why he would have nothing to do with it.

In spite of this conflict of opinions, smoking was

[1] *Epistolæ et judicia*, loc. cit., pp. 164 ff.

making its way in Holland, where Leyden would seem to
have been the chief centre of the cult; as early as 1622
we find one of its citizens, Thorius, writing a *Hymnus
tabaci*.

However, a revulsion of feeling soon set in; it was
obvious that the medicinal virtues of this tobacco were
not so great after all. Moreover, the practice of smoking
could be a great nuisance to those who did not themselves
indulge in it; many could not endure the new-fangled
habit, while others were deterred by the discomfort which
usually results from the first experiment. The consequence was that the use of tobacco, whether medicinally
or for pleasure, soon began to meet with fierce opposition,
particularly from those persons who had been confident of
complete recovery after using it and were proportionately
disappointed.

But the strongest antagonism came from the clergy;
always suspicious of innovations, in that age particularly
so, they hastened to describe the new custom as ' godless.'
In the newly discovered countries, where smoking was
an old-established custom, they had shown little sympathy
with the natural feelings of the natives, and were much
too premature in their endeavours to destroy their belief
in their old gods and force them immediately to adopt
the Christian faith. In the same spirit they attacked
every old custom and tradition, even their picture-writing,
which was certainly closely connected with their religious
system. The clergy were naturally horrified to see the
Indians smoking in the Christian churches which they
were compelled to attend, just as they were accustomed
to do in their own heathen temples, where smoking was

Qui nitet hic Phœbo Juvenis formosior ipso,
  Non minor herbarum est, non minor arte lyræ.
Hunc tenuit Sophiæ, Clariæ tenuêre sorores;
  Sed fuit Hippocratis maxima cura sui.
En nunc fumifici surgit cantata Tabaci
  Gloria: virtutes quas habet herba, legis.
Quid gaudes, Philocapne? tuo non istu palato
  Serviet, affectis sed, Panacea, locis. P.S.

Fig. 27. JOHANNES NEANDER OF BREMEN

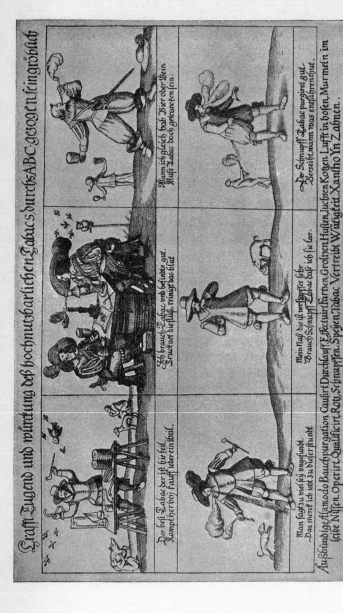

Fig. 28. Broadsheet showing the Virtues of Tobacco

regarded as part of the ritual. As early as 1575 a Mexican Council [1] issued an order forbidding the use of tobacco in the churches throughout the whole of Spanish America. Soon, however, the missionary priests from Europe themselves became so addicted to the habit that it was found necessary to make laws to prevent them from smoking or taking snuff during any part of the Mass or the Divine Office. In Lima, the capital of Peru, a decree was passed by the Provincial Council on October 7, 1588, by which the celebrant was forbidden, under pain of everlasting damnation, to use tobacco in any form whatever, whether for smoking, chewing, or snuff-taking.

In a manifesto issued by the Council of Mexico, October 27, 1589, we read:

> Out of regard to the reverence due to the Holy Eucharist, it is hereby commanded that no tobacco in any form whatever be taken by clerics before reciting Holy Mass, or by any person before receiving Holy Communion.

These measures were approved by the Holy See as applicable only to the districts in which they originated; in Europe at that time the practice was almost unknown, and consequently the necessity for such a prohibition did not arise till much later.

In Mexico, and especially in the newly discovered territories, it was only at first that these prohibitions were strictly enforced. To the great majority of the natives smoking was at once a pleasant enjoyment and an act of worship; their conquerors, on the other hand, however masterful, were comparatively few in number,

[1] Ferraris, *Bibliotheca canonica.* See Moroni, *Dizionario*, vol. lxxii, ff. 176–179.

and these all, laity and clergy alike, were in turn conquered by the fascination of tobacco. The more the
priests succumbed to the habit the greater difficulty they
had in enforcing the prohibitions, which, consequently,
as time went on, were either relaxed or forgotten.

Very different was the situation in Central Europe,
where the habit was destined to conquer the entire
population, though only gradually and intermittently, in
accordance with the fluctuating fortunes of the Thirty
Years War. It is true that in many districts, thanks to
the interference of the local authorities, progress was
hindered for a time; but it was already too late to enforce
actual prohibition, since, as a contemporary, Hans Jakob
von Grimmelshausen, remarks, smoking, or tobacco-
drinking as it was called, had become so common throughout Germany that by the end of the war nine day-labourers
out of ten smoked their pipes, and even apprentices and
boys were taking to the habit. To Grimmelshausen—
well known as the author of *Simplicissimus*—the thing was
incomprehensible; it made him furious to think that
there was hardly a peasant's hut but had its pipe-smoker :
" Some of them," he says,

> drink their tobacco, some eat it, others sniff it up through the
> nostrils—indeed, I am surprised that I have not yet found anyone
> plugging his ears with it. But the other methods I have myself
> seen practised by persons of all classes, from prince to bishop, from
> bishop to barber; and each of them is prepared to explain why
> he does it and how it benefits him. One man smokes because it
> enables him to see better; another because it disperses water in
> the brain; a third to ease his toothache; a fourth to stop the
> singing in his ears; a fifth will tell you it makes him sleep; a sixth
> that it quenches his thirst; a seventh that it neutralizes the bad

effects of too much water-drinking; an eighth that it expels evil humours; the ninth man smokes to pass the time; the tenth because he doesn't wish to be unsociable. . . . They will tell you it benefits the peasant who smokes it, the man who prepares it, the carrier who conveys it, and the merchant or shopkeeper who deals in it.[1]

We may also mention here a work by Carolus Stephan and Johannes Libaldo, *A True Description of the Noble Weed Nicotiana*, which appeared in 1643. This 'new mischief,' as tobacco was often called, is here condemned as being not only injurious to a man's health, but also highly dangerous to his habitation ; owing to their clumsy method of lighting their pipes—with flint, touchwood, live coals, or tinder—it very often happened that while men were smoking in the flimsy wooden dwellings of that period a spark would settle on the timber, and the whole house, sometimes a whole village, would be in a blaze. Thus, on August 26, 1642, in Görlitz, a town in Prussian Silesia, the whole of the Nicholas district, including church and tower, and about a hundred houses, was burned to the ground. Such incidents, naturally, did not make the authorities any more indulgent toward the new habit, and in certain parts of Germany and Central Europe it met with violent opposition. In all classes of society people were divided into two hostile camps, which fought vigorously either for or against the claims of tobacco.

Germany at that time was split up into countless petty princedoms, often of the most insignificant dimensions, and the attitude of the different governments toward the new custom naturally depended upon the personal predilections of the actual rulers. The highest personage of all

[1] J. C. von Grimmelshausen, *Satyrischer Pilgram* (1667), Part II, pp. 47–61.

—though more in name than fact—the Emperor, began to take an interest in the tobacco question soon after the Peace of Westphalia (1648), and caused inquiries to be made concerning the truth of the matter among the local rulers of those parts of Germany in which, according to his information, the custom first originated and had assumed the greatest proportions. Thus we find the Emperor Ferdinand III,[1] in 1649, addressing a questionnaire to the town of Cologne; the answer of the civic authorities in this case has not been preserved, but we may form some idea of what it must have been from the following edict issued by the Elector of Cologne on August 16 of the same year:

> WE, Ferdinand, by God's grace Archbishop of Cologne and Elector, do all and each to wit; Whereas it is shown by daily experience that tobacco-drinking, which in former years was used hardly anywhere, has now spread abroad everywhere, and is so mightily increasing not only among soldiers and common men, but even among children, insomuch that not only all manner of sicknesses, but also destructive fires have resulted therefrom (after credible reports that have reached us) both here and in other kingdoms, so that neighbouring princes and states have been compelled to forbid such abuse. Therefore We graciously and solemnly command all and every in Our Archdiocese, bailiffs, justices, mayors, cellarers, carriers, the burgomasters, aldermen, and councils in towns, and all other Our subjects in general, strictly to forbid the sale and purchase and use of tobacco everywhere, under penalty of incurring Our high displeasure and punishment, together with the confiscation of the tobacco and the pipes.
>
> FERDINAND

This edict was communicated by the town council to

[1] August Boerner, *Kölner Tabakhandel und Tabakgewerbe, 1628 bis 1910*, p. 11 (Essen on the Ruhr, 1912).

the citizens of Cologne, with the threat of a fine of fifty gulden, or imprisonment, and severer penalties in case of a repetition of the offence. We also find the Prince of Jülich-Berg consulting with his town councillors as to the best way of abolishing the smoking of pipes in view of the danger of fire and other evils resulting from it.

It was about this time that Johann Michael Moscherosch published his *Wunderliche und wahrhaftige Gesichte Philanders von Sittewald*. The author, who had lived through the stormy times of the Thirty Years War, and been the victim of every kind of misfortune and spoliation, depicts the miserable condition of that mad time, and speaks in most unfavourable terms of 'the poisonous weed,' the fumes of which he specially detested. In a description of the Court of Lucifer he introduces a devil who is perpetually blowing smoke from mouth and nostrils simultaneously:

"What ails thee, fiend?" I asked, and was told it was the tobacco fiend, at which I wondered not a little. In sooth I had long supposed there must be a fiend of some sort urging the people on to smoke tobacco, but now that I had seen him with my own eyes I was assured it was so. "Thus," said the fiend, "do I take revenge in full upon the Spaniards for all their cruelty to the Indians; since by acquainting their conquerors with the use of tobacco, I have done them greater injury than even the King of Spain, through his agents Columbus, Pizarro, Cortez, and Almagro, ever did his victims; for it is both more honourable and more natural to die by a pike-thrust or a cannon-ball than from the ignoble effects of poisonous tobacco."

They who smoke tobacco can be compared only to men possessed, who are in need of exorcizing. While their throats belch forth the stinking, poisonous fumes, they remain none the less thralls to the tobacco fiend to whom they cling with an idolatrous devotion, exalting him as their god above all others, and striving to entice all they meet to imitate their folly. One thing at least it teaches them, the better to endure the reek of hell.

Once as I watched certain men drinking their tobacco, the Lord spake to me, His unworthy creature: "O man! Seest thou how the Abomination of Desolation lies hidden in the hearts of mortals, and causes them to worship it as a god, by means of this perpetual and accursed sniffing up of tobacco? Yea, all men, without discrimination, have now, through the cunning wiles of the Devil, acquired this habit and do adore and worship this noisome idol."

Yet consider well, beloved mortals, brothers and sisters in your madness, how the Devil hath deceived you! For even as they who grow fat and fleshy through much gluttony do clearly show that their god is their belly, so you, who use the filthy weed, do fill yourselves with the spirit of fire, and belch forth from your mouths the smoke of perdition.

Although it was generally allowed that the plant had many virtues—for instance, it was known to have proved a safeguard against infection during the Great Plague in London—Moscherosch (*alias* Philander of Sittewald) was careful to place the tobacco plant under the protection of a special devil in hell, in which connexion he tells the following agreeable story.

In my young days when I was a soldier, my host, who hated tobacco, asked me if I knew why soldiers, more than others, were addicted to tobacco. I replied it was because they had to drink such a quantity of water; but he said "No! they do it in order to accustom themselves gradually to fire, smoke, and stench, so that when at last they go down to hell, where they are compelled to drink pitch and sulphur, it may not go so hard with them." . . . Thereby they always stink so horribly—like a smouldering heap of ruins—that no-one can bear to be in their company. . . . It is a common saying that if a man is not a lusty smoker he is no true soldier, indeed is hardly a man at all.

Fig. 29. BROADSHEET IN PRAISE OF TOBACCO

Fig. 30. Smoking as the Favourite Amusement of the
Dutch, about 1650

In the years immediately after the Thirty Years War every effort was made to stop smoking in Germany. Three of the Electorates began by proclaiming universal prohibition, and Bavaria followed suit on August 22, 1652. The distinguished and enlightened Elector Max I, who was just dead, had bequeathed to his fifteen-year-old son, or rather to the regency, a detailed programme in which everything was to go on exactly as in his own lifetime; this included various provisions for the speediest possible healing of the grievous wounds the country had suffered in the Thirty Years War, and also an entirely new edict [1] forbidding smoking. As the Electress, Maria Anna, informed the nation in a general edict, " tobacco-drinking was strictly forbidden to the peasants and other common people, and due penalties for each offence would be exacted from the transgressor."

When Max's son, Ferdinand Maria, took over the government he proceeded to carry out his father's instructions to the full, though the Electress's prohibition of tobacco seems to have made little impression on the nation, smoking going on just the same in spite of it. The new Elector was therefore moved to issue a fresh proclamation : "He was greatly pained," he said,

> to hear that the successive orders respecting the use of tobacco had been very carelessly observed, and in some cases criminally disregarded. He understood that on the occasion of the annual fairs tobacco in large quantities had been brought into Bavaria by merchants and tradesmen from Augsburg, Nuremberg, and other places, and publicly exposed for sale. For the future he

[1] The original edict (August 22, 1652) has been lost, but its contents are included in the general edict of July 9, 1853, to be found in the Munich Archives. See J. Micheler, *Das Tabakwesen in Bayern*, pp. 5 ff. (Stuttgart, 1887).

commanded that tobacco should be obtainable only in the towns, from apothecaries and druggists, on a doctor's prescription. Anyone disobeying these orders would be prosecuted.

In the Electorate of Saxony also about this time the authorities began to manifest a violent dislike to the smoking habit; in the town of Bautzen, for instance, in 1651, the worthy councillors were seized with such a detestation of it that they resolved to deal with it as severely as possible. Accordingly, on April 18 of that year the burgomaster and corporation issued an edict with the object of checking the abuses and disorders arising from tobacco-smoking, which had crept in as a result of the unhappy war. Those people who assembled in the smoking taverns inhaling "all the smell and reek, amid every kind of discomfort, misery, and horror at the same time," were bidden to beware of the evil thing; in any case it could do them no good, for had not their forefathers enjoyed good health and lived to a ripe old age in happy ignorance of this extravagant habit? Therefore the corporation decreed that all citizens found smoking or snuff-taking, whether in taverns or in their own homes, should be liable to a fine of five thalers, the same penalty to be enforced on all landlords who should offer tobacco to their customers, or bring them fire to light their pipes.

This particular edict was followed on May 19, 1653, by a general interdiction for the whole of Saxony. In this proclamation, issued by the Elector Johann Georg, we read that

Whereas the colonel of the fortress had given strict orders to his soldiers, as likewise the burgomaster to his citizens, that one and all should abstain from "the deadly tobacco habit," and whereas such orders had been so little regarded that on April 25, through the carelessness of certain smokers, a fire had broken out in the cellar of the town hall of Dresden, be it known to all that for the future not only is smoking absolutely forbidden to soldiers and civilians alike, both in beer-houses and cellars, but tobacco must no longer be sold except in apothecaries' shops, as ordered by a doctor's prescription.

These official enactments were seconded by certain high ecclesiastics and university professors in a manifesto in which we read:

It is both godless and unseemly that the mouth of man, which is the means of entrance and exit for the immortal soul, that mouth which is intended to breathe in the fresh air and to utter the praises of the Most High, should be defiled by the indrawing and expelling of tobacco smoke.[1]

Similar opinions are to be found in an oration delivered in 1653 by one Tappius, Professor of Medicine in the University of Helmstedt, *De tabaco ejusque hodierno abusu*. As the author says:

In every district, town or house, at the present day, you will find people, without distinction of age or sex, swallowing this mixture of dry and wet which they call smoke, and staggering about like men drunk with wine.

"Blood and brain," he thunders on,

become heated and dried up—the whole head is turned into a noxious furnace—it is fatal to all genius, and when taken with beer and wine the effects are doubly pernicious. Tobacco, in short, is one of Satan's crafty devices to dull the finest intellects, which might otherwise work against him; as is well known, it is the arch-deceiver's practice to turn the most wholesome remedies to base abuse.

[1] H. Pilz, *Über den Tabak und das Rauchen*, p. 148 (Leipzig, 1899).

Tappius concludes with some anatomical illustrations showing the sad effects of tobacco on the smoker's brain.[1]

Attempts at prohibition now spread rapidly throughout the country. In 1656 the people of Württemberg were forbidden, "because of the risk of fire," to sell, buy, or use tobacco, except for medicinal purposes. In Cologne—destined later to become one of the chief centres of the tobacco trade—by 1659 the scandal of smoking, according to the town council, had so increased that

> many citizens do thereby weaken their powers both of mind and body, at the same time exposing themselves and others to the risk of dangerous and dreadful diseases.

This edict, however, which was far vaguer than the one previously quoted, and which made no mention of penalties for the offenders, attracted little attention, and finally fell into oblivion—the more naturally as the sale, cultivation, and preparation of tobacco (tobacco-spinning, as it was called) were gradually developing into an ever-increasing source of wealth for the town and its inhabitants.

Meanwhile, in the very districts where smoking was prohibited, the custom had attained to extraordinary popularity in spite of all opposition. In Bohemia, for instance, in 1662 a general proclamation complained that, in defiance of all attempts to repress it, tobacco was now smoked by all—in taverns, in cottages, and even in the public streets. "The common people," it is stated,

> are so given up to the abuse that they imagine they cannot live without several pipes of tobacco a day—thus squandering in these necessitous times the pennies that they need for their daily bread.

[1] J. Tappius, *Oratio de tabaco ejusque hodierno abusu* (Helmstedt, 1653).

Fig. 31. THE GERMAN TOBACCO-DRINKER

116

Fig. 32. DUTCH SMOKING TAVERN IN THE SEVENTEENTH CENTURY

SMOKING IN CENTRAL EUROPE

In Nuremberg, in 1661, we find a certain Johann Lassenius complaining bitterly in his *Adeligen Tischreden* of the way in which the men of his day

> do chew and tipple their tobacco, that a man will even drink himself silly, since it dries up all the moisture of the brain which cannot live without it. Many a one becomes so used to the stuff that he cannot be parted from it neither day nor night.

There were some who would smoke forty, fifty, and even more pipes a day—truly a " right bestial habit, to hug to oneself a thing so contrary to nature, and so unnecessary."

> It is deplorable to see how many a man who has fallen a victim to this frivolous habit will smoke away his brain, his memory, his wits—is not such a man to be pitied, who can no longer control his natural instincts and faculties? For my part I could wish that this thing had never been heard of in Germany, a country which has borne itself so manfully for many hundreds of years before the introduction of tobacco and could most probably get on well enough without it in the future. It is degrading to have to mix with the smoking gang—they stink just like pigs and goats. . . . For my part I am determined to have nothing more to do with them.

Nevertheless, tobacco had its admirers—H. Bernstein of Erfurt, for instance, who in 1664 published a short work on its virtues. He and others were highly indignant when certain dignitaries of the Church decreed that in the reports of diocesan visitations, which at that period were made at frequent intervals, individuals who were found to be addicted to smoking should be mentioned by name. Thus in a report, in 1662, on a certain Christel Ledermann, he is described as a drunkard and a roysterer, and so strongly addicted to tobacco that on Easter Day, when he presented himself at the altar, he stank so of tobacco that the parson could scarcely bear it.[1] In other reports we read bitter complaints from the clergy that they could hardly breathe in church because the peasants reeked so of tobacco.

In that age of persecution and prohibition very few men of letters ventured to come forward in defence of smoking. Mention must be made, however, of Bartolomäus Schimper, who in the *Breslau Calendar* for 1660 wrote as follows :

> In the opinion of certain doctors and physicians, tobacco, when rightly used, is both wholesome and beneficial; applied externally it heals sores and wounds, taken internally it is very good for the brain; if the head be congested by a cold phlegmatic humour, a few whiffs of the best tobacco, mixed with aniseed and marjoram, will thoroughly clear all the passages, for the brain contracts and shrinks together just like a sponge when moisture is squeezed out of it.

At the same time the author does not omit to censure the glutton who smokes to excess.

On the whole, however, the literature of this reactionary period is on the side of the prohibitionists. The most violent antagonist of the new habit was Jakob Balde—a Jesuit, and a man of world-wide celebrity in his day; in his satirical indictment of tobacco, *Die truckene Trunkenheit* (*Drunk without Drinking*), the author, who is prodigal of ' splendid conceits ' and ' flowers of eloquence,' thunders against " the smoking fellows of Northern Germany who live only to smoke and who cannot live without it." For his part he cannot under-

[1] Report of the Baden-Durlach Consistory, in the Carlsruhe local archives. See Tiedemann, *Geschichte des Tabacs*, p. 167.

stand how people can throw away good money on such folly.

So soon as a ship with tobacco from overseas comes into port—they can scarce wait till the stinking cargo is unloaded—they take the first boat they can find, and off they go to the vessel. Then a box must be opened and a sample of tobacco cut off from the roll, that they may taste the nasty stuff, into which they stick their teeth as greedily as if it were the daintiest of morsels. If they find it to their liking, then they are all athirst to enjoy it, and quite beside themselves with happiness. After some gaping they begin to bargain and inquire the price; ducats or golden guineas, 'tis all one to them—they grudge no expense for an article like this : what is the good of money, they say, if it is to lie idle in the purse? Money, we know, is more precious than virtue, but unto them tobacco is dearer still.

Balde goes on to say that his countrymen are so infatuated that they not only smoke tobacco, but actually sniff it up.

" Judge for yourselves," exclaims our Jesuit,

which of the two kinds are the greater fools ! True, the latter seem in a sort to manage their stinking business more politely, in that they refrain from annoying other people's noses with their smoke, preferring to defile their own with the filthy dust.

The worthy Father then proceeds to invoke the powers of Hell to punish all who smoke tobacco.

"What difference is there," he asks,

between a smoker and a suicide, except that the one takes longer to kill himself than the other? Because of this perpetual smoking, the pure oil of the lamp of life dries up and disappears, and the fair flame of life itself flickers out and goes out all because of this barbarous habit.

The justification for Balde's attack on the widespread but dubious reputation of tobacco was, he alleged, the fact that, in spite of the number of its victims, so many men sympathized with his own detestation of it and with the object of his appeal. He declared that there were many who preferred smoking to all the pleasures of the table; he called the smoking taverns (*tabagies*) " schools of slavery," or schools for those who were desirous of learning the true nature of madness; he made fun of " the elaborate silliness " of those who frequented them, and " the grotesque depravity of those who could thus outrage nature."

He was no less violent against the snuff-takers, the worshippers of tobacco dust, which, indeed, like death itself, reduces mortals to dust; finally he scourges those women who indulge in this heathenish passion, " to the harm of their reputation, their fortune, their figures, and their offspring."

But however the clergy might protest against smoking this did not prevent the custom from finding numerous followers in their own ranks, and the ecclesiastical hierarchy was torn by frequent disputes on this question. Small wonder then if, in these circumstances, the new custom soon spread to the neighbouring countries; authorities might thunder as they liked, but their subjects came ever more and more under the spell of the novel enjoyment.

CHAPTER VI

PROGRESS OF SMOKING IN SOUTHERN AND EASTERN EUROPE, AND IN THE ORIENT

SLOWLY but surely the habit found its way into Switzerland. As early as 1616 we read of herbs that had hitherto been regarded solely as medicinal being used for smoking and snuffing up through the nose, though for some time this was done only by a few individuals and in strict moderation, as we see from a book published in Zürich, *Concerning Nicotiana, the Healing Herb*.[1] The author, while praising its manifold virtues, records with amazement that he had seen Englishmen ' drink ' tobacco for six or seven hours together without losing consciousness.

Following the introduction of leaf tobacco there came from Germany 'tobacco-makers,' as they were called, who 'span' the leaf, and pedlars who dealt in it. In every Swiss town, however, the authorities regarded the newfangled custom with grave misgivings. In 1643 one of these merchants who came from Lorraine was not allowed to settle in Basle, on the ground that " the town had no use for one of his trade." The following years brought many local prohibitions, and in 1652 came a general order that made smoking a penal offence for all, with a fine of two florins.

After the Peace of Westphalia the independence of

---

[1] J. Ziegler, *Tabac, von dem gar heilsamen Wundtkraut Nicotiana . . .* (Zürich, 1616).

[121]

Switzerland, which had actually existed since 1499, was formally proclaimed, and henceforth the various cantonal governments assumed greater prominence. In accordance with the strict moral code introduced by Calvin at the Reformation, the different governments were in the habit of issuing frequent official reprimands in which the sins of the inhabitants were brought to light and severely censured. One of these, dated September 9, 1656, complains bitterly of the growing iniquities of the people— cursing and swearing; staying away from church; the extravagant and frivolous ways of many young persons, even those of good family, who rose late and spent the rest of the day in eating, drinking, and gambling; the universal spread of 'tobacco-drinking' even among females, resulting in serious financial loss to the country—all these things aroused the indignation of the authorities.

Yet, in spite of their repeated admonitions, they were forced to recognize as time went on that the unnecessary custom of tobacco-drinking was steadily gaining ground. From many of the counties—Kyburg, for instance—came complaints that

> the abuse of tobacco had become so general that lads of twelve might be seen pipe in hand even in farm buildings, which were thereby exposed to serious risk of fire. Moreover, the rage for this commodity, of which our ancestors had no knowledge, contributed not a little to the present scarcity of money which was steadily on the increase; and especially was it to be noted that young people, who were by nature hot-blooded, were by this habit driven to reckless excess and became drunken and dissipated.

From the clergy also came many complaints of the behaviour of the people, among whom smoking, snuff-taking, and chewing of tobacco had become so common even in the streets and on the way to church, that the stench of it even penetrated into the sacred buildings.[1]

From all quarters came insistent demands to increase the severity of the present laws, which the great majority of smokers openly defied. One edict followed close upon another: thus in Zürich, in 1667, the burgomaster and town council, in their solicitude for the welfare of the citizens, endeavoured by solemn warnings and admonitions to reform "all dissolute and godless wastrels, especially those who were addicted to the pernicious habits of smoking and snuff-taking." Nor did the proclamation stop at sharp reproof; the "lazy, good-for-nothing crew" were warned that if they persisted in their impious course no innkeeper would be allowed to supply them with either meat or drink; they would be set to work at the ramparts, and, on repetition of the offence, would be ignominiously expelled from the city and the country, beaten with rods, branded, or, should they prove incorrigible, sentenced to perpetual banishment, "in order to rid ourselves and our people of any further annoyance."[2]

As these conflicts spread, and the canton of Berne became involved, the Swiss National Assembly took the matter in hand. It was a time of great excitement, caused by a new and severe edict issued by the authorities at Zürich against the "epidemic of smoking," which, in spite of all prohibitions, was constantly spreading. This practice not being necessary to existence, but rather

[1] Synodal Gravamina, May 9, 1616 (Zürich State Archives).
[2] Edict of the town of Zürich, June 3, 1667 (Zürich State Archives).

destructive to health, besides liable to cause fires, must be put a stop to; consequently a fine of fifteen livres would be imposed for each offence.

In the diet held in November 1670 it was plain that the passing of the prohibition was a matter of general doubt. "Although the injurious habit of smoking," we read in the decree,

> has been everywhere prohibited by order, we recognize that these orders have been met by a spirit of opposition which it is not easy to suppress. Nevertheless we have once more resolved not to recede from our position.

The town of Basle put up a special fight. Being, from its position, a clearing-house for the tobacco trade, it was already fully alive to the great financial advantages involved; the civic authorities, while admitting that "the too general habit of smoking among the common people was a great scandal," refused nevertheless to interfere with the sale and transport of tobacco.

In 1671 the Swiss delegates were obliged to report that the evil custom still flourished all over the country, in spite of all the edicts. Nevertheless they adhered to their policy of prohibition. On February 24, 1671, another sharp order was issued from Berne, where the feeling against tobacco was particularly strong, and later in the same year the cantons of Berne, Lucerne, Unterwalden, Fribourg, and Soleure decided to form a coalition to stamp out the 'iniquity.' This, however, proved to be just as ineffectual as all previous attempts. Still the Parliament stood firm for universal prohibition, in spite of an "urgent supplication" issued by the trade against all these repressive measures. Individual reports on the abuse of the herb still kept coming in; the county of Kyburg, in particular, raised its voice in protest, in 1674. "At the same time, worshipful sirs," wrote the author of the document,

> I cannot and ought not to refrain from solemnly protesting when I see how old and young, male and female, the poor even more than the rich, abuse this herb which was sent by God as a healing boon to mortals, and by snuffing, drinking, and chewing it, pervert it to the destruction of their health and the ruin of countless households.

This complaint, it appears, was written at the urgent request of all the clergy, magistrates, judges, and officials of Kyburg.[1]

In the Toggenburg proclamation we are told that the habit of smoking had grown to such an extent that servants, and even wives and daughters, used tobacco to a scandalous degree, to say nothing of the danger of fire, and that it was high time to take proceedings against such a useless and pernicious abuse. In the same strain Berne, the arch-enemy, issued a further and far stricter order, absolutely forbidding the practice of smoking to all men, without discrimination of rank or calling. They even set up a sort of High Court of Inquiry, a 'Tobacco Chamber,' consisting of seven councillors, who were to see that prohibition was strictly enforced. But even this proved equally futile. Such was the disagreement in Switzerland on the question 'to smoke or not to smoke' that no prohibition was able to check the spread of smoking, which had already extended beyond the southern and eastern boundaries.

[1] Report on the abuse of tobacco in the county of Kyburg, 1674 (Zürich State Archives).

After the Thirty Years War smoking spread eastward through the patrimonial dominions of the house of Habsburg in Austria. The first reports of this development belong to the year 1650, but in Bohemia, the chief seat of the war, the introduction and spread of tobacco can be traced to a slightly earlier date.

On the other hand, opposition and reaction set in much sooner in the Emperor's dominions than elsewhere. Scarce had the habit gained a footing after the Peace of Westphalia when the governments of most of the Imperial dominions felt called upon to protest, with threats of prohibition and penalties, against " the newly introduced vice of tobacco-drinking." [1] In Moravia the use of tobacco was forbidden as early as 1652 by a decree of the Diet, just at the time when the cultivation of the plant was introduced into Austria, particularly Neumarkt, by the Bavarian immigrant Hans Hertinger, and had spread thence over Upper Austria, Styria, and Carinthia. The time when it was grown merely in pleasure-grounds and botanical gardens was over; in accordance with a general demand large quantities had been imported into Germany, where it was extensively cultivated. The clerical authorities in Austria saw with disapproval that the subjects of the ecclesiastical state were beginning to smoke; worse still, in 1656, in the course of a diocesan visitation, it was discovered that even the priests had taken to the habit—a thing which the Prince Archbishop denounced as an offence against decency and morals. In the arch-

[1] Dr F. Wieser, *Über die Produktion, den Konsum und die Besteuerung des Tabaks im Kronlande Salzburg von 1657 bis zur Einführung des Tabakgefälles im Jahre 1817*, in *Fachliche Mitteilungen der österreichischen Tabakregie*, 8th year, Part I, March 1908.

bishopric of Salzburg the new custom was less popular, apparently because of the risk of fire resulting therefrom. On October 23, 1657, the Archbishop issued the following decree :

> Whereas the harmful and immoderate habit of smoking in this neighbourhood, as also in our worshipful diocese, has undoubtedly been the cause of many serious conflagrations, to say nothing of other damage and annoyance, with a view to the suppression of this evil we do hereby command that the use of tobacco be universally forbidden under pain of severe and certain punishment.

This order was never revoked, though later, owing to the changed ideas of the times, it was forgotten, and fell into desuetude. It is certain that these numerous prohibitions—for in Austria tobacco, from the very beginning, came under the laws which forbade the importation of all raw products from foreign countries—so far from checking the smoking habit, actually served as a fresh incentive, as is usually the case with 'forbidden fruit.' Thus we find the custom gradually spreading from Bohemia to Dalmatia—to Vienna itself—and so over the borders into Hungary.

Meanwhile the tobacco plant, which had reached Italy not long after its introduction into Europe, had penetrated into every part of the Peninsula. Spanish seamen had brought it to Naples and Sicily (which were still under the rule of Spanish viceroys); Portuguese and English sailors to the ports of Genoa, Pisa, Spezia, and Venice ; travellers from Germany and Switzerland to Lombardy. Exalted personages, like Cardinal Crescenzio, who had learned to smoke on their travels, brought the habit home with them, and taught it to the nobles and clergy at the minor Courts of Italy, as well as to those who made up the gorgeous retinue of his Holiness the Pope. Before the year 1615 smoking, in any form, was but little known among the masses in Italy, but in the next ten years it had spread like wildfire over all the land. At that time the nobles and the clergy set the fashion for all—their rule was absolute, what they did must be right, and the people followed them. That these two classes should be the first to adopt the new custom was only natural, for the new 'herb' cost much money, and the home production could not as yet be made to pay.

Thanks to the example of the sailors, and also of the Spaniards—all enthusiastic smokers—who occupied such a large part of Italy at this time, smoking now began to make considerable progress in that country, all the more because, in spite of the opposition of the *literati*, the attitude of the authorities was not so hostile as in Germany; indeed, they were concerned rather with the profits which they saw might be made by taxing tobacco, and which soon began actually to exceed their highest expectations. In the Venetian Republic in 1626 a tax of twelve *soldi* was levied on every pound of imported tobacco, and the example thus set was speedily followed by Mantua, Piedmont, and other parts.

Meanwhile the clergy both in Spain and Italy became so addicted to smoking, and later to snuff-taking, that they went even so far as to gratify their longing during the celebration of Mass. This naturally roused the indignation of their non-smoking brothers as well as the laity, and led to drastic action on the part of certain of

Fig. 33. Title and Frontispiece to J. Balde's Satire on the
Abuse of Tobacco, 1658

VRBANVS/VIII·   BARBERINVS
FLORENTINVS   PONTIFEX MAX·
CREATVS DIE VI·AV·   GVSTI AN·MDCXXIII·
Obijt die 29   *Iulij 1644·*

Fig. 34. POPE URBAN VIII (1623–44) (MAFFEO BARBERINI)

the bishops. Seville was a notable example; here the Cathedral Chapter seemed powerless to check the evil: chaplain, priest, and deacon either smoked or took snuff during Mass, with no regard for the sanctity of their office, defiling the sanctuary, the altar, and all other parts of the church by the tobacco they dropped, as well as by their spittle, thus setting an example which the congregation were not slow to imitate. As neither warnings nor punishments availed, the Chapter of the diocese of Seville decided at last to appeal to Pope Urban VIII to put a stop to these scandalous practices. The result was the Bull *Ad futuram rei memoriam*, given at Rome and sealed with the Fisherman's Ring, January 30, 1642.

Whereas the churches are houses of prayer consecrated to the service of God, and therefore in every way to be considered holy, We to whom the care of all the churches in the world has been entrusted are bound to see that all unseemly and profane behaviour be excluded from them; and whereas information has lately reached Us from the Dean and Chapter of the metropolitan church in Sevilla that in those parts the use of the herb commonly called tobacco has gained so strong a hold on persons of both sexes, yea, even priests and clerics, that—We blush to state—during the actual celebration of Holy Mass, they do not shrink from taking tobacco through the mouth or nostrils, thus soiling the altar linen and infecting the churches with its noxious fumes, sacrilegiously and to the great scandal of the pious . . . it therefore behoves Us, in order to purge our churches of this shameless abuse, to prohibit and interdict all persons of either sex, clergy or laity, collectively and individually, from using tobacco or snuff in any form whatever in the churches of the said diocese of Sevilla, their vestibules, vestries, or immediate surroundings; and all persons thus offending shall be punished by immediate excommunication, *ipso facto*, without further ado, in accordance with the terms of the present interdict.

In spite of the severity of this enactment, a special clause was inserted by which, almost as a matter of course, certain high personages were exempted and could be "dispensed at discretion." Through the loophole thus left the Bull eventually became more or less ineffective, though the immediate result was the enforcement of stricter discipline not only in the churches in the diocese of Seville, but throughout the country. Pope Urban VIII, who insisted on the sumptuous and artistic adornment of all sacred buildings in accordance with the sublime purpose for which they were intended, was especially indignant at the idea of their pollution. It was he who had employed Bernini to furnish the magnificent embellishments of St Peter's in Rome, and had erected the bronze *baldachino* and the four spiral columns on the high altar, at which none but the Holy Father has the right to say Mass. His successor, Innocent X, who also enriched St Peter's with a splendid pavement and pillars of precious marble, soon had his attention drawn to the fact that in various places, not only in Spain, the sanctuaries were filled with tobacco smoke, and the faithful would carry their irreverence so far as to defile the floor of the church by spitting on it. The result was that his Holiness found it necessary to issue a Bull on the same lines as that of Urban VIII; it bears the date January 8, 1650, and reads as follows:

> We have been greatly pained to learn that there are certain persons, clergy as well as laity, so unmindful of the reverence due to consecrated places that they do not hesitate to smoke or snuff up the herb commonly known as tobacco even in the church of the Prince of the Apostles, in the city to which the faithful of every

nation in the world are wont to resort from motives of devotion, thereby causing deep distress to all pious souls.[1]

In order to stamp out this abuse in the said churches the Pope, by virtue of his Apostolic dignity, goes on to forbid and interdict the use of tobacco in any form in St Peter's Church, its choir, chapels, nave, vestries, and porticoes, under penalty of instant excommunication, *eo ipso*, without further order.

But this Bull also provided for special exceptions in the case of Seville, and in the concluding paragraph we find a hint that little hope was entertained of any strict compliance with its conditions: " Concessions must be made in the general administration of justice similar to those enjoined in the case of the present interdiction."

A few years later, in 1655, a general permission to sell tobacco as well as brandy was granted to a contractor for a substantial payment, and henceforth similar transactions formed one of the most considerable sources of revenue for the Papal States. The statement of a superficial historian, which has been persistently copied by countless writers up to the present day, to the effect that a prohibition was promulgated affecting all Christians, including those outside the pale of the Church, is without foundation. It was probably invented to account for the delightful anecdote of the non-smoking Pope who excommunicated all smokers, and his successor who smoked and consequently, for obvious reasons, revoked the edict. The truth is that the use of tobacco was never actually forbidden to Christianity at large, nor even in the churches in

[1] *Collectio bullarum sacrosanctæ Basilicæ Vaticanæ*, vol. iii, p. 265 (Rome, 1752).

Rome, with the exception of St Peter's. Yet how necessary such restrictions were is evident from an incident which had occurred somewhat earlier at Capocelere, in the Kingdom of Naples, and which roused the faithful to the highest pitch of indignation.[1] One Sunday a priest who was celebrating Mass took a pinch of snuff just after receiving Holy Communion ; the fit of sneezing that ensued caused him to vomit, and throw up the Blessed Sacrament on to the altar in sight of the congregation. This shows that snuff-taking had already taken a strong hold in Italy, where numbers had become enslaved to the habit.

Soon after the publication of these two Bulls certain clerics, in their zeal and devotion to the sacred edifices, proceeded to interpret them as meaning that any prohibition affecting the first church in Christendom must naturally apply to all other churches, while Father Diana, the theologian, and Pascializo, the canonist, went so far as to assert that smoking in church must, in accordance with the aforesaid Bulls, be regarded as a deadly sin. This interpretation, involving as it did such large numbers of the clergy, naturally raised a storm of protest, which was allayed only by the official pronouncement of Cardinal de Lugo that smoking in church was not a deadly sin, but that " one ought not to do it." Such a weak and half-hearted statement looked very like surrender, while, on the other hand, little good was done by the manifesto of certain clerical fanatics to the effect that tobacco was simply an invention of the Devil, who had entered into a pact with the dusky savages in America to deliver the souls of the white men into his hand through its agency.

[1] A. Vitagliani, *De abusu tabaci* (Rome, 1650).

In the higher ecclesiastical circles the feeling was one of astonishment at the large proportion of priests who smoked or took snuff immediately before or even during the Liturgy. After the issue of the Papal Bull opinion was divided as to whether every individual bishop had the right to take restrictive measures against the alarming growth of this new evil. When it was asked why the custom was beginning to spread among the clergy the reason alleged was that they found it a safeguard for the chastity to which they were vowed; smoking expelled the humours from the brain and body, with the result that smokers were less liable than others to the temptations of the flesh. This was the answer given to a certain doctor [1] by Fra Giuseppe da Convertino, a Franciscan, who asserted that he spoke from experience —those ecclesiastics who smoked or took snuff usually found it easier to overcome such temptations than those who were ignorant of the habit. From this certain doctors—*e.g.*, Neander—argued that the aged should not use tobacco, since they were by nature dried up and so had no need of it.

Among the many bishops of that time who were firm opponents of both smoking and snuff-taking we may mention Bishop Sarnelli. Tobacco, according to him, was just a filthy weed that polluted both mouth and nostrils.

> Although it is permissible for a man to use it in case of necessity, it is certainly not decent to do so in all places and in general company; consider, for instance, that the act of snuff-taking is apt to result in so violent a sneeze that the hearer is moved to invoke the help of heaven!

[1] A. Vitagliani, *De abusu tabaci*, p. 70.

Here we see the origin of the custom, which has survived to the present day, of saying "Good health!" when anyone sneezes.[1]

"What a shameful spectacle," exclaimed an ecclesiastical writer of the time, Tesauro by name, in his *Moral Philosophy*,

> to see a man stick a piece of broken horn in his mouth, plugged with that smouldering sooty stuff the reek of which he first draws down his gullet and then puffs out through his nose, like the horses of Diomedes, or the bulls of Jason!

The attitude of the Italian men of letters of the time toward smoking was decidedly adverse; they offered little opposition to its moderate employment as a medicine, reserving their thunder for those who smoked to excess. The titles of some of their works are sufficient indication of the author's opinion—*e.g.*, Santorini's *Polvere schernito ovvero invettiva contro il tabacco* (*The Accursed Weed: an Indictment of Tobacco*) (Florence, 1654). It was only toward the end of the seventeenth century that Italy fell into line with the rest of Europe in accepting the change of attitude toward smoking as originated by the authorities and men of learning.

Meanwhile the habit had made prodigious strides. Ships from Holland and Spain, Venetian galleons, and the English merchant vessels, which had brought the first coffee to Constantinople about the middle of the sixteenth century, were responsible later for the introduction of the smoking habit, which speedily became popular. The Turkish Empire had already entered upon that decline

[1] Bishop Sarnelli in his ecclesiastical letters. See Moroni's *Dizionario*, vol. lxxii, fl. 176-179.

which began with the death of Suleiman II (the Magnificent), the victor of Mohács. He was succeeded in 1603 by Sultan Ahmed I, in whose reign the secret influence of the harem and the eunuchs, the "Guardians of the Gate of Happiness," assumed even greater prominence. With the general spread of smoking in Turkey the country was soon divided into two opposing camps.

The *Mufti* (priests) maintained that it was contrary to the teaching of the Koran, and in consequence it was strictly forbidden in Ahmed's reign. Some accounts, not too well authenticated, tell us that those who were detected in the act had a pipe-stem thrust through the nose, and were paraded on donkeys through the streets of Constantinople as an awful warning to the others. Such cases, however, were rare, and the penalties for disobedience were in any case not so severe at that time as they were later, in the reign of Ahmed's son, Murad the Cruel. Succeeding to the crown as a boy of fourteen, Murad soon showed himself to be the most forceful but at the same time the most bloodthirsty tyrant the Ottoman Empire has ever known.

At that time the followers of the Prophet, to whom wine was forbidden, had become so attached to the stimulating and soothing effects of coffee and tobacco as to find them indispensable to existence; while the Turkish poets, in defiance of the Koran, were in the habit of praising coffee, tobacco, opium, and wine too, as the 'four elements' of the world of pleasure, the four cushions of the divan of delight. The scholars of the new age, however, wavered in their description of the 'four elements' —sometimes they were the "supports of the temple of

luxury," at others the "agents of the Devil." Sultan
Murad, who punished wine-drinking with death, though
he himself drank to excess, could find no enjoyment in
smoking. This young ruler, with big scowling eyes and
a pale face framed in coal-black hair, had many difficulties to encounter at the beginning of his reign. A
disorderly people, an army without discipline, janissaries
in open mutiny, an empty treasury—such was the heritage
to which he succeeded. With these problems he proceeded to grapple with a brutal severity, which he extended
further to all such things as personally displeased him,
among which was the habit of smoking as practised in
the coffee-houses and smoking taverns of his capital. The
Sultan had already dealt severely with isolated cases when
on August 7, 1633, an appalling conflagration, which
laid half Constantinople in ruins, led to a ruthless and
persistent campaign against smoking. The birth of the
Sultan's first son—after six disappointments in the form
of daughters—was being celebrated with general rejoicing,
including the usual illuminations and fireworks, when a
ship at anchor in the harbour caught fire; the flames
spread with amazing rapidity to the town itself, until
houses, palaces, mosques, and barracks were all ablaze
in one gigantic conflagration. In two quarters of the
town only two houses were left undamaged, while the
number of wooden buildings burned to the ground was
over 20,000. The result was a great outburst of indignation among the people against the Sultan and his
careless officials, whom they held responsible for the whole
catastrophe. The malcontents would meet in the coffee-
houses and smoke their pipes while they discussed the un-

happy condition of the realm—a fact of which the Sultan, who was in the habit of going disguised, like Haroun al-Raschid, among his people, took advantage. While visiting certain tobacco-houses he overheard several vigorous denunciations of his own misgovernment, with the result that, under the pretext that the outbreak was caused by smokers, he gave orders that all places where people met to smoke tobacco should be razed to the ground, as being, in his opinion, mere hotbeds of rebellion.

The next step was an edict forbidding the use of tobacco under penalty of death. Though anonymous epigrams were circulated among the populace imploring the Sultan to banish the sighs of an oppressed people rather than the fumes of tobacco, his orders were carried out by his agents with blind and slavish obedience; before long the tobacco-smoker came to be dealt with as severely as a criminal of the lowest class. The Sultan continued his secret visits by night to the various resorts in the town, and anyone caught smoking over his coffee was marked for death; the next morning his corpse would be found in front of the house in which he had been detected, a gory witness to the tyrant's wrath.

The Sultan's lust for slaughter once excited, it gradually assumed a sadistic character, quite independent of his hatred of tobacco. Nor did he fail to profit by it at the same time, since the estate of the victims passed in every case into the Imperial coffers; indeed, countless numbers of those condemned to death on a charge of smoking were actually the victims of the Sultan's avarice. "This is my high behest, which if thou failest to fulfil, thy head shall be cut off!"—such was the invariable formula employed by Murad, who was no respecter of persons. Even French interpreters were impaled and hanged, while in the case of certain ambassadors from Persia he had their noses and ears cut off and sent the wretched victims away with their dispatches nailed to the gaping wounds thus made. Having given his own physician a fatal dose of opium, he made him sit down with him to a game of chess, in order the better to watch and enjoy the sight of his struggle with death. Whenever the Sultan went on his travels or on a military expedition his halting-places were always distinguished by a terrible increase in the number of executions. Even on the battlefield he was fond of surprising men in the act of smoking, when he would punish them by beheading, hanging, quartering, or crushing their hands and feet and leaving them helpless between the lines. The climax of his barbarities was reached during the campaign against Persia: he had a thousand prisoners drawn up in front of his tent, each of them accompanied by an executioner; at the instant that the Sultan appeared at the entrance the whole thousand were simultaneously put to death. The atrocious excesses of this blustering tyrant created such an atmosphere of terror among his immediate entourage that they received his every word and gesture as if they were the decrees of fate. In his presence all men trembled and were silent, and all vied with one another in instantly carrying out his savage orders.

Nevertheless, in spite of all the horrors of this persecution and the insane cruelties inflicted by the Sultan, whose blood-lust seemed to increase with age, the passion for smoking still persisted. The sway of the monarch was not co-extensive with the bounds of his empire, and even the fear of death was of no avail with the passionate devotees of the habit.

Murad IV, under whose bloody tyranny 25,000 victims are said to have been put to death in only the last five years of his reign, died in 1640, and was succeeded by Ibrahim, a profligate sensualist, and the abject slave of his own harem. During his reign Murad's prohibitory laws remained in force, but during the last years of that ruler and throughout the reign of Ibrahim many who dreaded the consequences of smoking turned to snuff-taking, and the habit became general. Not till the reign of Mohammed IV, who came to the throne in 1648, and was defeated at the siege of Vienna, 1683, were the savage laws against smoking repealed. This Sultan was himself a smoker, and from this period we note the enormous increase of the habit in every place where Turks were to be found. Moreover, the climate and soil of the Ottoman Empire were so peculiarly favourable to the cultivation of tobacco that the trade in the commodity, as well as the habit of smoking, soon became of considerable importance—a fact which has led superficial observers to conclude that both the plant and the habit actually originated in these regions and spread thence to East and West.

Meanwhile smoking had made its appearance in the north-east of Europe ; Turkish ships carried it to the coastal cities of the Black Sea, English sailors to the Baltic and the shores of the North Sea ; travellers from Germany and Poland had introduced it to inland Russia, where, however, it met at once with stubborn resistance, especially on the part of the clergy.

Michael Feodorovitch Romanoff, the first of his line, after the freeing of Moscow from Polish rule in 1613, had been elected Tsar, as representative of the ancient dynasty of Rurik. Michael's father, the patriarch Philarete, who during his lifetime had a sort of share in the sovereignty, was a bitter opponent of smoking—all the more so as, in the course of the Thirty Years War, the custom had assumed alarming proportions, people smoking quite shamelessly in the churches, even during the services. Both Philarete and his successor in the Patriarchate convinced the Tsar that the practice was profane and abominable, besides being accountable for the enormous increase in the number of fires in Moscow; moreover, it was intolerable that the citizens should approach the shrines and sacred icons with their clothes stinking of poisonous tobacco smoke. Michael was therefore moved to publish an edict to the effect that smoking must be regarded as a deadly sin; no one, whether national or foreign, was to be allowed to have tobacco in his possession, whether for smoking, snuff-taking, or for the purpose of trading in it; offenders would be treated as criminals, sent to the 'New Quarter,' and severely punished. Persistent offenders were sometimes exiled to Siberia, and the Emperor, following the Sultan's example, appropriated their property. A special court for dealing with smokers was next established, where the punishment inflicted was usually slitting the lips, or a merciless flogging.

Adam Olearius, who visited Moscow in 1643 and

Fig. 35. SULTAN MURAD IV (1623–40)

140

Fig. 36. WOODEN HOUSES IN MOSCOW IN THE TIME OF THE
FIRST ROMANOFF TSAR

published an exhaustive account of the country and its customs, gives the following description :

> The Russians have long been addicted to smoking, even a poor man preferring to spend his last penny on tobacco rather than on bread. However, it soon became evident that the people, so far from being benefited, got great harm from the practice. The ordinary citizen, his servants, his serfs, all alike would neglect their work; owing to the carelessness of smokers many houses were burned to the ground, while even in the churches the sacred icons, which should be honoured only with incense and sweet perfumes, stank of tobacco smoke. Consequently in 1634 the sovereign, at the instigation of the Patriarch, issued an order strictly forbidding the use or sale of tobacco, as well as all private traffic in brandy and beer. Offenders are usually sentenced to slitting of the nostrils, the bastinado, or the knout; those convicted of taking snuff have their noses torn away. We ourselves have met with many victims of each of these forms of torture, which were inflicted alike on men and women.
>
> The knout seemed to me a barbarous method of punishment; I saw it inflicted, in September 1634, on eight men and one woman who had been convicted of selling tobacco and spirits. These persons were made to strip to the loins, in the presence of the tribunal; then one after another was hoisted on to the back of the executioner's assistant, around whose neck the culprit's arms were fastened, his legs being tied together by a rope held by another attendant, so that he could move neither hands nor feet. The executioner then took his stand behind the victim at a distance of three paces and plied the long stout whip with such force that the blood flowed freely after every stroke; at the end of the knout are three thongs, the length of a finger, made of hard untanned elk-skin, which cut like a knife. In the case of grave offenders the victims are sometimes whipped to death; in this instance each man received from twenty to twenty-six strokes; the woman endured sixteen, after which she lost consciousness. Not a finger's breadth of skin was left on their backs, which looked like the flayed carcase of an animal.

Then came the turn of the tobacco-sellers and the traffickers in spirits; after a small ticket bearing the word for tobacco had been hung round the necks of the former, and a little flask round those of the latter, they were bound together two by two, by the arms, and thus under escort were whipped around the courtyard and back again into the castle.[1]

Yet even these prohibitions and penalties (confined for the most part to the city of Moscow) failed to stop the growth of the habit among the Russians; the warmth created by smoking was some slight protection against the extreme cold they had to endure, while its soothing effects were invaluable for inducing sleep. A smoker would often fall asleep with his pipe still alight, with the result that numbers of the flimsy wooden houses of Moscow were burned to the ground, till at last it became customary to blame the users of tobacco for all the more serious conflagrations. Accordingly, the Tsar Alexis, the second of the Romanoffs, who succeeded in 1645, published a ukase forbidding smoking altogether, and threatening those who were caught with the most terrible penalties, including torture and exile.[2]

In the part of Moscow known as the 'New Quarter' the criminals were racked and tortured in public. The Civil Code of the time appointed a special body of vigilants whose duty it was to search for contraband tobacco. Their instructions included the following:

Should a tavern-keeper, tobacco-seller, or anyone in the possession of tobacco offer the inspectors a suitable bribe, say

[1] Adam Olearius, *Beschreibung der Moskowitischen und Persienischen Reise*, pp. 100 and 140 (Hamburg edition, 1696).
[2] From K. Lettenbaur, *Rauchverbote*, in the *Deutsche Tabakzeitung*, June 7, 1894.

from five to thirty roubles, so as not to be taken to the New Quarter . . . they may take the money; but if, after receiving it, they let their man escape, they can be punished with the knout and expelled from office.

In Russia, as elsewhere, the literature of the time was bitterly hostile to the new custom; in 1630, for instance, a violent attack was published, in Russian, denouncing smoking as a deadly sin, the clerics who were responsible for it basing their argument on the text in the Bible, " The things which come out of him, those are they that defile the man " (St Mark vii, 15).

But all the prohibitions in Europe were helpless against the power of tobacco. Scandinavia was the next country to capitulate: the soldiers of Gustavus Adolphus, on their return from the Thirty Years War, introduced the custom into the interior, while the seaports learned it from English and Dutch sailors. As early as 1633 a treatise on the virtues of the wondrous herb *Nicotiana* was published at Uppsala,[1] and in 1641 came the first royal proclamation from the King of Sweden dealing with the regulation of smoking. In the remote north, however, there was never such serious opposition as in other quarters, though in Denmark we meet with an enemy of the habit in King Christian IV, who commissioned his Court physician, Simon Pauli, to write a severe denunciation of it.

The sailors and merchants of the coastal towns, whose business took them across the sea to distant lands, had discovered that the traffic in tobacco was extremely

[1] Johann Franken, *De præclaris herbæ nicotianæ sive tabaci virtutibus disputatio* (Uppsala, 1633).

lucrative, and, once introduced into a country, it created a strong and growing demand; consequently they lost no time in taking a store of it with them wherever they went, and thus they introduced smoking to nations which had hitherto been ignorant of it. First in importance came Africa, a country largely unexplored, of which only the shores of the Mediterranean and the west coast were known. The inhabitants of the former were the first to learn the use of tobacco, which they got from the Spaniards, French, and Italians. Meanwhile Spanish and Portuguese sailors, who controlled the slave trade on both the east and west coasts of the continent, brought their tobacco with them, and the caravans conveyed it into the interior. The negroes, peculiarly susceptible to narcotics of all kinds, seemed to find in tobacco some consolation for their oppressed condition; they took to it with enthusiasm and soon became the most intemperate of smokers. The Dutchmen brought it to the Cape of Good Hope, whence it spread northward to the peoples of the districts known to-day as British South Africa, and also to the Hottentots. Finally, the Portuguese and Dutch, rounding the Cape, crossed over to the coast of India, taking their tobacco with them.

But the habit of smoking had already penetrated into Asia by various other channels. The campaigns of Murad IV were instrumental in bringing it to Persia, where at first it was punished by heavy fines, or occasionally by death. Meanwhile the more central regions had been approached from two directions—eastward from Turkey and Russia, westward from Eastern Asia and Japan, to which it had been brought at the end of the

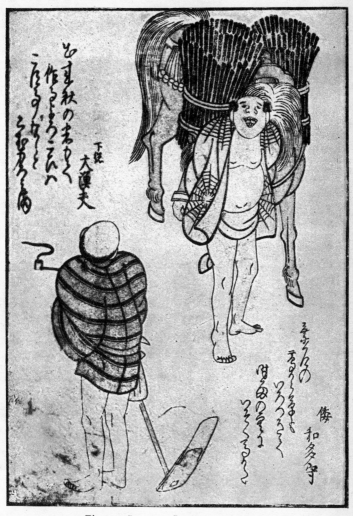

Fig. 37. Japanese Labourer smoking

Fig. 38. A Geisha smoking

sixteenth century by Portuguese and, later, Spanish sailors coming from the Philippine Islands. Landing on the coasts of India and Siam, Portuguese sailors contributed their share, till the habit had penetrated finally to the Court of the Emperor of India, the Great Mogul, at Delhi.

Japan, however, was the first Eastern nation to practise it extensively. Here again, as is well known, the introduction was due to some Portuguese on board a Chinese pirate ship, who, about 1542, were driven out of their course by a storm, and forced to land on the south-western extremity of the islands. This rediscovery of Japan—known hitherto only through the account of Marco Polo, who had spoken of it as " Zipangu, rich in gold "—proved the beginning of a lively commercial intercourse between Portuguese merchants from India and the Japanese. Jesuits and missionaries from Portugal followed in the train of the merchants, and all were received in the most friendly manner by the Japanese, and especially by the Daimio of Satsuma, one of the most powerful princes of Kiushiu, an island at that time practically independent of the central government. Japanese accounts [1] still exist describing how the Portuguese merchants and seamen brought tobacco-leaves with them and taught the inhabitants of Kiushiu to smoke. By 1595 the habit was well established in that island, but no attempt was made to grow their own tobacco. It was in 1596 that Shimatsu, the head of the princely house of Satsuma, received the first consignment of seeds, which he sent to the Emperor at Kioto, at that time the capital of Japan, who had them

[1] See a letter from Mr H. Nomura of Tokio to Professor O. Comes describing his researches in the Japanese Archives. Reprinted by Comes in *Histoire, géographie, statistique du tabac*, p. 249.

planted in the royal gardens. With this exception the cultivation of tobacco was naturally confined at first to the seaports, particularly in the south, such as Nagasaki; a doctor of that town, named Saka, has left us an account of how the *Nanbans* (the Japanese name for Portuguese) brought tobacco-leaves and taught them how to smoke.[1]

About that time the bold and powerful Emperor Hideyoshi, the Napoleon of Japan, who died in 1598, had managed to bring all the islands under one strong central government; his dreams of conquest embraced the whole of China, and he actually succeeded in annexing Korea. In the reign of his son, Hideyori—whose guardian was the great Jeyasu of the house of Tokagawa, appointed Shôgun in 1603—the practice of smoking had grown to such an extent as to provoke opposition: the regent, Jeyasu, issued a prohibitory edict affecting the whole of Japan, although 'smoking-clubs' already flourished in the capital itself. As no notice was taken of this edict, still severer measures were taken in 1607 and 1609, by which the cultivation of tobacco was made a penal offence. Finally, in 1612, Jeyasu decreed that the property of any man detected in selling tobacco should be handed over to his accuser, and anyone arresting a man conveying tobacco on a pack-horse might take both horse and tobacco for his own. Yet in spite of all attempts at repression smoking became so general that in 1615 even the officers in attendance on the Shôgun—at that time residing at Yeddo, the modern Tokio—had acquired the habit. The result was a sterner warning, to the effect that

[1] See Satow, *The Introduction of Tobacco into Japan*. (Cf. *Transactions* of the Asiatic Society of Japan, VI, i, 68.)

anyone in the army caught smoking was liable to have his property confiscated. In 1616 the penalties were made still more severe : to a sentence of imprisonment a fine was added, in many cases equivalent to an increase of from thirty to fifty days on the original term. But it was all of no avail; the custom spread rapidly in every direction, until, as we read in an Imperial poem of the time, many smokers were to be found even in the Mikado's palace. Finally even the princes who were responsible for the prohibition took to smoking, and the great land-owners and rulers of the Daimios, the military and feudal aristocracy, who were all devotees of the habit, were glad to let the laws fall into abeyance. In 1625 permission was given to cultivate and plant tobacco, except in ricefields and vegetable gardens. By 1639 tobacco had taken its place in polite Japanese society as an accompaniment to the ceremonial cup of tea offered to a guest. Thanks to the temporary annexation of Korea, and the subsequent wars, it was introduced into Korea, and thence to Central China and what we now call Manchuria; the Manchus took kindly to the habit, and spread it throughout the north and north-eastern parts of China.

The south and south-west, on the other hand, got it from the Portuguese who landed at Macao and founded a small colony in Canton in 1567. At the beginning of the seventeenth century a brisk trade was carried on between Canton and the Philippine Islands, which had already got their tobacco from the Spaniards. With surprising swiftness the habit penetrated into the very heart of China, so that the Emperor Wan-li, of the Ming Dynasty, who flourished from 1573 to 1620, was surprised to see that the new habit had grown to be as much an institution as tea-drinking itself.

In 1641 Tsung Cheng, the last ruler of the Ming Dynasty, attempted to prohibit smoking by an edict, but this had merely the same futile results as all the others. The Manchus, who conquered Peking after the revolution of 1644, revoked all existing prohibitions, and henceforth the Chinese, encouraged by the example of the Court, became greater smokers than any other nation.

The last country to welcome the tobacco plant was Australia, whither it was imported by navigators from Europe and Japan. In so sparsely populated a region the progress of smoking was naturally slower than elsewhere; but, with this exception, within little more than a century after the introduction of tobacco into Europe the cultivation of the plant and the habit of smoking, in spite of all obstacles and all attempts at prohibition, had spread over the whole world, and soon began to exercise so irresistible a sway over all men that neither emperors, kings, Popes, doctors, nor *savants* could stand against it.

CHAPTER VII

THE GOVERNMENTS' SURRENDER TO TOBACCO

DURING Louis XIII's reign a noteworthy change took place in the fortunes of tobacco in France. Smoking offended the taste of the upper circles, the Court, the nobility, and the clergy; it was considered hardly consistent with aristocratic dignity or feminine charm to be always puffing out tobacco smoke. Fashion favoured another way of enjoying the magic herb: snuff-taking was pronounced a far daintier and more elegant method, and spread widely among the higher classes; the lower classes of the population went on smoking pipes, but their betters took more and more to snuff. In the early part of the seventeenth century tobacco was very costly in Paris, and high prices were asked for it in the so-called *tabagies*, or smoking taverns. Richelieu, who became the Chief Minister in 1624, and was always on the look-out for fresh sources of revenue, thought that in tobacco he could find an inexhaustible spring of wealth. He advised the imposition of a duty of thirty sols [1] on every pound of tobacco imported. Personally the Cardinal objected to smoking, and thought that this growing habit might be checked by making it expensive; a heavy duty on tobacco would probably be better than unprofitable prohibition, and would be more effective in setting limits

---

[1] Sol = sou, five centimes, or a halfpenny. The value of money was, of course, far higher in the seventeenth century than it is now.

to the use of tobacco. A royal edict of November 17, 1629, imposing a duty of thirty sols on every pound of tobacco imported runs as follows : " As We have been informed [1] that of late great store of *petum* or tobacco had been coming in from abroad, without paying duty," the duty is imposed, " as otherwise this free importation would have led to the bringing in of very great quantities ; when Our subjects, seeing the cheapness of tobacco, would use it continually, whereby no small hurt should come to their health." [2] Only the West India Company, in which the Court and High Society were interested, had the privilege, according to this edict, of importing and selling tobacco from its plantations in the Antilles without paying duty.

Smoking, however, had not been fully approved by the authorities, and occasionally we meet, even after 1630, with isolated cases of prohibition. In a Naval Order, 1634, we find the Port Commander forbidding anyone *de pétuer* [3] after sunset—no doubt on account of the danger of fire. In March 1635 a Lieutenant of Police, apparently ignorant of Richelieu's financial schemes, issued an Ordinance forbidding many things, and among them the sale of tobacco except by apothecaries, when prescribed by physicians. This regulation, which would have cut down the revenue from Richelieu's tobacco duty, was not in force for long, and by 1636 the duty brought in over 50,000 livres. Richelieu's main idea of either checking the new habit by a tax, or at any rate making a profit for the State, was

[1] By Richelieu.
[2] See F. A. Isambert, *Recueil général des anciennes lois françaises*, vol. xvi, No. 169, p. 347 (Paris, 1829).
[3] To smoke, from *petum*, the Brazilian name for tobacco.

taken up in Italy, where a still more effective means of
making money for the State was discovered. The Duke
of Mantua, of the house of Gonzaga, hit on the plan
of granting a certain Giovanni Tugnoni the monopoly of
spirits and tobacco for a yearly rent of 16,900 lire. At
the same time he forbade anyone else to import tobacco.
That was the beginning of the tobacco monopolies which
were to become so mighty in every country of the world,
and are still powerful in many states. In Lombardy the
Government claimed the control of the tobacco trade in
1637, and on September 20, 1647, the Duchess-Regent
of Savoy granted the exclusive right of selling tobacco to
Count Galliani and certain corporations in Piedmont.

The republic of Venice was most successful in profiting
by the new habit. In 1626 it taxed tobacco, and in 1651
began to limit its cultivation and sale, while granting
certain communes, especially in the Brenta valley, the
privilege of growing tobacco. In 1659 was founded the
first tobacco *appalto*, a contract whereby the exclusive
right to import, manufacture, and trade in tobacco was
farmed out to a private person for a certain consideration.
The payment for a three years' lease of the monopoly at
Venice was 8000 ducats. Only the ' Seven Communes '
were any longer allowed to grow tobacco, and they had
to regulate their supply by the demand of the Venetian
appalto. Their tobacco could be sold only to the *appalto*
at Venice. This method became a model monopoly,
imitated in most European states. Its brilliant financial
results induced emperors and kings, nobles and clergy,
feudal lords and governments of all sorts to raise their
ban on tobacco, and in course of time to reverse their

former policy ; .for the vast increase of smoking in later centuries, and the ever-rising revenues from tobacco taxes and monopolies, led governments to urge their subjects to consume more and more.

The methods of Northern Italy were very soon followed in the south. In Rome Pope Alexander VII issued an edict on September 22, 1655. In virtue of his anxious search for means to relieve the misery of the poor he now forbade all persons under his rule—clergy or laity; even barons, princes, dukes; bishops, archbishops, or cardinals —to import or grow tobacco, under a penalty of six scudi for every pound weight. At the same time the monopoly of spirits and tobacco was farmed out as at Venice. This *appalto* was in force at first only in Rome and its neighbourhood, and a Papal decree granted the right of preparing tobacco to the Jews at Ferrara, in 1657, because " they are more skilled in trading therein than others."

The countries outside Italy now adopted similar methods. Some began with ' tobacco taxes.' In Silesia in 1657 the princes and the estates imposed a duty on tobacco, and in 1664 this was done in Bohemia. In 1665 the Bohemian Diet farmed out the duty to a contractor for a payment of three gulden on the hundredweight. In 1668 the estates of Bohemia were allowed to levy a gulden and a half on every hundredweight of imported tobacco, for constructing fortifications. An *appalto*, a monopoly like those already existing in Italy, was first started, naturally, in the lands bordering on Venetia—*i.e.*, Görz, Gradiska, and Tyrol—by Archduke Ferdinand Karl.[1]

[1] *Verleihungsurkunde* ('notice of the grant '), October 24, 1662, Innsbruck. See Dr Franz Wieser, *Zur Geschichte der Tabakproduktion in Tirol*, in *Fachliche Mitteilungen der österreichischen Tabakregie*, 5th year, Part III, October 1905.

"We, Ferdinand Karl, by God's grace Archduke of Austria, Burgundy, etc., Ruler of the County of Tyrol, etc.," so runs the edict,

> be it known to you that we have graciously given and granted to Gideon May, the Jew, the trade and business in tobacco and snuff in this our County of Tyrol, to him solely and alone. Wherefore it is our command that no one whosoever shall henceforth sell, import, bring, or furnish any snuff or tobacco in this our County of Tyrol, but anyone that deals or desires to deal in tobacco must purchase or procure the same from the aforesaid May.

In the same year the Counts of Fürstenberg, who had grasped the possibilities of profit in tobacco, presented a petition to the Emperor, asking for the exclusive right to import tobacco into the hereditary Austrian dominions, at a moderate rental; but as the Emperor had just issued a prohibition for Tyrol, and the Estates of Lower Austria were strongly opposed to such a monopoly, the request was not granted. The Tyrolese Estates, too, thought that Archduke Ferdinand's edict favoured this new vice, and to some extent approved of it; and they approached the Emperor Leopold I, requesting him to forbid the smoking and importation of tobacco altogether. The Imperial Court was just then ready enough to grant such a petition. In February 1668 a fire had broken out in the Hofburg at Vienna, caused, it was said, by smoking. It seems that a soldier of the guard had used a live coal to light his pipe, and by his carelessness started a fire near the rooms of the Dowager Empress Eleonore. The whole of the so-called 'Leopold' suite on the first storey was destroyed, and some of the archduchesses hardly escaped with their lives: the private chapel was burned down.

The Emperor answered the Tyrolese with an edict, of August 21, 1668, in which it was stated that it was proved by experience that the abuse of smoking " injures the health of man, and often shortens his life, takes much money out of the country, and causes many fires." Therefore, in answer to the representations of the Estates, it was his Imperial wish and command that tobacco should be neither bought nor sold in Tyrol, except at apothecaries' shops for medicinal purposes. This decree makes it quite clear how the Emperor Leopold regarded the new habit of smoking; but his private financial interests were soon to prevail over his moral principles.

In the summer of 1670 the Emperor wanted to have a *Gesperrtes Geiayd* in Upper Austria—*i.e.*, a *battue*—in which the game was driven into a certain area of the woods, and prevented from escaping by enclosing the woods with planks or strips of linen. When the sovereign told his Chief Huntsman, Count Franz Christoph Khevenhiller of Franckenburg, to make due preparations for the hunt the Count was startled at the suggestion that he should fence in so large a space with strips of linen, and answered that the cost of such a business would be so enormous that the ordinary revenue could not stand it. But Leopold was not to be put off so; he would have his hunt in Upper Austria, and wrote to his Chief Huntsman that he must think of some plan to bring in the necessary money.

Khevenhiller thought and thought, and finally hit on an idea by which he could kill three birds with one stone. He wanted to fulfil three conditions—the hunt must take place as prescribed, the Imperial revenues were not to be lessened, and, last of all, Khevenhiller might as well make a trifle for himself. His plan was to get for himself an *appalto* for the exclusive right to import and sell tobacco, as in Italy and Tyrol; pay for the Emperor's hunt out of the proceeds; and possibly save something for his own pocket. With this view the Count proposed[1] that the Emperor Leopold should graciously grant to "a certain person" the right to import tobacco into Upper and Lower Austria, and forbid all others to do so, since tobacco was a commodity brought from abroad, and merchants of Ratisbon and Nuremberg and other foreigners had hitherto made a profit out of it—which went out of the country. The customs duty would be paid to the Emperor as before, and his revenue would not suffer in the slightest. Khevenhiller closed with these words:

> So I venture to nominate myself for the purpose, and humbly to petition for the grant of this right of importation, solely in order that the fences may be prepared, and the Upper Austrian Hunt may be brought to perfection during the time of my service to Your Imperial Majesty.

Count Khevenhiller undertook to supply the country with tobacco at his own risk and with his own capital, and not to ask exorbitant prices.

He goes on:

> Considering that the yearly supplies will be large in the manner aforesaid, I am humbly of the opinion that a certain amount may be drawn therefrom, as an extraordinary fund for the purpose of the proposed fencing, and any such expenses may be from time to time so defrayed that not a penny of Your Imperial Majesty's ordinary revenue need be spent thereon. Moreover, the customs

---

[1] Count Khevenhiller to Emperor Leopold I; no date, but certainly before April 13, 1669 (Vienna Exchequer Archives).

officers must be informed and ordered that henceforth no one, whether subject or foreigner, is to deal in tobacco, and anyone who transgresses this order shall have his goods confiscated.

FRANZ CHRISTOPH KHEVENHILLER

The Emperor two years previously had issued an edict forbidding the sale of tobacco in Tyrol, but by this time he must have realized that very few obeyed his command, and that smoking was spreading more and more; now Khevenhiller proposed a method by which he could gratify his passion for sport without its costing him anything. First, however, the provincial Estates had to be dealt with, and they were absolutely opposed to the Chief Huntsman's proposal. They presented a memorial stating that a monopoly of a commodity " used by the common people " would soon develop into a crushing burden on the country. If the Sovereign was so keen on hunting his subjects would far rather pay a contribution, without abandoning tobacco-dealers and consumers " to the arbitrary will of a greedy monopolist." [1]

But sport was Emperor Leopold's ruling passion, and the monopoly was granted " to our Chamberlain and Chief Huntsman in Upper Austria, Count Khevenhiller, to pay for the hunt in Upper Austria." The Count surrendered his monopoly after a time in return for a money payment.

The first tobacco monopoly for Upper Austria expired in 1682, but it was the beginning of many similar grants in the hereditary states of the Habsburgs. These were sometimes made to great nobles, like Count Königsegg,

---

[1] Josef von Retzer, *Die Tabakpachtungen in den österreichischen Ländern von 1670 bis 1783* (Vienna, 1784).

sometimes to Jewish dealers and Italian contractors, and thus marked the transition to the universal State monopoly which was established in the Austro-Hungarian monarchy, and still exists in the present republic of Austria. It is interesting to read a report of the *Hofkammer* (Exchequer) of August 20, 1677, on a tobacco *appalto* which an Italian named Donadoni applied for in the case of Styria, Carinthia, and Carniola.

> The contractor will not pay the agreed sum from his own purse, but squeeze it out of the people, and out of anyone who uses tobacco, by unduly raising the price, or taking some other advantage . . . the which, as is easy to guess, may cause great lamentation and complaint in all the land. For although tobacco be not necessary to the sustenance of man, yet have matters gone so far that many are of a mind that they would rather lack bread than tobacco, and some are so greatly given thereto that they use continual smoking as their medicine—whence this monopoly could not be brought in without singular vexation and general lamentation.

As was only to be expected, the monopolists in the various hereditary states used their privilege to make the greatest possible profit for themselves, and thus especially oppressed the lower classes, who were defenceless, and could not get tobacco from any other source. There were continual remonstrances from the provincial Estates, asking for " the defence of the poor and heavily oppressed inhabitants of the land, and the common people." [1] " Truly," one of these documents runs,

> we consider this tobacco *appalto*, like all monopolies and *appaltos*, hateful, hurtful to the common weal, and drawing with it an

[1] Complaint of the County of Carinthia to the Emperor Leopold I, May 17, 1686.

enormous, usurious, and intolerable profit, which goes to the monopolists alone, while the weight thereof falls on the already burdened commonalty.[1]

But Leopold had tasted the sweetness of the money brought in by the monopoly; and, much as he personally disliked smoking, he had no notion of giving up the income derived from farming out tobacco. He issued letters patent to establish his right to the monopoly of tobacco for all future time.

"Following the example of other sovereigns and republics," the edict declared,

for the good of Our general Treasury, We have graciously determined, in virtue of Our Imperial, royal, and princely power and sovereignty, and the *jus præmptionis et vectigalis* attached thereto, to draw a revenue from tobacco, whether smoked or taken as snuff. This commodity is not needful for the sustenance of mankind—rather has it become an arbitrary though almost universal habit. For this purpose we have determined, through Our Imperial Exchequer, either Ourself to take over the trade in such tobacco, or, according as We may think most profitable to our Treasury, to lease or farm it out to one or more persons.

Henceforth all official interference with smoking was aimed only at averting and minimizing the danger of fire. The spread of smoking in the hereditary Austrian states during the latter part of the seventeenth century can be inferred from a passage in the scheme for a tobacco monopoly in Bohemia: "in the Kingdom of Bohemia, among nobles, townspeople, and peasants alike, there is hardly one in a thousand who does not use tobacco."

The news that princes and governments might find a

---

[1] Report on the *appalto* petitioned for by Liscutin and Donadoni for Styria, Carinthia, and Carniola, July 30, 1686.

gold-mine in tobacco spread far and wide; gradually the prohibitions were annulled, and one State after another imposed duties or established monopolies. The princes of that age led a life of luxury, and were given to building; many had a load of old debt remaining from former wars; all of them needed money, vast sums of money— the Elector Ferdinand Maria of Bavaria, for instance, who was driven by poverty on January 2, 1669, to summon the Bavarian Diet, which had not met since 1612. At this session various taxes were discussed, including a duty on tobacco, and prince and people were agreed on this point; but they veiled their real motive under the pretext of supporting the Government in the fight against the insidious herb.

We may note that the Estates in Bavaria, unlike the similar assemblies in the Austrian lands, shared in the profits of the tobacco trade, which accounts for their being less rigid in condemning smoking. We can see from the various laws regulating the tobacco taxes in Bavaria that "the decrees issued against tobacco-smoking, on account of its evil consequences, have hitherto met with small success." [1]

Taking a hint from the *appaltos* in neighbouring states, the Electress Henrietta Adelaide proposed to grant the exclusive right of dealing in tobacco, for all Bavaria, to one of her favourites, a certain Baron von Simeoni, " in consideration of his faithful service, and so that he may profitably employ the fifty thousand thalers that he has earned with grievous labour and trouble." [2]

---

[1] Josef Micheler, *Das Tabakwesen in Bayern*, p. 9 (Stuttgart 1887).
[2] *Ibid.*, p. 13, etc.

But the clergy at that time had a good deal to say on political matters, and the Elector thought it best to get them on his side beforehand; so he asked the Electress's confessor, a Theatine monk, Father Spinelli, whether he could agree to this arrangement with a clear conscience. The confessor, supported by the clergy, who mostly hated tobacco and had private quarrels with Simeoni, declared with all solemnity that such a business was not to be done. Simeoni's scheme fell through, but the idea of drawing public revenue from tobacco was soon taken up again. In 1674 the Elector again asked Fathers Frey and Spinelli the question whether, "to restore the public credit, and to stop the leaks in the finances, a tobacco monopoly could not be established, whether in the name of a private person or of the State." As the unpopular Simeoni was now out of the way, the two Fathers answered the question affirmatively, and on December 2, 1675, the first tobacco monopoly for Bavaria was given to an Italian. It was followed by many others.

This method of farming out the tobacco trade was imitated in France, and Louis XIV, in an edict dated at Versailles September 1674, said, almost apologetically, that this system had been introduced into so many other countries that France was bound to adopt it.

"Seeing that the use of tobacco," the edict runs,[1] has become so general in all Our dominions, that it has given occasion to most of the princes Our neighbours to make this business a chief source of their revenues, We have thought that We might draw a similar profit by introducing the tobacco monopoly; and We have considered the plan laid before Us the more reasonable, in that tobacco is not a food needful for health

[1] Isambert, *op. cit.*, vol. xix, No. 785, p. 145.

or nourishment, and may be a means of making it easier for Our people to bear a part of the extraordinary expenses of the present war.

The King, in this edict, reserved for himself the privilege of manufacturing and selling tobacco; this privilege was then farmed out to contractors, of whom Jean Breton was the first; it was elaborately regulated by Colbert in July 1681. In France also this system brought a golden stream into the coffers of the State. Other countries hastened to follow the example of France, and in 1676 a certain Daniel Hartwich asked the Great Elector for the privilege of trading in tobacco in Brandenburg. Frederick William, himself a snuff-taker—we still have his silver shell-shaped snuff-box—on May 18 of that year granted Nathan David and Daniel Hartwich, two Jews, in return for a cash payment, the right for twelve years, " to them alone and none else," to grow, twist, and sell tobacco.

Everywhere the policy of prohibition was giving way before the policy of taxation. Oliver Cromwell was opposed to tobacco, and would not allow it to be grown in England, but he went no further, and did not dare to engage in a struggle which he would have found harder than the Civil War.

Most of the tobacco consumed in England still came from Virginia and the other English colonies gradually springing up around it. The great success of the tobacco plantations in Virginia, which enriched the settlers there, induced enterprising nobles to ask Charles II for charters to found similar colonies—one of them was the settlement called " Carolina " in honour of the King. Those who left England on account of religious persecution swelled the number of the colonists, and a long series of small settlements arose on the New England coast. The new-founded states and colonies north and south of Virginia were interrupted by stray Dutch and Swedish settlements. The Swedes soon gave way to the Dutch, but the latter, who founded New Amsterdam at the mouth of the Hudson river, were a foreign element among the English colonies. The Virginians and other British settlers found the Dutch colony a thorn in their flesh, for tobacco-smuggling from the Dutch settlement was most hurtful to the trade of the Virginian planters. The war with Holland, forced on Charles II by his Parliament, was welcome to the Virginian planters, who had used all their influence in Parliament to attack New Amsterdam; now they had their chance, and one day a British squadron of four ships appeared off the Dutch colony. The Governor, terrified, surrendered the settlement without firing a shot. The King, left in possession of New Amsterdam by the Peace of Breda, 1667, gave it to his brother James, Duke of York, afterward James II; thus New Amsterdam was newly christened New York. The obstacle to the prosperity of tobacco planters and dealers was now removed, and colonization went on extending.

As the colonists pressed inland and westward they came into relations, friendly or hostile, with the Indian tribes of this district, who were all confirmed smokers. Alternating with many murderous encounters there were long palavers at which the pipe of peace, the calumet, played its part; these again might lead to the signing of treaties ceding territory to the ' pale faces ' on very unequal terms. The simple Red Indians did not realize the value of their land, and would accept the most worthless presents in return. These gifts nearly always included pipes and tobacco; among the goods which were exchanged for Indian territory between Rankokas Creek and Timber Creek, in New Jersey, on September 10, 1677, we find 120 pipes and 100 jews' harps.[1]

The Quakers, who were persecuted in England owing to their refusal to take the oath or serve in the army, settled on former Dutch territory in North America. William Penn, the son of a vice-admiral who had done good service to his country, had inherited from his father certain claims on the crown which Charles II settled by granting him the district between New York and New Jersey on one side, and Maryland on the other. Penn determined to found in this territory a state where religion should be free and all class distinctions abolished.

It was necessary to come to terms with the Indian tribes settled in the forest country afterward called Pennsylvania, and it frequently happened that Penn had to smoke the pipe of peace with the chiefs. They met him with the calumet, a large bowl of polished red stone and a long stem decked with gay feathers. The chiefs smoked choice tobacco in the pipe, and blew the first puff of smoke toward the sun, where, they thought, the Great Spirit, the lord of life, dwelt, asking him for help and guidance. The Great Spirit seems to have advised them ill, for when they settled the bargain for the sale of the land, at a final smoking conference with Penn, the price for the whole rich territory was ridiculously low—a collection of cheap

[1] Samuel Smith, *History of the Colony of Nova Cæsaria, or New Jersey* (Burlington, 1765).

articles, including 300 pipes, 100 baskets of tobacco, twenty snuff-boxes, and 100 jews' harps. Still, on one point aborigines and colonists, conquerors and conquered, Puritans, Quakers, and Sun-worshippers, were all agreed —they were all inveterate smokers. A few only, including Penn himself, had no liking for tobacco, but were glad enough to have the profits of the tobacco trade for themselves and their communities.

Meanwhile tobacco was taking its place in English politics. Hardly had Richard Cromwell abdicated and General Monk restored the Stuarts, in 1660, than the duty on tobacco was raised and regulated: the word appears for the first time in the statute-book for that year. The King objected to tobacco cultivation in England, as the imported Virginian tobacco was easier to control for customs duty. He stated in his decree that the cultivation of tobacco in the home country deprived him of a large part of his revenue; and as, moreover, the prosperity of the American planters depended on the sale of their tobacco, he must in their interests wholly prohibit tobacco-growing in England and Ireland. Charles II was honest enough to admit that he was taking this step on his own account, as well as for the Virginians.

These provisions against tobacco-growing in England were not obeyed, and in 1670 Charles II was compelled to pass an Act [1] giving full powers to the officers of his army to uproot and destroy all tobacco plants growing anywhere in England or Ireland, except those in a physician's garden, so that his Majesty's plantations

---

[1] Tobacco Acts of Parliament 1670 to 1869. Act to prevent the planting of tobacco in England and for regulation of the plantation trade, 1670.

overseas should suffer no damage. This order was carried
out by galloping regiments of horse over the unauthorized
tobacco-fields, which entirely ruined the plantations.

It was important to take steps beforehand to secure the
revenue, for in the succeeding years snuff-taking came in
from France, conquered the upper classes, and increased
the consumption of tobacco. Macaulay[1] describes the
fashionable coffee-houses in London, near St James's
Park :

> The atmosphere was like that of a perfumer's shop. Tobacco
> in any other form than that of richly scented snuff was held in
> abomination. If any clown, ignorant of the usages of the house,
> called for a pipe, the sneers of the whole assembly and the short
> answers of the waiters soon convinced him that he had better
> go somewhere else. Nor, indeed, would he have had far to go.
> For, in general, the coffee rooms reeked with tobacco like a guard
> room, and strangers sometimes expressed their surprise that so
> many people should leave their own firesides to sit in the midst of
> eternal fog and stench.

Smoking and snuff brought in revenue, and in 1685 the
customs duty on tobacco was again regulated, on the proposal of a forerunner of Adam Smith. In the "Glorious
Revolution" of 1688 the tobacco revenue was pledged to
the Dutch Government to pay the expenses of William's
expedition.

With the far from disinterested change of attitude of
governments toward tobacco came a corresponding
change in the tone of literature. Writers in the middle of
the seventeenth century had been hostile; in the last
thirty years of the century they were not only friendly to

[1] Lord Macaulay, *The History of England from the Accession of James II*,
vol. i, Chapter III.

tobacco, but broke forth into pæans and panegyrics, as in the palmy days when tobacco had been thought a panacea. A professor at the University of Paris, Magnenus, a famous and learned physician, devoted an elaborate study to the plant, dealing with all the uses of tobacco, medicinal and other.[1] An old work of H. Bernstein was reissued in 1673 under a new and expressive title, *Miraculum tabaci* (*The Magic Herb Tobacco*). A certain Baillard, in 1667, wrote a history of tobacco, with special reference to snuff, owing to the growth of snuff-taking in fashionable circles in Paris.

Very significant of the interest that governments now took in increasing the consumption of tobacco—and their own revenue—is the fact that Louis XIV, who personally objected to smoking and snuff-taking, allowed the Marquis de Prade to print and circulate all over the kingdom, *avec privilège du roi*, a book absolutely in praise of tobacco.[2]

The glory of tobacco was heightened by the notion that it gave protection from infectious diseases. In the latter part of the seventeenth century first one and then another country of Europe lay under the terror of the plague. Great cities suffered especially—as London did in June 1665. Physicians were helpless to stop the mortality; for lack of any better remedy they recommended smelling, chewing, or continually smoking tobacco. The boys at Eton had to smoke every morning as a means of disinfecting themselves; the people who were busy tending the sick, or carting the corpses of the dead out of the city, smoked incessantly, to ward off

[1] Magnenus, *De tobaco* (Pavia, 1669).
[2] De Prade, *Histoire du tabac* (Paris, 1677).

infection ; the doctors, including the then famous Richard
Barker, earnestly recommended tobacco, since he and
others thought they had noticed that in former outbreaks
of disease tobacco-dealers in their shops had escaped. A
contemporary, Samuel Pepys, bears witness to this practice in his *Diary*. During the plague time, on June 7,
1665, a terribly hot day, he was reluctantly forced to go on
pressing business through Drury Lane to the West End,
and saw on two or three houses, where the plague had
been raging, great red crosses on the doors, with the
inscription, "Lord have mercy on us ! "—a sign to warn
men from entering the houses. Pepys tells us how he
suddenly felt ill at the sight of these crosses, and hastily
bought a roll of tobacco to smoke and chew. As soon as
he had done so his sickness and his fright left him, and
he went home safe and sound. Probably imagination had
much to do with this, but it is possible that tobacco smoke
had a slight effect as a disinfectant, though far less than
was expected.[1]

Vienna in 1679 was terribly ravaged by the plague.
We have a memorial of this in the penitential sermons of
the famous imperial preacher, a reformed discalced Augus-
tinian monk, Father Abraham a Santa Clara, collected
in a pamphlet entitled *Mercks Wienn. Desz wütenden
Podts eine umständige Beschreibung*.[2] The preacher puns
lugubriously on the name of the city. *Wienn*, as he calls

[1] Scientists seem still to differ on the question whether tobacco is a disinfectant or not. In a work called *Tobacco and Physical Efficiency: a Digest of
Clinical Data* (New York, 1927), by Pierre Schrumpf-Pierron, dealing with the
medical properties of tobacco, and including an excellent bibliography of the
subject, Chapter XII discusses the disinfectant effects of the plant, and cites
nearly as many physicians who believe in them as those who do not.

[2] Printed at Vienna, 1680.

it, begins with a W, pronounced in German Vay like *Weh*, the German for woe; and he goes on in a similar strain. He writes:

> Anyone who was living in Vienna in September 1679 must own that the misery was beyond the power of any painter to picture, for Death was raging in such fashion that many believed it was the end of the world. In Lord Street was Death Lord, in Singer Street Death hath sung a requiem for many, in Heavengate Street, Death hath sent many a man to Heaven, . . . on the Brandstatt hath Death made ashes of many, like burned-out brands. In fine, there is no street or lane, be its name fitting or not, in Vienna or in the suburbs, where Death has not passed. All that month in Vienna nothing was to be seen but carrying away the dead, shrouding the dead, burying the dead,

till at last no one dared to perform the sorrowful and perilous duty. In this time of need Abraham a Santa Clara speaks of the protective virtues of " tobacco, the soldier's familiar sweetmeat." He goes on:

> I wonder that among the hundredfold names of this plant no one has called it *herba militaris*, or the soldier's herb, since no others use it so commonly. As has been found by experience, the plant has a most wholesome working against the plague, and tobacco steeped in wine for an hour is given with lemon-juice to the plague-stricken with good result; especially is tobacco smoke at this time serviceable against foul air, wherefore our good soldiers here have used it more than their wont, and many have found it a well-proved means of defence. Yet many have been carried off by raging Death, as though he would show that he will leave no order of men unscathed, for Death can scale or undermine all the bastions and ramparts of the city, wherever he can catch a soldier.

Certainly the plague that ravaged Europe set many people smoking, for what was at first prescribed by doctors as a medicine or a disinfectant became a habit which was continued for pleasure after the fear of plague was gone, and the number of smokers grew mightily, as did the glory and dignity of tobacco as expressed in the literature of the time. Only old-fashioned farmers saw with anxiety that the plant was in many parts driving corn out of cultivation, and they now and then protested against excessive tobacco-planting. One of these writes, in 1682, that it is doubtful

> whether in Germany at the present time the growing of tobacco does not do more harm than good; it mostly comes from the fact that the common peasantry, during the long times of war, have caught the way of smoking from the soldiers, till it is an obstinate habit. The fields are greatly exhausted by this crop, and less fit for corn and wheat; and it were much to be desired that the prince's government should in some measure limit, if not altogether forbid, this abuse of tobacco-growing. Yet is it a wholesome and excellent herb, profitable for use in medicine; only it is blame-worthy that wide fields should be ruined by it, more for wanton snuffing and smoking than for the sake of health.[1]

In Austria, too, alarm was felt lest the new culture of tobacco should drive out cereals. The Exchequer agreed with the farmers in attacking unlicensed tobacco-growing. "The lower classes," it wrote,

> consider it as their inalienable right to grow tobacco, and assert that it is the most profitable of crops, and cannot be given up if they are to pay the charges on their land. The peasantry, with its usual stupidity, forgets that it is only through the *appalto*, the customs duties and expenses, that tobacco fetches so high a price; without these it would hardly fetch six gulden the hundredweight.

One of the most enthusiastic panegyrists of tobacco about this time was Cornelius Bontekoe, a celebrated

---

[1] Hohberg, *Georgica curiosa* (1682), Part II, p. 68, etc.

physician in Holland. In his book, *A Short Treatise on Man's Life, Health, Sickness, and Death*, he glorifies tobacco and recommends it "to all who love life and health." He repeats the doctrine that tobacco is a panacea; declares that it is the surest means of prolonging life, and should be used every day. "There is nothing so good, nothing so estimable, so profitable, and necessary for life and health as the smoke of tobacco, that royal plant that kings themselves are not ashamed to smoke." Bontekoe proceeds to name the three great achievements of his time: the first is the discovery of the circulation of the blood; the second the circumnavigation of the earth, which has led to the third achievement—the bringing of that priceless herb tobacco to Europe.

Another enthusiast was Beintema von Peima, who in 1691 expressed his views in the title of his book, *Panacea oder das allgemeine Hilfsmittel; oder, Lob des Tabaks*. He ended his book with the wish that all men and women might be encouraged to smoke, that they might enjoy a long and happy life.

Voices were raised on the other side by certain of the clergy, who did not agree with such ideas. One of these, the preacher Kaspar Hoffmann, pastor of Quedlinburg, in the Harz, in his fiery orations (1684) always spoke of smoking as the work of the Devil. But it was in Switzerland that the opposition to tobacco was most persistent. The population at large, and especially the traders, were strongly against the official prohibition of smoking, and in March 1686 certain merchants who were fined bluntly declared "that they are not minded to pay the fine." They said that of late all the traders in the

world had been free to deal in tobacco, and they wanted
" all to stand and act together so that this ban on tobacco
may be repealed."

The Town Council of Zürich wished to take strong
measures against such "unheard-of insubordination."
Individual citizens might be drastically dealt with, but
what could be done with the innumerable refugees from
Piedmont, who had taken refuge in Switzerland? They
were all great smokers, and, as the Council thought,
risked setting the town on fire, and were a bad example
to others.

Gradually the Councillors begin to realize that there
are people who are so used to smoking that they cannot
do without it. A milder tone is employed in admonishing
the Piedmontese emigrants. "They must take care,"
says the order,

> not to smoke in public inns and in the public streets, and if some
> of them are not able to abstain from this vice they may satisfy
> their desire by themselves outside the walls of the town, so that
> those who have a natural aversion from this ugly habit may not
> be annoyed.[1]

Gradually another idea penetrated into Switzerland—
that if prohibitions were unsuccessful some revenue at
least might be got from smoking.

The Zürich Town Council, whose heads were beginning
to yield, grudgingly but of necessity, and the Bailiff of
the City of Baden, proposed that, instead of prohibiting
smoking, "every one who smokes tobacco should pay a
fine, and the money should accumulate," and "weapons

[1] Notice to the "Piedmontese Exiles," November 10, 1687 (Zürich State
Archives).

of war should be bought therewith to distribute to our poorer subjects " in case of need.[1]

Berne was the last to yield to tobacco. In 1693 the city issued a tobacco decree, complaining that the prohibitions were disregarded, and threatening " smoking and chewing " with heavy penalties. The sale of pipes and tobacco was forbidden, and such goods, if met with, " must be burned by the town sergeant in a public place, and the pipes broken."

The following years in Switzerland were filled with a fierce clash of opinions as to smoking. Those in favour of tobacco slowly but surely gained the upper hand, as persons in authority themselves fell victims to the new habit. In 1702 the Trade Council officially proposed to permit tobacco-growing in the country, to prevent so much money going abroad for imports. In 1705 Freiburg asked Berne if that city would not co-operate in a new and general prohibition of tobacco ; but the Freiburgers themselves were doubtful if this was practicable, as " the Committee for repressing excess " ended its report with a rider, suggesting, " not a complete prohibition, which is thought impossible, but merely some limitation on smoking."

In the edicts of 1706 we can trace the slow retreat of the city authorities ; though still hostile to smoking, they no longer forbid it entirely, and put forward the danger of fire as their chief objection. Still smoking is described as " unprofitable, lewd, and aimless," and the statement is made that it is only through " God's gracious providence "

---

[1] This was left for further consideration in the session of the Baden Council, July 2, 1702 (Zürich State Archives).

that all the houses, villages, and towns have not been burned down by the carelessness of men; but a fine is imposed on smoking only where there is danger of fire.

In February 1709 the Lesser Council repealed the order prohibiting tobacco, recognizing that it could not be enforced, and on April 25, 1710, a tobacco toll of seven and a half batzen was levied on every smoker or snuff-taker. Hardly a month later this resolution was rescinded, for the free Swiss would not submit to it. There was great discontent aroused by the tax in town and country alike. "Manifold threatening movements are taking place among the citizens, and have found their way into the local courts," is the statement in a report; and the Government had no desire to arouse a revolution. They therefore gave way along the whole line, "so that this evil spark may be quenched in time, and not arouse a dangerous fire." The surrender was complete. The authorities did not even dare to draw a revenue from tobacco in Switzerland, as was done in other countries, and shortly after permission was given to cultivate tobacco in the country. Smoking had a free course.

The conflict of opinions still raged. One of the most amusing points was the debate, in which many clergy-men and doctors took part, on the portentous question whether a smoker's brain was coated with a black film, as some said they had proved by dissecting the bodies of smokers. Even Neander, in the course of his inquiries, stumbled on this point, and asked his colleagues what they thought about it. Most of them denied that the brain would be blackened by smoke, but Hadrianus Falckenburgius took the view that a man's brain could get as sooty as a chimney. It seemed that various experiments in the dissection of executed criminals had settled this point.[1] Many men, including Kaspar Hoffmann and the physicians Paw and Rolfink, seriously believed this, and declared that they had seen the proof with their own eyes. The question was taken so seriously that Adam Hahn, a doctor at Jena, felt compelled to add, in a new edition of a *Tabacologia* of 1667 which he published in 1690, a chapter of his own which gives a history of this quaint discussion, and elaborately proves that smoking does not encrust the brain with soot. The whole story was clearly made up by tobaccophobes to scare the public off their new habit.

Of what use, however, was any private opposition, when tobacco was conquering princes and potentates? It was an age of Absolute Monarchy, and if the sovereign lit his pipe all his subjects could puff theirs freely. A striking instance is the case of Russia, where Peter the Great's autocracy began to make itself felt toward the end of the seventeenth century. In 1689 he had become sole ruler of Russia, the greatest original that ever wore a crown, thirsting for knowledge and eager to teach others. Tsar Peter wanted to catch up the march of progress which had left Russia lagging in the rear for centuries ; he wanted to make his nation a civilized power at one stroke. From the start he associated with the better-educated foreigners in Moscow, such as the versatile Scot Gordon, and Lefort from Geneva, and was introduced by them to other foreigners who lived in the

---

[1] *Epistolæ et judicia clarissimorum aliquot medicorum: De tabaco* (Utrecht, 1644).

German suburb of Moscow, the Sloboda. A vigorous intellectual life prevailed there, arts and sciences were studied, and men busied themselves with mathematics and astronomy as well as with handicrafts; many Englishmen and Dutchmen dwelt there, as well as Germans. The young Tsar, hungering and thirsting for knowledge, came under the influence of this society, without giving up his taste for drink and debauchery. His way of life soon led to a quarrel with the Patriarch, the head of the Orthodox Church, which had hitherto been a state within the State. In 1690 the Patriarch Joachim tried to expel the foreigners from the Tsar's Court, and forbade "the heathen," Gordon, to dine at the Kremlin. As a crowning outrage this stranger, like other foreigners, dared to disobey the Patriarch's prohibition of smoking, and ventured to tell the Tsar, only too ready to listen, of the profit and pleasure of this new vice. Peter did not yet feel strong enough to set himself openly against the Patriarch, so he bided his time, and went on drinking, and associating with foreigners just as before. When he travelled to Archangel, at that time the port for goods from Western Europe, he met merchants and sailors from England and Holland, and indulged his passion for learning all about shipbuilding and navigation. All these strangers were smoking pipes, like Gordon and his other friends in Moscow. He soon took to smoking himself, and the middle-sized Dutch pipe which was then in common use became the Tsar's inseparable companion. To the great wrath of the Patriarch, Peter not only himself smoked, but allowed his subjects to smoke. The Patriarchs of Moscow had soon to recognize that their independence in other more weighty matters could not be maintained : the Church became a department of the State, instead of a state within the State. Soon Tsar Peter could be seen in Archangel dressed like a Dutch skipper, pipe in mouth, drinking and smoking in the taverns, while the pilot Timofei Antip talked to him about the latest pattern of ship.

In 1697 Peter started on his famous trip to Western Europe, intending chiefly to study all the latest achievements of industry, especially shipbuilding, in the countries where they were most highly developed. Holland was the nearest stage, and he worked as a carpenter in a shipyard at Zaandam. Here, of course, he met mostly sailors and ship's officers, and if he had not been a great smoker already he would certainly have become one here, or in England, where he next stayed. William of Orange, the new ruler of England, shook his head at the uncouth manners of his Imperial guest, though he was pleased when Peter said that, if he were not lord of Russia, he would like to be an Admiral of the English fleet. William was not pleased, however, when the palace which had been lent to the Tsar was turned into a pigsty, where the Tsar, dressed like a workman and smoking his pipe, ate and slept at unseemly hours and indulged in occasional orgies. Admiral Lord Danby, afterward Marquess of Caermarthen, was told off to be bear-leader to the Tsar. It was said that Danby was quite as hard a drinker as his Imperial pupil, who always reeked of spirits. The Marquess was quite an original, and the two got on excellently. Danby entered into Peter's wildest plans, and not only gratified his taste for pretty women and drinking bouts, but took his ward to factories, hospitals, shipyards, in fact, everywhere where there was something to see and something to learn. There was never in all the world a more eager scholar than the Tsar. In England Peter saw high and low all smoking, and was confirmed in his opinion that the ban laid on smoking by the Russian clergy was wanton oppression. English merchants, knowing the young Emperor's modern ideas, determined to profit by them. One day a deputation appeared in Peter's London residence and requested the Tsar, in the presence of Admiral Caermarthen, his mentor, to allow tobacco to be imported into Russia. Peter thought this was a chance of getting a revenue for the State, as other countries had done, and gave the required permission, on payment of duty. The Admiral expressed a fear that the Patriarch of Moscow would oppose the importation of tobacco, but Peter answered that the clergy were concerned only with divine matters, and he would not let them meddle in worldly affairs. The Patriarch, he said, was not a customs officer, and had enough to do to look after the spiritual health of his flock. Later, on April 2, 1698, Peter made a contract with his bear-leader, giving him the sole right to import 10,000 hogsheads [1] of tobacco into Russia every year, paying the Tsar £2000 annually. Peter had a threefold purpose in making this agreement : firstly, he enabled the English merchants to trade with Russia ; secondly, by including Admiral Caermarthen in the contract he let his friend make some money out of the tobacco trade ; and, finally, the Tsar himself got the annual payment, like manna from heaven. When he returned to Russia he confirmed the permission to import tobacco and to smoke,

---

[1] A hogshead contained about 140 litres, or 30 gallons measure.

and introduced the tobacco monopoly, which he farmed out to his favourite and former playmate, Menschikov, who had risen from a pastrycook to be the Tsar's friend.

All this was done in scorn of the spiritual head of the Church at Moscow. The Patriarch Joachim had other insults to bear from the Tsar. He had once threatened to excommunicate any Russian who shaved, as was the fashion in England, instead of wearing a beard. Now the Tsar himself came home clean-shaven from England, and when the assembled boyars, generals, and high officials welcomed him, in his palace, he suddenly pulled a pair of scissors out of his pocket and with one snip cut off the beards of the Commander-in-Chief, the Viceroy of Moscow, and other magnates. But there was worse to come. At a wild drinking bout the Tsar ridiculed the head of the clergy by bringing forth a burlesque "High-priest of Bacchus," offering him the incense of burning tobacco, and puffing smoke into his face. Anybody could see who was meant by this Bacchic Pope. Peter the Great no longer feared openly to override the prohibition and smoke in the street. It was a sign that he was independent of the clergy, formerly omnipotent in Russia. He was especially fond of smoking when he received foreign ambassadors, who well knew his reason. In these seeming trifles, smoking and shaving, there was a real meaning. A man with a beard was to Peter the symbol of tradition and reaction, and was therefore an enemy. In the matter of smoking, as in so many others, he opened the way for new customs, and the habit spread mightily in Russia from that moment.

The tobacco habit was now so universal that, even when

an absolute monarch personally disliked smoking, unlike Peter, his people were not to be hindered from enjoying it. Autocracy in its extreme form prevailed in France under Louis XIV, "*le Roi Soleil*," who carried it to its highest point, with greater refinement than Peter the Great, but hardly more morality. He was not only the mightiest, but the finest and most elegant, monarch of his age. The splendour, luxury, and extravagance of Versailles were unique—so was its immorality. Naturally French society was given to smoking and snuff-taking no less than the masses of the people. The greatest authors dared to celebrate the new pleasure, and to extol it in their writings. In 1665 Molière's comedy of *Don Juan* appeared in Paris. The poet makes Sganarelle say:

> Whatever Aristotle and all the philosophers may say, there is nothing like tobacco; it is the passion of all proper people, and he who lives without tobacco has nothing to live for. Not only does it refresh and cleanse men's brains, but it guides their souls in the ways of virtue, and by it one learns to be a man of honour. Do you not see how readily men offer their tobacco right and left, wherever they are? No one waits to be asked; he anticipates another's wish; so true is it that tobacco begets honourable and virtuous sentiments in all those who use it.

Thomas Corneille, the lesser brother of the great dramatist, but himself no mean poet, turned these words into rhyme when he versified Molière's comedy in 1677 and published it as *Le Festin de Pierre*.

> Whatever Aristotle's school declare,
> Tobacco is divine, beyond compare,
> And to employ aright an idler's leisure,
> No sport is there that gives so great a pleasure.

A HISTORY OF SMOKING

A new-found medicine, a heav'n-sent gain,
It cleanses, brightens, and restores the brain,
Of melancholy it is purgative ;
Who lives without tobacco does not live.
Tobacco, O tobacco, that I love !

This glowing appeal of the two poets sounds seductive, but Louis was deaf to its charm. He hated tobacco in any form, and was restrained from forbidding its use only by financial considerations. His chief pleasure was good eating, and he had the finest appetite in his kingdom. We know from the Duc de Saint-Simon, the keen observer of his age, that it was not unusual for the King to consume at one meal four platefuls of various soups, a whole pheasant, a partridge, a dish of salad, two large slices of ham, roast mutton with garlic sauce, a dish of pastry, then fruit, and hard-boiled eggs to wind up. As he would not allow smoking in his own neighbourhood, his courtiers had to do it privately ; that was the least of their vices. The clearest view of the manners of the Court is given by the description of the famous Princess Palatine Liselotte,[1] who had married the King's misogynist brother, Philip of Orléans, in 1671. She came in all her natural simplicity into the most artificial Court that could be imagined, and shocked it by her unique originality. She was never given to be " mealy-mouthed," as she says herself in her own blunt but expressive style. She never got on with her husband, who could hardly read or write, and was generally idle and lazy—except when he gambled away vast sums ; but this gave her a clearer insight into the

[1] Duchess Elisabeth Charlotte of Orléans, born Princess Palatine, *Hof und Gesellschaft in Frankreich am Anfang des 18. Jahrhunderts*, selected letters, edited by Paul Volkmar (Stuttgart).

Fig. 39. Interior of Old Chinese House, with Lady smoking

Fig. 40. Elisabeth Charlotte of Orleans (Liselotte)

181

ways of the French Court, which she despised from the bottom of her heart—as she did smoking.

" All the women in Paris," she once wrote to her aunt, the Electress Sophia of Hanover,

> go stripped (*i.e.*, with neck and bosom bare) and it disgusts me—you can see almost down to their waists; you have never seen anything madder than the way they go on; they all look as if they were just out of a madhouse. They could not be worse if they did it on purpose to look frightful. I don't wonder that the men despise the women; the women are too contemptible with their dress, their drinking, and their tobacco, which makes them smell horribly.

Another time she is still harder on the habit of smoking and snuff-taking.[1]

> This snuff is a disgusting affair, I hope you don't take any, dear Louise! It puts me in a temper when I see all the women here, with dirty noses, as if they had rubbed them in the muck—excuse the word!—come and stick their fingers into any man's snuff-box—it makes me sick, it is so disgusting.

She breaks out violently in another letter to her stepsister Louise.

> There is nothing in the world that I hate like snuff; it gives people dirty noses, makes them talk through their noses, and smell horribly. I have seen people here who once had the sweetest breath in the world, and after they took to snuff, in six months they stank like goats. There is nothing, I think, nastier than taking snuff and getting one's nose just as if—excuse the phrase—one had tumbled into a muck-heap. Our King likes it no more than I do, but all his children and grandchildren take to it, without caring for displeasing the King. It is better to take no snuff at all than a little; for it is certain that he who takes a little will soon

[1] *Op. cit.* p. 335 : Liselotte to the Raugräfin Louise, Marly, August 6, 1713.

take much, and that is why they call it ' the enchanted herb,' for those who take it are so taken by it that they cannot go without it; so take care of yourself, dear Louise ! [1]

After reading these samples we must admit that Liselotte was not " mealy-mouthed," for one could hardly believe that a woman's soft lips could utter such language. But this was sweetness itself compared with other expressions in her letters, especially when she spoke of her bitter enemy, Madame de Maintenon, whom she called " old beast," " old ragbag," " she-devil." This was partly due to jealousy, for the Duchess, in all honour, had a great admiration for Louis XIV. The amusing part of it was that the King was the only one who always came off well in her letters, while all the others were treated in the most unflattering style—and the King had the letters shown to him by his Minister of Police. At first he was amused at her frankness, and felt flattered that he was so well treated ; moreover, he was well content that Liselotte shared his opinion of smoking and snuff-taking. Later, when French troops conquered and devastated the Palatinate, Liselotte's own country, there were terrible quarrels, and the Duchess was too severe on Madame de Maintenon, soon to be the King's wife. One day Louis told his wife about these letters, and war broke out between the two ladies—an unequal fight, for the King leant to Maintenon's side.

The King and his sister-in-law were alone in their hatred of smoking and snuff-taking. All the rest of the royal family, even the King's daughters, had no idea of sharing his aversion. One day the King was late at cards in his

[1] *Briefe der Herzogin Elisabeth Charlotte von Orléans*, p. 335 (edited by Hans F. Helmolt, Leipzig, 1924).

drawing-room. When Philip of Orléans was going to his rooms he noticed the smell of smoke coming from a neighbouring room. He went in and found the King's daughters smoking pipes which they had brought from the guard-room of the Swiss Guard. He advised them to stop at once, for the King was just coming ; but the smoke was still there, and Louis XIV gave his daughters a good scolding next day.

High dignitaries who were given to smoking or snuff-taking, and had often to hold long conferences with the King, suffered from his hatred of tobacco. Marshal Count d'Harcourt, a good soldier and beloved by his men, who was a friend of the Maintenon, and knew well how to blend the soldier with the courtier, was a passionate de-votee of snuff—though he was more cleanly than Marshal d'Huxelles, whose clothes and cravats were always soiled with it. Harcourt noticed, when he was with the King, that Louis greatly disliked the smell of tobacco. He was afraid that this might have unpleasant consequences for him, and might stand in the way of his ambition. He was a man of energy, and resolved to break himself of his habit forthwith. Soon after he had a stroke which partially paralysed his body. The doctors let him smoke and take snuff again, thinking that this ailment might be caused by his sudden change of habit ; but this did no good, and the Marshal died soon after in great pain.

The reckless follies of Louis XIV's courtiers sometimes ended tragically. Canon Jean de Santeul was a welcome guest at the Court, for he was a well-known Latin poet and a great wit. One day, in 1697, he was dining with the Prince of Condé at Chantilly. The revelry became fast and furious, and host and guests were deep in wine. The Prince forced Santeul to go on drinking, and finally shook his snuff-box into a goblet of wine and compelled Santeul to drink it off, to see what would happen. The poet was at once taken ill, and died in agony within forty-eight hours, with every sign of poisoning. Louis XIV must have been very angry at such occurrences, but the omnipotent "*Roi Soleil*," dreaded by the whole world, was powerless against smoking. His hands had been tied since Colbert had told him of the rich returns from the tobacco monopoly ; and he was compelled even to sign decrees protecting the tobacco trade. After Colbert's death his policy of drawing a rich revenue from tobacco was still continued. An abuse had sprung up through soldiers and sailors smuggling in tobacco from abroad and cutting out the expensive article supplied by the monopoly. In consequence of this a royal ordinance was issued on October 13, 1688, forbidding soldiers to smoke any tobacco except from the licensed shops, under penalty of imprisonment for the first offence, and of running the gauntlet for the second.

But apart from his financial interests Louis XIV was a lifelong hater of the weed, and when he appeared snuff-boxes vanished into pockets, and pipes up sleeves. Only one man at Court was still fiercely opposed to tobacco, though some said he took up this attitude to please his royal master ; he was Fagon, Louis XIV's body physician. The Academy of Science, which had been founded at Paris in 1666, discussed three years later whether the ever-growing use of tobacco injured the brain. De Courtigi, an Academician, maintained the view that smoking was

not only not injurious, but actually helpful. His chief
opponent was Fagon, the royal physician, a little crooked
man who could hardly balance himself on his lean legs.
He was always ill, always coughing, but good humoured
and witty; he lived to be eighty, and had great influence
with Louis XIV.

Though tobacco had overrun the whole world Fagon
and his King were unconquered, and before the whole
Academy he answered De Courtigi by stating, from the
results of his experience, that the frequent use of tobacco
shortened human life. The same question was discussed
on March 26, 1699, in the Paris School of Medicine, of
which Fagon was president.

"America, conquered by the Spaniards," Fagon began,[1]

triumphed over the arrogance of her conquerors by infecting them
with her own vices; she hastened on the death of her new masters
by giving them venereal disease—and tobacco. Well would it
have been if this plant had remained undiscovered. A man of sense
who has good breeding, good manners, and good health, who has
received God's good gifts, and is wise enough to use them aright,
must shun the deceitful lure and never defile his mouth with the
stench of a pipe.

"Who is the rash man," Fagon goes on,[2]

that first tasted a poison that is more dangerous than hemlock,
deadlier than opium? When he opened his snuff-box, did he not
know that he was opening Pandora's box, from which would spring
a thousand ills, one worse than another? Assuredly, when we try
it for the first time, we feel an uneasiness that tells us that we
have taken poison.

[1] See E. Cardon, Le Musée du fumeur (Paris, 1866).
[2] Nicolas Andy, De la Génération des vers dans le corps de l'homme, p. 235
(Amsterdam, 1701). In the Appendix to this book, which is on a different
subject, Fagon's speech is given.

Fagon described, with gross exaggeration, the ill consequences, sickness and dizziness, fever and palpitations, of the first trial of tobacco. "When, unfortunately," he went on,

> against all advice, he falls under this dangerous habit, all reasoning, all warning, is in vain. He cannot shake off his enemy. . . . All other pleasures bring satiety, which weakens their ill effects; tobacco alone becomes a fatal, insatiable necessity. It has been said that love is a brief epileptic fit, but smoking is a permanent epilepsy.

Fagon admits, indeed, that tobacco has some uses, but only to add the classical tag that enemies are most to be feared when they bring gifts. His remarks aroused great opposition among the learned assembly, in spite of the King's influence. The general impression produced is shown by the anecdote, which was current during Fagon's lifetime, that in the middle of his fiery philippic he thoughtlessly seized a snuff-box and took a pinch, amid universal laughter. The truth seems to be that Fagon was unable to attend a meeting at which the question was again to be discussed, and asked one of his assistants, who was given to snuff, to read a manuscript address expressing his views. It was the reader, not the author, of the speech who took the incongruous pinch of snuff; but naturally Fagon himself got the credit of it.

CHAPTER VIII

SMOKING IN THE EIGHTEENTH CENTURY:
PIPE VERSUS SNUFF-BOX

BY the beginning of the eighteenth century the whole world had surrendered to tobacco. Every one smoked, and the stern prohibitions of the seventeenth century dwindled down into regulations forbidding smoking in places where there was danger of fire, and in public, on the ground of decency. The change was inevitable, for the princes and rulers who had issued the prohibitory edicts were now slaves to the tobacco habit themselves. Hitherto all over Europe most people had smoked middle-sized Dutch clay pipes, and the upper classes provided themselves with artistic china pipes. Now snuff-taking began to be fashionable in France, and from thence, as well as from Spain, spread far and wide among the upper classes of Western Europe. The habit took such a hold of the Court and the governing classes, the nobility and clergy, in France and England, that it almost entirely supplanted smoking. Snuff was fashionable; smoking was relegated to the middle and lower classes. Tobacco was still sovereign, but under another form, as was noted by the Italian Baruffaldi,[1] who saw the spread of snuff-taking in his own country, and called tobacco the food of the brain. Snuff was introduced into England by the courtiers and officers who had been with Charles II in France.

[1] *La Tabaccheide*, p. 104 (1714).

[187]

When the Stuart monarch came back in triumph in 1660 the snuff-box followed in his train. Under the last two Stuart kings, and then under William and Mary, and under Queen Anne, the last Stuart sovereign, snuff-taking was the only fashionable way of using tobacco, and dainty snuff-boxes were handled by all the gallants and ladies of the Court. Smoking was tabooed in High Society, though the other classes were still faithful to the pipe. Snuff-taking was brought to Germany at the end of the seventeenth century by the Huguenot refugees from France. Thus, as Boerner [1] states, the first snuff-dealers, and especially the first snuff-manufacturers, nearly all came from France to Cologne, a city which soon became the centre of the trade in pipe-tobacco as well as snuff.

In Germany, where smoking was relatively a new habit, snuff took a long time to become general in good society. The first two kings of Prussia, Frederick I and Frederick William I, were great pipe-smokers, and their nobility mostly followed their example. In 1701 the Elector Frederick III of Brandenburg took the title of King Frederick I of Prussia. Smoking played a considerable part in the new royal Court, though it was still hedged in with elaborate etiquette. King Frederick I was the first to hold so-called tobacco-parties, where great dignitaries and their ladies appeared in full Court dress. Fig. 42 shows one of these functions, at which the Queen, with powdered hair, and wearing a long train and ermine mantle, goes up to the King, who is wearing all his orders, and lights his long clay pipe with a spill. Round him in the wreathing smoke sit, strictly in order of rank,

[1] *Kölner Tabakhandel und Tabakgewerbe, 1628 bis 1910*, p. 25.

[188]

Quoy qu'en dise Aristote, & sa digne Cabale,
Le Tabac est divin, il n'est rien qui l'egale
C'est dans la Medecine un reméde nouveau,
Il purge, réjoüit, conforte le cerveau,
De toute noire humeur promptement le délivre,
Et qui rit sans Tabac n'est pas digne de vivre.

B. Picart delin: et ex. 1715.   Moliere.

Fig. 41. LADY TAKING SNUFF

Fig. 42. Frederick I of Prussia's "Tobacco Club" (1701–13)

generals and Ministers of State in full-bottomed wigs and full uniform; pages and footmen wait at table. There were, too, big official banquets, which were called 'tobacco-meetings,' merely because the King, who himself wanted to smoke, allowed his guests to indulge in the habit—which was usually thought improper at table. Frederick I's successor was an obstinate, overbearing, impulsive man, with simple and soldierly tastes. Frederick William I (1713-40) kept up the 'tobacco-parties,' but completely changed their character. They became far more free-and-easy. Whenever the King was at Berlin, Potsdam, or Wüsterhausen he gathered his friends round him every day at five o'clock in the afternoon, when official functions permitted. At first they numbered only seven or eight, chiefly generals and staff-officers. At Potsdam they met either in a room of the palace or a summer-house; at Wüsterhausen, when it was fine, they sometimes occupied a Turkish tent that was pitched on a little island near the old castle. It was called the Tobacco Club, for every one there either smoked, or if he was not a smoker, pretended to be. Gradually the King added to the list of guests; for though he liked to talk about his giant guard of " big, strong fellows," he wearied of mere military conversation. Gradually he asked in men of learning, travelling foreigners, the ambassadors of other states, if he liked them, and even buffoons and boon companions. The King was a great eater, but a still greater drinker, and old Rhenish and foaming beer were always on his table. At the Tobacco Club every one had merely beer and a short Dutch clay pipe of the commonest kind; the King alone had a silver-mounted pipe. The tobacco, Dutch leaf, was on the table in wicker baskets, with little pans of glowing peat to light the pipes. The servants, when the room was ready, were sent away and forbidden to enter till the Club meeting was over, so that the members could talk freely and crack jokes to their heart's content. Before every guest stood a huge white jug of beer and a glass, and on a table by his side bread and butter, cheese, and cold meat. Each had to help himself and carve for himself. Sometimes the King prepared a dish of fish with his own august hands in the sight of his guests, and made the salad himself. But the chief business of the evening was smoking, and the King sometimes—especially when his friend Stanislaus, the ex-King of Poland, was there—smoked all night. In 1735 they used to smoke thirty pipes and more, from five in the afternoon to two o'clock next morning. Frederick William I, whose health was none too good, envied King Stanislaus, whose 'leathern mouth' could stand smoking to any hour. The Imperial ambassador, Count Seckendorf, was anxious about the King of Prussia. " I took occasion," he writes,

to advise him, for his health's sake, to moderate his way of living. He seems to see himself that too much smoking is injurious to him, and has abstained from it for some days; it would be well if he could do the same with regard to drink.[1]

It was torment for members of this society who did not smoke to sit in a cloud of smoke. The Old Dessauer,[2] who could never bring himself to smoke, sat among the guests with an unlighted pipe in his mouth, and by

[1] Seckendorf to Prince Eugène, February 23, 1731 (Vienna Archives).
[2] Field-Marshal Leopold I, Prince of Anhalt-Dessau.

his side Count Seckendorf, the Imperial ambassador, a regular member of the Tobacco Club. They often discussed important matters of policy. Both of them, in order to satisfy the rules of the Club, puffed away like thorough smokers. The King liked to appear as an ordinary person, forbade any ceremony, and no one even rose when he came in. The royal princes usually came into the Tobacco Club in the evening to bid their father good night. They thought it such fun that it was hard to get them back to the Queen's rooms, where they were not allowed to romp. The fun at the Club often grew fast and furious. The King and his guests played the wildest tricks on an odd figure, the historian Gundling, who was given to drink too much. But, apart from this horse-play, the most important business of State was discussed at the Tobacco Club, and individual members of the company, as they could talk more freely, tried to win over the King to their side. That was the time when the differences between the King and the Crown Prince Frederick came to a head over the marriage question. Two parties, the Anglo-Hanoverian and the Imperialist, were struggling to influence the Prussian Court, and each tried to get the King on its side.

Queen Sophia Dorothea, a cousin of Princess Caroline of Hanover (whose son was heir-apparent to England), and the English party sought to unite Prussian and Anglo-Hanoverian policy by a double marriage. The Prince of Wales was to marry the Crown Prince's elder sister, Friederike Sophie Wilhelmine (afterward Margravine of Bayreuth), and the Crown Prince was to marry Princess Amelia of Hanover. The Imperial Court at

Vienna was doing its best to foil this plan, which included the further idea of installing the Crown Prince Frederick as the English Viceroy of Hanover. With this aim Count Seckendorf, a friend of the King of Prussia, was appointed Imperial ambassador at Berlin, and was well furnished with money. The Count soon won the King's favour by his charm of manner, and as a mark of distinction was admitted, as we have seen, a member of the Tobacco Club. Seckendorf won over General von Grumbkow, the King's confidant, who was also a regular member, gave him a pension, and secured his help in opposing the double-marriage plan. Three months after the Imperial envoy arrived there was a change in the aspect of affairs : King Frederick William seemed to be dropping the treaty with Hanover, and taking the Emperor's side. Still nothing was yet settled, and for the next year or two this weighty affair was warmly debated in the Tobacco Club, or, as Carlyle calls it, " the Tobacco Parliament." Seckendorf's reports to the Emperor and Prince Eugène tell us how the Club was the focus of political intrigue, how Grumbkow supported the Count, and on those days when Seckendorf could not be present furnished written reports of the proceedings. It was not easy to get the King completely under his thumb, as Seckendorf himself admits. In one of his reports to Prince Eugène he gives a view of his relations with Prussia. He writes :

You will see by all my reports that I have continually sought to confirm the King of Prussia in his determination to make a close and friendly alliance with his Imperial and Royal Majesty, according to his assurances given to me verbally and in writing ; but the King is of such a secretive, false, and fickle temper that

Fig. 43. Aristocratic Smoking-Party, about 1720

192

Fig. 44. The "Tobacco Club" in the Time of Frederick William I of Prussia (1713–40)

it is impossible even to guess at his real views, and we can only rely on conjecture.

"At the Tobacco Club," Seckendorf's report goes on to say,

more emphatic language is used, and lately, when Major-General von Marwitz and Colonel Tokkum had had too much wine and spoke rather more freely on the Hanoverian side, the King declared that any Prussian who was for Hanover was a rascal.

The Crown Prince, who was present, heard all these speeches and reported them to his mother. As is known, the marriage affair was ended by the attempt of the Crown Prince to escape.

Frederick William, with his personal taste for smoking, was the last to want to hinder his subjects from following his example, but he was not going to give up the revenue from tobacco. Carlyle says he had a genius for economies, and his system of taxation and his measures for saving expense—so different from his father's ostentation and extravagance—served as a model for his age. In granting out the tobacco monopoly, which was a heavy blow for the merchants, who had been free to deal in tobacco before 1719, he followed no new plan. On August 14, 1719, he granted two Jewish commissaries, Moses and Elias Gompertz, the sole right for twelve years to manufacture the tobacco which hitherto had been imported from abroad. In return he got 2000 thalers for the recruiting chest and one of his beloved giant grenadiers, whom the two Jews valued at 1300 thalers. But this held good only for foreign tobacco, and apart from that the King left " every farmer and householder free as beforetime to continue growing tobacco in Our dominions, and increase the same at will." [1]

Afterward the King, with a just estimate of his own interests, tried to take the monopoly away from the contractors and make it a State affair; but his officials took more narrow views, and nothing was done for the moment. The royal "Tobacco Parliament" continued one of the chief consumers of tobacco.

Even in his last days the King could not tear himself away from his beloved Tobacco Club. In 1740, a few weeks before his death, the members assembled in the great hall of the palace, and had their pipes and tobacco as usual, but it was noted as an ill omen that the King, the greatest smoker of them all, never touched his pipe. They were all sitting, as at the Tobacco Club, in a circle, when the Crown Prince entered rather late, having been kept by inspecting one of his regiments. As soon as the Crown Prince appeared all stood up and bowed, thinking that the King's rule that no one should be saluted at the Tobacco Club did not hold for a palace hall. This highly offended Frederick William; he angrily exclaimed that they were bowing to the rising sun, but he would show them that he was still alive, and still the master, and dismissed the company with every sign of annoyance. After a time the guests were invited to the palace again, but they were not long to have a chance of meeting, for on May 31 the King died. Frederick II, who had never cared much for the Tobacco Club, abolished the institution.

Meanwhile smoking and snuff-taking were continually

[1] See E. P. Reimann, *Das Tabaksmonopol Friedrichs des Grossen*, p. 20 (royal edict, Berlin, August 14, 1719).

increasing in other European countries, and the monopoly system was altered and improved. The Emperor Leopold I, in a decree of May 20, 1701, enforcing his sovereign right and power over the tobacco monopoly, called smoking "a habit that has crept in and become well-nigh universal."

The *appalto* system still prevailed in Austria, and the Emperor Charles VI, who recognized the great possibilities of revenue latent in the tobacco trade, attempted, between 1723 and 1726, to change the private *appalto* into a State *Regie*. The attempt failed owing to a lack of proper organization—and no wonder, when an Imperial *valet de chambre* was thought capable of filling the post of managing director of the *Regie*.[1] The Government had to go back to the old system of farming out the monopoly to private contractors, who used their privileges oppressively, for their own advantage.

Complaints came from all quarters; popular discontent often took a violent form, as when an angry mob once attacked the Vienna office of the *appalto*. Especially loud complaints came from Bohemia to the officials at Vienna, stating that "these appaltists are getting all the public trade, or at least the best part of it, into their claws, and as a necessary consequence are ruining all the other traders."[2]

The monopolists tried to suppress smuggling and unlicensed trade by spies and inspectors, to the great wrath of the people. The Styrian Provincial Council in 1751,

---

[1] See *Fachliche Mitteilungen der österreichischen Tabakregie* (1912), p. 86, *Die Monopolgesetze und die Besteuerung des Tabakskonsums von 1683 bis 1783.*

[2] *Historisch, Politisch, Juridisch, und Cameralische Reflexions über die dermahlige Landes Verfassung des Königreiches Böheimb.* (1718).

in the name of the population, declared that it was forced to make known "after how cruel and so to speak un-Christian a fashion the poor inhabitants and peasants are continually handled by the inspectors set over them . . . and robbed of all their possessions."[1]

The countless complaints of the Lower Austrian population against the oppression of the revenue officers, who imposed "excessive fines and punishments" for slight offences, end with a warning against driving the people to insurrection by the arbitrary acts of these officials.

The old prohibitions against smoking were now fading away. They were in force only "in those places where great damage might be wrought by carelessness." Sometimes it was considered that smoking interfered with work, and for this reason the City Council of Cologne forbade workmen to smoke at work, or in the public streets, or other public places, since they "are led into great excess by continual smoking of tobacco, whereby not only is valuable time wasted, but also fire is to be feared."

Similar regulations were often issued at that time in innumerable towns of Europe, and with good reason, considering that timber was still in general use for building houses. In most towns and villages smoking in the streets was forbidden, and the watchmen were ordered to stop it. Smoking in public was still regarded as an offence against propriety. But no one could say that there was any danger of fire from snuff-taking, which needed no flint and steel, and tinder; this helped to spread the new fashion.

As the question of propriety had been raised, writers

[1] Dr Franz Wieser, *Zur Geschichte des Tabakgefälles und der Tabakkultur in Dalmatien, 1700–1884*, p. 145, etc.

of the time came to discuss of women smoking in society. In 1715 a very ' advanced ' lady,[1] who considered tobacco to be the secret of long life, wrote a short book advocating smoking for women, with the pleasing title *A Sound and Pleasant Proof that a Respectable Woman may sometimes enter a Coffee-house without Damage to her Good Name, and moreover she may, and should, treat herself to a Pipe of Tobacco. Further it is also explained why Women go first, and why Men wear Beards. All most briefly and pleasantly proved, and maintained by Incontestable Reasons.*

Not only women claimed the right to smoke for their sex; they were supported by men—whose motives for this championship it is vain to conjecture. Dr J. J. W. Beintema, probably a descendant of the writer who waxed enthusiastic over tobacco in 1690, wrote a *Vernünftige Untersuchung* on the question " whether ladies of pleasure and other ladies may not be permitted to smoke like men, and whether it is good for their health?" The Doctor concluded,

> that tobacco is invaluable, and that he pities those who drag on a miserable life without it. I will merely state at the outset that it is a glorious venture when a woman takes heart to smoke a pipe of tobacco. Her charming sex has an equal right with men.

We see what advanced opinions tobacco fostered. The gradual spread of snuff-taking was also echoed in literature. One author wrote a satire on the *Lust of the Longing Nose*.[2] From this we can tell how seriously snuff-taking was competing with smoking. The writer says:

[1] Mme Leucorande, Lindenstadt, 1715.
[2] Johann Heinrich Cohausen, *Satyrische Gedancken, von der Pica Nasi; oder, Der Sehnsucht der lüsternen Nase, das ist von dem heutigen Missbrauch und schädlichen Effekt des Schnupftabacks* (Leipzig, 1720).

The world has taken up a ridiculous fashion—the excessive use of snuff. All nations are snuffing. All classes snuff, from the highest to the lowest. I have sometimes wondered to see how lords and lackeys, High Society and the mob, woodchoppers and handymen, broom-squires and beadles, take out their snuff-boxes with an air, and dip into them. Both sexes snuff, for the fashion has spread to the women; the ladies began it, and are now imitated by the washerwomen. People snuff so often that their noses are more like a dust-heap than a nose; so irrationally that they think the dust an ornament, although, since the world began, all rational men have thought a dirty face unhealthy; so recklessly that they lose the sense of smell and their bodily health. They snuff without need, at all times, in all places, without rest, as though their fate and fortune, their name and fame, their life and health, even their eternal salvation depended on it.

Do but notice what grimaces snuff-takers make, how their whole features are convulsed, how they dip into their snuff-boxes in measured rhythm, cock up their noses, compose their mouths, eyes, and all their features to a pompous dignity, and, as they perform the solemn rite of snuff-taking, they look as if they scorned the whole world, or were bent on some enterprise of which they might say, like Bouflet, " I will make the whole world tremble! "

I have found by certain experiments that such men have the idea that, in the moment when they sniff the snuff up their noses, they are as men inspired, transformed into mighty kings and princes, or at least made royal and princely at heart.

The clergy, too, fell under the spell, and owned that, as a puzzle of the time states, " The answer is tobacco, which now rules the whole world." Innocent X, in 1650, had threatened those who smoked in St Peter's with excommunication, but his edict was a dead letter. Pope Benedict XIII, of the Orsini family, was himself first given to smoking and then to snuff-taking.

Every day the Pope could not help noting some of the

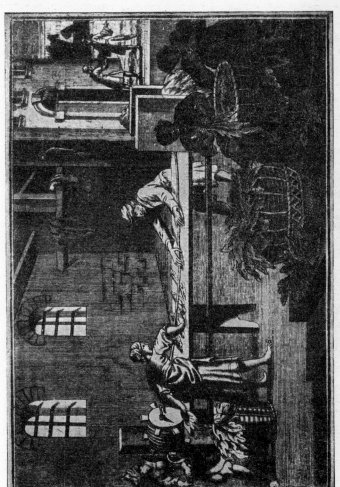

Fig. 45. Preparing Tobacco, about 1750

Fig. 46. Tobacco Harvest, about 1750

clergy leaving the chancel in the middle of the services, and disturbing the congregation. They could no longer restrain themselves from indulging in their beloved habit. Accordingly, the Holy Father addressed a letter to the Cardinal Archpriest of the Vatican Basilica.[1] In view of the circumstances, and by the advice of physicians, he permitted the use of snuff in the aforesaid church and all parts of it, and repealed the former Bull of excommunication. At the same time the Pope expressed his hope that, in spite of this permission, no one would fail in due reverence, since such is fitting in a cathedral famed over the whole Catholic world, whereto all nations of the earth made pilgrimage from the farthest parts, to do honour to the holy bodies of the glorious Apostles Peter and Paul. Accordingly, Innocent X's Bull was " withdrawn, annulled, and utterly repealed, as though it had never been issued and proclaimed." The Cardinal, who had to make known this ordinance,[2] admonished

the whole clergy of the aforesaid cathedral, earnestly, in the name of the Lord, that not only were they to take snuff within the precincts of the church so discreetly that no scandal or offence might be given to any of the congregation, but no one, especially when taking part in the holy ceremonies, should openly or covertly offer the box or casket wherein he keeps the tobacco dust to any beside or around him.

But snuff-taking was now free of St Peter's.

Thus one barrier after another fell, and the victory of tobacco could not be made plainer to all men than by

[1] Ordinance of Pope Benedict XIII, January 10, 1725.
[2] Order of the Cardinal di San Clemente, Chamberlain and Archbishop of the Vatican Church. Hannibal, *Literæ executoriales chirographi* (Rome, 1725).

the fact that the chief Shepherd of Christendom himself had surrendered, and permitted clergy and laity to enjoy the once proscribed herb in St Peter's, the centre of the Catholic Church.

The repeal of Innocent X's Bull had an effect far beyond the limits of St Peter's. It was taken in Germany as a solemn approval of snuff-taking. Since Frederick II, afterward the Great, came to the throne of Prussia in 1740, snuff-taking, like other French fashions, spread widely. Frederick, with his well-known love for the French language and manners, set the example. He never smoked, but was all the more addicted to snuff. His contemporaries all agree in reporting that he was often to be seen with his face and clothes soiled with snuff. Although many men declare that he carried his snuff loose in his waistcoat pocket, yet the French fashion of wearing and giving away finely wrought snuff-boxes flourished most in his reign. A snuff-box in pure gold, studded with diamonds, often was presented to a foreign ambassador, as a daintily disguised bribe—and bribery was common enough in official and diplomatic circles at that time. Some contemporaries declared that certain Ministers of State were quoted as costing two, three, or more snuff-boxes. All the museums of Europe possess fine examples from the Courts of Louis XV and XVI, Peter the Great, Frederick the Great,[1] and others. If a sovereign wished to honour or bribe a man he gave him his portrait enamelled on a splendid snuff-box, with his initials in diamonds. These exquisite snuff-boxes were

[1] See some fine specimens in Martin Klar, *Die Tabatieren Friedrichs des Grossen* (Berlin, not dated).

sought after by collectors. Prince Louis Ferdinand of Bourbon Conti, who died in 1776, left 800. Frederick the Great, too, had a large collection of fine specimens.

The King, though he himself never smoked, had financial reasons for not hindering the practice in his dominions; but he issued a stern edict against careless smoking in town or country. A spark might easily catch the corn or the barns, and smoking in harvest-time was punished with a month's imprisonment on bread and water.

In spite of the popularity of snuff and smoking there were still people who were alarmed at the increased consumption of tobacco in particular countries. A book, very popular at the time, called *The Wise and Law-abiding Householder*, protested not so much against the use of tobacco as against excesses in that use.

" It would be well," the author says,

> if the German nation would use the fruits and plants derived from the Indians moderately, and would distinguish between use and abuse. But now things have come to such a pass (Lord have mercy on us !) that we poor people of the Old World get something from the New World which right soon packs us off into the next world. Especially is this true of the beloved herb tobacco, a noble plant, but sore misused among us.[1]

In Germany smoking was still trying to come out into the open, though this was forbidden in most of the German states. It soon became evident that it was impracticable to prosecute all who dared to smoke in the

---

[1] Franciscus Philippus Florinus, *Œconomus prudens et legalis; oder, Allgemeiner kluger und rechtsverständiger Hausvatter*, Book III, p. 604 (Nuremberg, Frankfort, Leipzig, 1750).

street. Yet the habit was still forbidden, and all through the eighteenth century, right down to the Revolution of 1848, we meet with innumerable notices issued by the authorities prohibiting, or at least limiting, smoking in public places. For instance, we read in the drill-book of the Hamburg City Guard, in 1752, that the officers had to take care that the men did not smoke pipes on the march. On April 24, 1750, the Hamburg General-in-Command repeated the order to all the sentries, that no one should be allowed to stay on the bridges, at the gates, and near the trees " smoking, and with pipe alight." In the neighbouring town of Altona the laws were stricter still, and no inhabitant could dare to look out of the window with a pipe in his mouth without incurring a fine. These rules were at first imposed to guard against fires; but they often served as a pretext for a prince who objected to tobacco to harass his smoking subjects. Prince Leopold III of Anhalt-Dessau, for instance, who ruled from 1758 to 1817, permitted his subjects, if they saw anyone smoking in the streets, to knock the pipe out of his mouth without fear of consequences.

In spite of all this, smoking increased daily. In the eighteenth century the students caught the habit, and soon no member of a university was complete without his pipe and his mug. At that time the word *Knaster* (canister) came into use; it was derived from the Spanish *canastro*, a wicker basket, as tobacco from the Spanish colonies was generally sent over in such baskets. On arrival in Europe the leaves were put up for retail sale in little packets, decorated with various woodcuts or prints, and marked with the name of the firm that sold

Fig. 47. SNUFF-BOX BELONGING TO FREDERICK THE GREAT

Fig. 48. Soldier smoking a Pipe

them. All sorts of pictures, such as " the smoking Indian " or " the Cossack," appeared on these packets.[1]

Frederick the Great had chosen as his financial adviser a certain Gian Antonio di Calzabigi,[2] one of the notorious adventurers who infested the Court at that time; and Calzabigi nominated one François Roubeaud, a bankrupt Marseilles merchant, as director of the tobacco monopoly. On May 4, 1765, Frederick signed an agreement with Roubeaud giving him the monopoly for all the Prussian dominions, and embodied this in an edict of July 17. This inevitably led to oppression by the inspectors of the monopoly, the so-called " tobacco grubbers." Popular indignation arose against these officials, and the Lord-Lieutenants and Councils of Brandenburg asked, in rather plain language, that they alone should be allowed to enforce the royal edict.[3]

The oppressive tobacco police might be replaced by the district officials, local magistrates, and publicans, which would be cheaper than hundreds and hundreds of spies. The provinces protested against search made without notice. . . . Such practices could not be approved by his Majesty, for every man should be at peace in his own four walls, and protected from having his house raided and arbitrarily ransacked by strange soldiers, not in the King's service. The action of the tobacco police was a breach of the peace. The nobility would never submit to the jurisdiction of the tobacco company, but would repel force with force. . . . Most of the tobacco was grown on the estates of the nobility, on public lands, and on village fields. . . . The nobility was not under

---

[1] These packets were often collected. In the *Historische Braunbuch Tabakanekdoten*, published by Josef Feinhals (Cologne, 1914), and dedicated to all friends and enemies of tobacco, there are many amusing stories, and numerous illustrations of the packets.

[2] See for details E. P. Reimann, *op. cit.*

[3] Reimann, *op. cit.*, p. 83.

the jurisdiction of the excise, and it would be monstrous if the excise officers dared to carry out a search in the houses of nobles or public officials. If they did, the resident landowners would be forced to take refuge in the towns to escape these armed raiders.

The King's experimental contract with the two foreigners was unsuccessful; they grew rich at the expense of his country. He broke with them altogether, and introduced a State monopoly of tobacco, which he tried to extend to Denmark and Sweden. He was successful in Sweden in 1786. Frederick issued directions [1] for carrying out this plan, which are characteristic of his anxiety to get the highest possible returns from his monopoly:

> In answer to your further report about the tobacco trade with Sweden, I say that we will first see how best it can be arranged, and I think you will be able to carry the business through successfully, especially if we give the King of Sweden some money, for he will do anything for money. The first point is to find out where the Swedes get their tobacco now, what it is like, and what are their favourite kinds; next I think that the tobacco we are sending to Sweden should preferably be manufactured at Stettin, and if Virginia leaf is wanted, you can have it sent straight there. If we can sell the Swedes tobacco a trifle cheaper than the others do, we shall get the whole trade into our hands. . . .

The Prussian State Monopoly doubled the price of the coarsest tobacco, and made the finer sorts much dearer. Toward the end of Frederick's reign no more edicts were issued against smoking, even in places where there was danger of fire; on the contrary, premiums were given for growing tobacco—which had to be sold to the monopoly. The King displayed a very modern desire to

---

[1] Draft orders of the King, October 2, 1785, to Count Schulenburg: Reimann, *op. cit.*, p. 225.

Fig. 49. SILHOUETTE OF A PIPE-SMOKER

JUGEMENT
SOUVERAIN,
Du 19 Décembre 1771.

Rendu en la Commission établie à Reims par Lettres Patentes du 21 Novembre 1765.

Qui condamne JEAN ALAVOINE, Employé des Fermes du Roi au Poste de Cléry, à être pendu; pour avoir favorisé le passage de plusieurs ballots de faux Tabac, à un endroit où il étoit de garde.

Fig. 50. Death Warrant for Infringement of the Tobacco Monopoly

205

stimulate the consumption of tobacco for the benefit of the public finances.

Frederick the Great's chief enemy, Maria Theresa, was, as one might expect from her character, opposed to smoking and snuff-taking; but as during her reign the tobacco monopoly, farmed out in the Austrian territories, brought in a large revenue, and her Chancellor, Prince Kaunitz, was an inveterate snuff-taker, she could not well attack tobacco, as she did immorality with her notorious Chastity Commission. The 'tobacco dues,' as they were called, were generally farmed out to Jewish contractors. The Emperor Joseph II, a great innovator, was the first to take the monopoly out of the hands of private persons. On January 14, 1783, he established the State *Regie*, which developed into a vast organization, and still brings in a large revenue in a sadly diminished Austria.

All countries drew enormous sums from tobacco monopolies and duties, and the money was often used to finance far-reaching political schemes. When the United States of North America proclaimed their independence they found much sympathy in France, though at first more or less unofficially. In 1777 Benjamin Franklin, who had taken a share in drawing up the Declaration of Independence of 1776, came to France as envoy for the new republic, and succeeded in getting money for the War of Independence from the *fermiers général*, who held the French tobacco monopoly. In an agreement dated March 24, 1777, Franklin undertook to deliver Virginian tobacco in return for 1,000,000 louis paid down by the *fermiers général*, and stipulated for another 1,000,000 louis when the tobacco was delivered. The delivery was long delayed, and the transaction could not be completed with the *fermiers général*, as they were swept away by the French Revolution. The money not covered by tobacco was afterward repaid to the new French Government, which took over the rights of the *fermiers général*, but it is worth noting that the money from smoking and snuff-taking helped to win the colonies their independence.

Toward the middle of the eighteenth century snuff-taking so increased that some people thought smoking was dying out. Dr Johnson said in 1773, " Smoking has gone out. To be sure, it is a shocking thing, blowing smoke out of our mouths into other people's mouths, eyes, and noses, and having the same thing done to us."

About 1786 smoking was ' out of fashion ' at Cambridge, even among undergraduates. No doubt Johnson generalized too freely from the habits of his own class and the upper circles, but, as we can see from other sources, snuff-taking was growing so fast that people could talk seriously of the dying out of smoking. At the end of the eighteenth century, however, a new form of smoking came from America and Spain and overspread all Europe. Hitherto Europeans had smoked only pipes. We have seen that in the earliest ages, in the West Indies and Mexico, a kind of cigar was smoked, consisting of a sheath of palm-leaves or some other material filled with tobacco. While Europeans were developing their method of smoking along independent lines Americans were improving the primitive cigar into a roll of tobacco-leaf, with nothing else except perhaps a straw down the middle. In Spanish America these rolls were called *Cigarros*, in English America *Segars*, and about the end of the

Fig. 51. Madame Vigée-Lebrun (1755–1842) smoking

Fig. 52. JOHANN GOTTFRIED HERDER (1744–1803)

eighteenth century cigar-smoking began to spread widely in all parts of America. Now and then it was forbidden for fear of fire, but this did not last. From Spanish America the cigar came to Spain, and thence spread, slowly but surely, over all Europe. In 1779 Peter Wendler, a German, secured from the Papal government the sole right for five years to manufacture 'tobacco sticks' (*bastoni di tabacco*) at his factory. Wendler was a versatile man. He had come to Rome first as a painter, and, finding that there was too much competition at Rome, became a pioneer of the cigar, without any fear of rivalry. France gradually became acquainted with the cigar, and the factories supplying the new form of tobacco were modelled on the Spanish. In 1788 the first cigar factory in Hamburg was founded, on the Spanish model, by a certain Hans Heinz Schlottmann. At first the new style did not catch on, so Schlottmann sent the German cigars on a six hours' voyage to Cuxhaven, and brought them back as 'genuine imported'; then they found acceptance. The good man had no idea that in the next hundred years the cigar would almost supersede the pipe and the snuff-box, and rank high above all other uses of tobacco, till it had to yield pride of place to a new mode, the cigarette.

CHAPTER IX

THE NAPOLEONIC PERIOD AND THE AGE OF CIGARS

WHILE the cigar was making its first appearance in Europe the storm had been gathering that broke loose in 1789 and hurled Europe into twenty-five years of almost incessant war.

The real causes of the French Revolution were largely economic. The French Court and aristocracy were insanely extravagant, and the money for their expenditure, and for the cost of a ruinous foreign policy, had to be furnished by the poorer unprivileged classes of the people. The middle and lower classes were overburdened with taxes, made more oppressive by being levied by *fermiers général*. Especially grievous were the so-called five great *fermes* for salt, spirits, customs, market-tolls, and, last and most unpopular, that for tobacco. The *fermiers* used the authority of the State arbitrarily, and earned the hatred of the people. When the Revolution came these barriers to trade were the first to be swept away. Tobacco, especially, it was thought, might well become cheaper, for the provinces annexed by France in recent wars, such as Alsace, grew tobacco, and were not under the monopoly. Their produce was now admitted free into the whole kingdom. The whole system of the *fermes* was swept away by abolishing the interior customs barriers and by refusing to obey the excise officers when they tried to stop free trade in tobacco. This change menaced the State revenue, which, in the hundred and fifty years since the creation of the monopoly, had risen from 4,000,000 livres to no less than 32,000,000 livres. The people fancied that by destroying the existing system and sweeping away all restrictions they would get all the tobacco and snuff they required easily and cheaply. They were soon to learn their mistake. The revenue disappeared; but the general disorder and insecurity affected the supply, and tobacco became scarce and dear. Mirabeau, the greatest statesman of the Revolution, had foreseen this development. The National Assembly at Paris, which was to decide the future fate of France, had to consider this serious question. Many and various schemes were advanced for abolishing the monopoly, but securing at least a part of the revenues for the pressing needs of the new Government. For instance, there was a proposal that every one who smoked, chewed, or took snuff should pay a duty, just as every one who appeared in a powdered wig had to possess a card stating that he had paid the proper hair-powder duty, which had formerly been farmed out. The difficulties in the way of this plan proved too great. Mirabeau was the only one who recognized that in the present circumstances it was as much in the interests of the population as in those of the State to maintain the tobacco monopoly in France and keep it for the nation. A few concessions would wipe out the memories of past oppression.

Mirabeau developed this view on January 29, 1791, in a great speech in the National Assembly. He was opposed on February 12, 1791, by the deputy M. Röderer. Röderer talked about the earth which would now be fertilized by freedom, of the profits of industry which fall to a few, and not to those who have laboured. The 32,000,000 livres of the tobacco *ferme* could have been wrung only from an enslaved country; the tree of the *ferme*, whose roots were watered with blood, could flourish only on the despair of the poor. No doubt the monopoly would not bring in anything like as much under the new *régime*, but in three years, as the deputy rather rashly prophesied, the finances of the country would be so firmly established that so great a sum would not be needed. Therefore he proposed that the Assembly should pass a decree giving every one in France full liberty to grow, manufacture, and sell tobacco.[1]

The Committee of the National Assembly worked out a compromise between these two contradictory proposals. The result was, as Creizenach very truly says, "an impracticable system of half measures, which offended all interests while affecting to consider them." They wanted to impose a duty which, according to their forecast, would bring in 12,000,000 livres. When the law came into operation, during the Revolutionary War, the revenue sank to 5,000,000 livres. Thus the tax that was the most easily borne of all had fallen away to nothing at a time when the State had far heavier burdens to bear than Röderer had foreseen.

Napoleon was the first to take up the matter, with his usual energy. He himself was not a smoker, and his first experience of the habit was unfortunate. In Egypt, where everybody smoked, and where the plague was raging in his army, he was told so much about the disinfectant

[1] Speech of M. Röderer on the prohibition of tobacco-growing and the exclusive privilege of manufacture and sale, delivered at the sitting of February 12, 1791.

Fig. 53. Smoking Club in England at the Time of the French Revolution, 1792

Fig. 54. A Modern Night's Entertainment

properties of tobacco that he resolved to try it. A Persian envoy had given him a richly mounted narghile, or water-pipe; with the help of his trusty mamelukes he screwed up his courage and boldly started. The smoke went the wrong way, and made him cough till he lost his breath. It is said that he exclaimed, "Take it away! How foul! You pigs! It makes me sick!" Whether or no this was Napoleon's only attempt to smoke, it is certain that not only did he never adopt the habit, but all his life objected to the smell of tobacco smoke. The fact is confirmed by his remark that smoking is only good to occupy the idle.

When the Emperor received the German princes at Frankfort in September 1804 he asked the Hereditary Prince of Hesse-Darmstadt, whom he had noticed smok-ing, if that was a habit with him. The Prince answered, "Certainly, Sire." "Well," answered Napoleon, "if you come to Paris with your clothes smelling of smoke not a woman will look at you."

Though Napoleon had no use for smoking he was from his youth up a mighty snuff-taker. He consumed seven pounds of snuff a month. Masson tells us that the Emperor never left his rooms without his eyeglass, his comfit-box with little lozenges of liquorice and aniseed, and his snuff-box. The lozenges were to freshen his mouth.

Napoleon owned countless snuff-boxes. On his Italian campaign of 1796 he used a box with the portrait of his beloved Josephine on the lid, and he was filled with superstitious fear when the lid was broken. When he lost the box, in October 1796, he was unhappy, and begged Josephine to send him another box with a lock of her hair. Besides this, Napoleon used a tortoiseshell snuff-box, set with four silver medallions, representing Regulus, Sulla, Pompey, and Cæsar—a rather characteristic collection. If one could collect all Napoleon's snuff-boxes in one room and arrange them in chronological order they would form a picture history of his life. Later on, when he married Marie Louise, the Austrians gave him a snuff-box with the Archduchess's portrait. After the birth of his son, the King of Rome, he long carried a snuff-box with a charming miniature of the boy by Isabey. Besides these, he owned numberless boxes set with medallions representing other great rulers—Alexander the Great, Augustus, Peter the Great, the Emperor Charles V, Charles XII of Sweden, or Frederick the Great. Of the ancients, he preferred those who, like Mithridates, Demetrius Poliorcetes, and Antiochus, had founded dynasties. According to the not very trustworthy memoirs of the Emperor's *valet de chambre*, Napoleon's life was attempted by means of snuff while he was still First Consul. At Malmaison, where he was then living, repairs had to be made in the fireplaces of his private rooms, and outside workmen were called in for the purpose. When they were gone a snuff-box was found on the First Consul's desk exactly like one he generally used. As Napoleon never put his snuff-boxes there his suite were suspicious ; they had the snuff in this box tested, and found that it was poisoned.[1]

Napoleon's campaigns, and his great economic measures, such as the Continental System established by the Berlin Decrees of 1806, affected every smoker. Owing to the

[1] I have never found any mention of this occurrence that is not taken from Constant's *Memoirs*. It is quite possible that Constant made up the whole story in order to enhance his reputation for faithfulness.

difficulty of importing tobacco the price went up; and as the supply continued short the cultivation of tobacco was taken up in such parts of Europe as were not ravaged by his campaigns. Some tried to find substitutes for tobacco, and in England and on the Continent various grasses or cherry-tree leaves were smoked. Napoleon, who needed huge sums for his Continental wars, thought of making tobacco and snuff serviceable to the State. In spite of the increased population, and the continual raising of the taxes and duties on tobacco, the revenue in 1809 amounted only to some 14,000,000 francs. Mirabeau had prophesied in 1791 that in less than twenty years the tobacco monopoly would be re-established. Napoleon did not consider the plan merely from the financial standpoint; he saw in such an immense organization an inexhaustible means of bestowing favours. The Emperor proved his foresight when he told his incredulous Minister of Finance that in time the monopoly would bring in a revenue of not 24,000,000 but 80,000,000 francs, because tobacco was an article that could bear taxation better than any other. The monopoly was re-established in France by an Imperial Decree of December 29, 1810. We shall see that Napoleon's estimate was fully realized in 1845, and that in our time the tobacco revenue has risen far beyond Napoleon's wildest dreams.

Though the Emperor himself did not smoke he was not so stern to those around him as Louis XIV had been. Many of his generals, such as Vandamme, Lassalle, and Oudinot, smoked. After one of Oudinot's exploits Napoleon presented him with a jewelled pipe worth 12,000 francs. When the Emperor was a prisoner at St Helena he not only retained his fondness for snuff, but the nervous state induced by his enforced idleness made him take more snuff than in the days of his power. On November 9, 1816, the Emperor had a bad fit of coughing, and went to bed directly after dinner, which was very unusual with him. " I must have taken too much snuff without thinking," he said. " I am such a creature of habit. The animated conversation prevented me from noticing it. You, *mon cher*, ought in such a case to take away my snuff-box; it is the office of a friend." [1]

Such were the views of the hero of war and policy. Goethe, the Napoleon of literature, was, as we must needs own, a bitter enemy to smoking. He never had any taste for it at home. His father, as far as we know, did not care for tobacco in any form. His mother in her youth and during the first ten years of her married life indulged in snuff, then gave it up, and in 1807 took it up again. On May 16, 1807, she writes to her daughter-in-law Christiane :

> This long, beautifully written letter, on which I have used up two pens, you owe to several causes. In the first place Doctor Melber has put things right again and skilfully mended up your old Granny ; secondly I have taken to snuff again—with excellent results. Without a pinch of snuff my letters were as dry as invoices, but now ! they go like greased lightning—not a pretty simile, but it is the only one I can think of.[2]

But her son, from his youth up, never cared for anything of the sort. Goethe often expressed himself severely about smoking, and compared tobacco with the things

---

[1] Las Cases, *Mémorial de Saint-Hélène*, vol. ii, p. 410 (Paris, 1823).
[2] *Die Briefe der Frau Rath Goethe*, 6th edition, p. 155 (Leipzig, 1923).

Fig. 55. Tobacco-wrapper, with Portrait of
Napoleon Bonaparte as First Consul, 1799

214

Fig. 56. Field-Marshal Prince Blücher von Wahlstatt, one of
the Most Ardent Smokers of the Napoleonic Age

he hated most in all the world. We see in his *Venezianische Epigramme,*

> Many ills can I bear with, and most of the things that displease me
> Quietly, bravely I meet, bowed by the will of a God.
> Yet are there some that I hate, that are worse than the venom of serpents,
> Four : tobacco the first, bugs then and garlic and . . .

This temper was naturally reflected in Goethe's attitude toward his friends, according as they were smokers or non-smokers. We can see this clearly in his remarks on two of them—the free-thinking schoolmaster, Johann Basedow, the founder of 'philanthropinism,' and the learned and refined physiognomist and theologian Lavater ; he had met them both in Frankfort and had travelled with them. Goethe was much interested in Basedow's plans, but could not entirely agree with his views. It was otherwise with Lavater, with whom he was personally in sympathy. The comparison between them which Goethe draws in his *Dichtung und Wahrheit* is all in Lavater's favour—and tobacco had something to do with this. "What a difference I found," Goethe writes, after some not very kind remarks about Basedow,

> when I thought of the charm that radiates from Lavater. Everything around him was as spotless as himself. In his presence one is purified, from fear of offending his purity. Basedow, on the other hand, was too much wrapped up in himself to notice anything outside. The most unpleasant part about him was that he was perpetually smoking rank tobacco ; and it was made worse by the fact that he used a filthy sort of tinder, very inflammable but smelling foully, and as soon as he had finished one pipe, lit his tinder, and poisoned the air with the first puff of smoke. I called

the stuff 'Basedow's Stinker,' and suggested that he should put it into a natural history under this name. He was greatly amused, and gave me an elaborate description of the disgusting way in which his tinder was prepared, taking a spiteful pleasure in seeing me sickened by his account.

Goethe was of opinion that a really well-bred man could not smoke ; yet he was forced to see all around him—his patron, Duke Karl August, Schiller, and nearly all his friends—smoking or taking snuff. He was said to feel unwell the moment he entered a room where there was tobacco smoke.

In his *Italienische Reise* we see a passage dated "Rome, February 9, 1788," in which the poet speaks of the attitude of the public toward artists, and compares the effect on himself of hasty and unfair criticism with what he liked least, the smell of tobacco. "How happy are the lookers-on ! " he says ;

> they think themselves so clever, they must be right—so do amateurs and connoisseurs. When I hear a man who can do nothing himself criticize others, it fills me with unspeakable disgust. Such talk makes me feel ill, just like tobacco smoke.

Oskar Meister [1] tells us of an amusing episode in Goethe's life. The poet too had experience of the servant difficulty. He had a cook called Charlotte Hoyer, and, after having been exceedingly ill served by her for two years, gave her a very bad character, written in his own hand. The police had just issued a notice that in giving characters to servants employers should be truthful rather than kind. Goethe complied with this order, and

[1] Oskar Meister, *Auch eine Goethehandschrift*, in *Der getreue Eckart* (Vienna, 2nd year, 1925, vol. ii, Parts 11 and 12).

wrote, " The cook has been bad-tempered, impertinent,
rude, fidgety, and spiteful, and has finally made life
intolerable for me." The cook, who as a crowning crime
was secretly given to smoking a rank pipe, tore up the
character, threw it at Goethe's feet, and raged round the
house like a wild beast. " When Goethe," Meister
writes,

> had left his study for a short time, at midday, he was met on his
> return by a dense cloud of acrid smoke. The cook, who was
> secretly given to the vice of smoking, had puffed her pipe into the
> sacred room, knowing that the poet hated tobacco and could not
> stand either smoking or smokers.

Goethe quite agreed with Alexander von Humboldt,
who said, " Two most important plants come to us from
America, one as a blessing, the other as a curse. The
blessing is the potato, the curse is tobacco."

Goethe often expressed his views on the point to
Major von Knebel, himself a poet, and tutor to the
Weimar Princes, and the latter reproduced what he said,
at length, in the form of a dialogue with Heinrich Luden,
the historian.

" Now, do take a pinch of snuff," said Knebel, offering
Luden his box,[1]

> it's so refreshing! The motto on the packet, " Schneeberger's
> Powder, for the blood, the head and the brain," is excellently true;
> it quickens the understanding and strengthens the memory. I
> advise you to try snuff. You are quite right not to smoke; but
> snuff is wonderfully wholesome, especially for the eyesight.
> (Goethe condemns both smoking and snuff-taking.) He is right
> about smoking; I only smoke one or two pipes a day. " Smoking,"

---

[1] Wilhelm Bode, *Stunden mit Goethe.* See also *Goethes Gespräche*, Flodoard
Freiherr von Biedermann, Insel edition, p. 196, etc.

he says, " stupefies a man, and makes him incapable of thinking or writing. It is only fit for idlers, people who are always bored, who sleep for a third of their lifetime, fritter away another third in eating, drinking, and other necessary or unnecessary affairs, and don't know—though they are always complaining that life is so short—what to do with the rest of their time. Such lazy Turks find mental solace in handling a pipe and gazing at the clouds of smoke that they puff into the air; it helps them to kill time. Smoking induces drinking beer, for hot mouths need to be cooled down. Beer thickens the blood, and adds to the intoxication produced by the narcotic smoke. The nerves are dulled and the blood clotted. If they go on as they seem to be doing now, in two or three generations we shall see what these beer-swillers and smoke-puffers have made of Germany. You will notice the effect on our literature—mindless, formless, and hopeless; and those very people will wonder how it has come about. And think of the cost of it all! Fully 25,000,000 thalers a year end in smoke all over Germany, and the sum may rise to forty, fifty, or sixty millions. The hungry are still unfed, and the naked unclad. What can become of all the money? Smoking, too, is gross rudeness and unsociability. Smokers poison the air far and wide and choke every decent man, unless he takes to smoking in self-defence. Who can enter a smoker's room without feeling ill? Who can stay there without perishing? "

Goethe is quite right in what he says; but he is wrong about snuff. He likes to be different from others. He has never tried snuff, but he sniffs up eau-de-Cologne and other perfumes instead. Well, we all like to smell anything that smells good, but if I were to snuff up that Cologne stuff it would kill me. He has nothing sensible to say against snuff. It's a dirty habit, he says. That is silly. Every sensuous enjoyment has something dirty about it at the start or the finish. That adds to the charm of it. The greatest of men have been great snuff-takers. Old Fritz always kept his waistcoat pockets full of snuff, except when he had just emptied them; and that other fellow, what's his name? Bonaparte, Napoleon, has always got his snuff-box open in his hand. It's

Und wärst du auch am fernsten Ort
Zur kleinsten Hütte durchgedrungen
Was hälf' es dir? du fändest dort
Tabacks und böse Zungen

Töplitz d. 20 Juli 1812.

Fig. 57. Pen-and-ink Drawing by Goethe, 1812

Fig. 58. SCHILLER IN CARLSBAD, 1791

natural, it's necessary! You would forget heaps of things and be often at a loss if a pinch of snuff didn't refresh your memory and sharpen your sense.

Knebel's remarks prove that he was by no means impartial; he himself took snuff, therefore Goethe ought not to condemn it, but the latter's views on smoking were quite right. The poet always considered smoking as one of the unpleasant features of life, which one could not escape. Mixing in society as he did, he was often in despair at not being able, do all he would, to escape from smoke, as he has said in a verse which he wrote under a sketch of his own (Fig. 57),

> Though to the furthest land you fare,
> And seek the hut of some outlander,
> What profit? You will find them there—
> Tobacco smoke and slander.

Goethe's attitude was quite the opposite of that taken up by his friend Schiller, who was devoted to tobacco, and used it in both forms, though he much preferred snuff. At the Military Academy of Stuttgart, where Schiller was studying medicine, tobacco was strictly prohibited; it was 'forbidden fruit,' and was smuggled in by an obliging servant. The pupils called such articles 'sins,' and each of their 'sins' had a number. It was enough to mention the number to get what you wanted. The lieutenant in charge, who had to supervise the conduct of his flock, soon found that Schiller was numbered with two classes of sinners: he both smoked and took snuff. He was often reproved, but with no effect; and when Schiller became a full-blown regimental surgeon his room always reeked of tobacco. When he was free to devote himself to poetry he retained his old habits. During his stay at Gohlis, near Leipzig, in September 1785, his friends noticed his excessive use of snuff, and the two great German poets must often have argued over the virtues or vices of tobacco. About that time tobacco became much cheaper, for King Frederick William II, immediately after Frederick the Great's death, abolished the hateful tobacco monopoly. When, however, the French Revolutionary War deranged the finances of Prussia the monopoly was restored, in June 1797. A few months later, on November 16, the King died, and his successor, Frederick William III, again abolished the monopoly in Prussia, on December 15, 1797. Thus it disappeared finally from Prussia, and soon after from all Germany.

The great war that ravaged Europe at this time promoted smoking, though it made it harder to get tobacco. Field service in war, with its intervals of waiting or mounting guard, its irregular succession of strenuous action and idle leisure, gave soldiers the opportunity and the desire for smoking. Troops from all the nations, marching over strange countries, brought their habits with them. British and French armies fought over Spain, and learned there the habit of cigar-smoking, which was only beginning to be known in their own countries. French campaigns brought the soldiers into new fields, and the cigar went with them, till this new habit began to spread over Europe. New cigar factories were started, and in a few years the cigar was driving out not only the pipe, but the familiar snuff-box. The pipe held its ground more obstinately, for meerschaums and fine china pipes, designed by artists like Wedgwood, were fashionable. The Duc de Reichstadt [1] was forbidden to smoke a pipe bearing his father's portrait, or at any rate had to do so in secret, as his mother did not like it. " Spanish snuff," she wrote to the Prince's tutor, Count Dietrichstein, " is a disgusting habit. I should like to know whether my son takes it out of Anglomania, or to imitate his late father." [2] The Prince's premature death proved that his mother and his tutor were right in trying to make him give up his favourite habit (see Fig. 60).

In 1805 cigars were still a novelty in Germany. When Windischgrätz, afterward Field-Marshal, was staying with his mother's relatives, the Arenbergs, a Spanish diplomatist gave him cigars, which he took home to Austria. They were the first that had been seen there.

In Brockhaus's *Konversationslexikon* (1809) the cigar is described as a novelty. The book states :

> We must mention here a new style of smoking, namely *cigarros*; these are tobacco-leaves rolled into hollow cylinders of the thickness of a finger. One end is lighted and the other put in the mouth. This is how they are smoked. This method, which is used in Spanish America instead of the pipe, is beginning to be common in our parts also; but whether it makes tobacco taste better or no is hard to determine, for it is—a mere question of taste.

Now the cigar started on its triumphal march through Europe, and especially through those parts occupied and ruled by the French. In a large part of this territory smokers were supplied with cigars by the French *Régie*.

[1] Napoleon's only son, formerly the King of Rome.
[2] The Empress Marie Louise to Count Moritz Dietrichstein, Piacenza, July 21, 1831 (Dietrichstein Papers).

In Austria they first appeared as *Zigari* in the retail price-list of 1818.[1]

Cigars soon became so popular that in England and France they won back for smoking its old social position, which had been almost eclipsed by snuff-taking. In Great Britain the lowering of the duty on cigars in 1829 caused many to try this new form of smoking, and the Members of Parliament set the example. As a concession to propriety, ' smoking rooms ' were set apart ; the House of Commons had one toward the end of the twenties. Smoking went on increasing, although Queen Victoria loathed tobacco in any form, especially when smoked, and never relaxed in her aversion during her long reign. Those were hard times for smokers at Court. Royal guests at Windsor had to smoke into the fireplaces, so that the smoke should go up the chimney.

The Queen had an ally against tobacco—the Duke of Wellington. In 1845 Wellington issued an order restricting smoking in the army.

> The Commander-in-Chief has been informed that the practice of smoking, by the use of pipes, cigars, or cheroots, has become prevalent among the officers of the Army, which is not only in itself a species of intoxication occasioned by the fumes of tobacco, but, undoubtedly, occasions drinking and tippling by those who acquire the habit; and he intreats the Officers commanding Regiments to prevent smoking in the Mess Rooms of their several Regiments, and in the adjoining apartments, and to discourage the practice among the Officers of Junior Rank in their Regiments.[2]

[1] In June 1812, in the Illyrian provinces occupied by the French under Marmont, cigars were sold for the first time, for 4 francs 25 centimes a hundred. See Franz Wieser, *Die Einrichtungen des französischen Tabaksmonopols in den illyrischen Provinzen 1809 bis 1830*, in *Fachliche Mitteilungen der österreichischen Tabakregie*, October 1910, vol. iii.

[2] Apperson, *op. cit.*, p. 176.

COMMIT NO NUIS-ANCE

Fig. 59. Popularity of Cigar-smoking in London, 1827

Fig. 60. THE DUKE OF REICHSTADT SMOKING A PIPE IN DEFIANCE
OF THE DOCTOR'S ORDERS

Smoking was still unfashionable in the streets and in public places that were not set aside for the purpose. In Germany men were far more strict. In most of the German states sentries and policemen were instructed to prosecute anyone smoking in the street. Heavy fines were enforced on breaches of the law, and as the law was continually being broken it was a constant source of strife between the people and the authorities, and in no small degree fostered the resistance to absolute monarchy.

At the time of the French Revolution the old decrees against smoking in the public street in towns and villages still existed in Prussia. Frederick the Great's edict of January 19, 1764, founded on the common law, was in force; according to this, an arbitrary penalty could be inflicted for smoking in dangerous places, and the informer was to receive a reward of no less than twenty-five thalers. Frederick William III enforced this law far more strictly than the great King, though he considered the informer's share much too high. He was especially angry when anyone smoking went past a sentinel, for he thought it showed contempt for the royal army.

" Every sentry," he wrote to one of his generals, " is to be respected like Myself, for he stands at his post in My name," and so no one must dare to smoke in his neighbourhood.

The police and gendarmes, eager to earn the rewards, instituted a regular hunt after people smoking in places where there was risk of fire. The Berlin joiners were sorely harried, for the chips from their work served as a pretext for declaring their workshops to be dangerous. There were many prosecutions of master-joiners and their men during the last years of the eighteenth century. This procedure often missed its aim and increased the danger of fire. For instance, on November 7, 1793, a police officer reported that in Lindemann's workshop, in the Taubenstrasse in Berlin, he had found a workman smoking, with shavings lying all round him. As soon as the man saw the policeman he threw down his pipe behind his bench among the shavings, thus increasing the danger of fire.[1]

The authorities thought of issuing a general prohibition of smoking to all workers in wood, but an urgent protest was handed in to the police headquarters, stating that to many workmen smoking had become 'a second nature'; that they and their masters all smoked together at their work, and the men would rather emigrate than submit to such a rule. When the French occupied Berlin in 1806 the rule forbidding smoking in the streets lapsed, for the French soldiers did not heed Prussian laws; but hardly was the French garrison withdrawn, in December 1808, than on May 28, 1809, the old prohibition of smoking in public was published again, so that the people might not think it was repealed. As the police and gendarmes were not enough to enforce this rule the garrison was ordered to see to the observance of the decree. The soldiers had to be warned not to give cause for complaint by smoking themselves. Some among the police and soldiers displayed a personal hatred of smoking and smokers. A police official named von Eckert was indignant that the police did not act with enough severity, and were

---

[1] Reports by the police officers Böhme and Neuendorff, November 7 and 8, 1793, in the Prussian Secret State Archives, Berlin-Dahlem.

often content when people merely took their pipes out of their mouths while in sight of an official. He declared that " it is necessary to aim at suppressing this unseemly habit." [1]

" It is indescribable," he reports soon afterward,[2]

> how far this unseemly practice of smoking has gone; last evening three young men were sitting on the promenade each smoking a long pipe; I sent Constable Schultz to stop them, but they made off as soon as they saw him.

The population waged a silent but stubborn war against the law. At last the Prussian police had to post up at every street corner of Berlin a bill threatening all who smoked in the street with a fine of five thalers or eight days' imprisonment, and to publish the same notice in the famous *Berliner Intelligenz-Blatt*. Soon after a police report announced [3] that the prohibitory edict " had been posted up at all the street corners, but unfortunately had been torn down everywhere next day by mischievous persons, and people were still indulging in this unseemly practice." There were constant affrays on account of smoking between the population on one side, and the military and the police on the other—and sometimes between soldiers and police. The citizens laughed at the soldiers for merely taking their pipes away; and on December 22, 1809, there was a fight between four hussars smoking in the street and the police, who came off worst in the fray.

As all the reports agreed in stating that smoking was

[1] Police report, Berlin, July 10, 1809 (Prussian Secret State Archives).
[2] Police report, Berlin, July 23, 1809 (*ibid.*).
[3] Berlin, August 13, 1809 (*ibid.*).

still spreading, the Chief of Police at Berlin issued the following order on June 8, 1810:

> Seeing that public smoking in streets and on promenades is as indecent as it is dangerous, and contrary to the character of an orderly and civilized city, the same is hereby strictly forbidden, not only for Berlin, but in Charlottenburg and the Tiergarten, and may only take place in the two latter places at the doors of houses, on the part of those who sit and stand there. Anyone transgressing shall be arrested, his pipe shall be taken away, and he shall be punished with a fine of five thalers, or corresponding imprisonment, or corporal punishment.
>
> These penalties shall be increased on a repetition of the offence, and insubordination will involve instant arrest. As the present prohibition, often issued in the capital, has been frequently broken, it is now to be enforced with all strictness, and the Government is requested to support this by military aid.

The soldiers told off to act as watchmen disobeyed the law themselves so often that the citizens complained.

"You cannot blame the citizens," was the despairing report of a police official,

> for smoking in the street, for the soldiers take the same liberty and stroll round in numbers with pipes alight. If the soldier has the right to do this I submit that so has the citizen. If I forbid the soldier to act so I must expect to meet with much unpleasantness, which I shall generally have to pass over in silence, since the army cares nothing for the police.[1]

When in 1813 a wave of enthusiasm swept over Germany, rousing the people to war with the hated French, and every one hurried to join the colours, the rule against smoking was ignored. A police report of May 2, 1813, states that a sergeant, trying to stop a man who was

[1] The police official Hunnel to the Chief of Police, February 25, 1812 (Prussian Secret State Archives).

smoking in the street, was at once surrounded, insulted,
and assaulted by a mob. He had tried to take the man's
pipe away, but four other " creatures with lighted pipes "
rushed on him. The people abused him, saying, " It's
nothing to do with the police, everybody smokes now,
and smoking is free, for everybody is a soldier." Then a
score of militia men came by, all with pipes, who insulted
and threatened him " till he finally ran away." The police
felt that they were unprotected, in peril of life and limb ;
the law was openly broken, but still they would not yield.
The *Intelligenz-Blatt* of August 25, 1813, repeated the
order against smoking, though the fine was reduced to
two thalers. King Frederick William III confirmed this
on August 31, 1815, reducing the informer's share to half
the fine. Afterward there was much argument on the
question where smoking might start outside the walls of
Berlin, and on what main roads the prohibition still held.
Outside Berlin, in Germany and elsewhere, more liberal
views prevailed. It was not plain, however, whether the
Berlin rule did not hold good for all Prussian towns—a
point which the Burgomaster of Magdeburg, on February
25, 1825, wanted to have cleared up.

He maintained that " most of the streets in towns are
not places where smoking is likely to cause a fire." He
even ventured to describe the prohibition as illegal and
not founded on common law, but Berlin argued against
his view and reminded him of the rule.

The wish to be freed from these petty restrictions contributed largely to foster the longing for political liberty.
Both found expression in 1830, when the French Revolution of July was followed in Berlin by aimless disturbances

by workmen, tailors, and apprentices, usually known as the "Tailors' Revolution." For several evenings the people crowded on to the Palace square, and voices arose from the crowd, calling for lighter taxation, the abolition of the rent tax and dog tax, and free smoking in the Tiergarten; but their demands for liberty, political and other, were unsuccessful.

In the summer of 1831 cholera broke out in Berlin, and spread with terrible swiftness. In a pamphlet that appeared in June 1831 smoking was recommended as an effective precaution against the disease. As the authorities did not object to the publication of this pamphlet many thought that smoking was now allowed and the rule against it repealed. Thereupon the police announced that smoking was still forbidden as formerly, and contradicted the opinion that the danger of fire was the sole reason for the prohibition. It was maintained in the Berlin *Intelligenz-Blatt* of June 15, 1831, that other considerations had been taken into account. "Among these we may mention," the paper states,

> the maintenance of public propriety. As all but a few will admit, in orderly and civilized cities, among which Berlin takes a leading place, it is quite inconsistent with propriety to allow smoking in the streets and on public promenades.

The prohibition, therefore, remained in full force. The decree was signed as usual by the Chief of Police, and also—which was unusual—by the royal Governor, von Tippelskirch, who afterward displayed a bitter and obstinate hostility to all smokers. Among the population this latest official notice caused great indignation, owing to the cholera, and a stream of protests, rather mildly expressed, flowed into the police headquarters. One citizen of Berlin [1] declared that, in view of the epidemic that was threatening the city, it was very desirable to allow smoking in public, for not only

> is it clear as day that tobacco smoke purifies foul air, but smoking itself makes the greater part of the public feel secure against infection. And as for the supposed impropriety and danger of smoking, this plea falls to the ground when we see that during a time of infectious disease smoking in public is allowed everywhere. . . . In Paris, Vienna, Hamburg, etc., where there is no lack of propriety and decency, people have long ceased to object to smoking in public, any more than they do to smoking in private houses.

Another Berliner addressed an almost identical petition to the King,[2] who handed it to the Chief of Police. But the bureaucracy was not inclined to yield. As the argument of protection from infection was not so easy to dispute, the police authorities proposed that as long as the epidemic lasted the existing regulations should not be enforced with the former strictness, but they were entirely opposed to any public announcement that smoking was allowed,

> since the public might infer from this that the practice is free everywhere, even in places where there is danger of fire, and in those localities . . . where it must remain forbidden owing to the risk of offending propriety and decency.[3]

In public, however, the prohibition was generally

[1] Letter of Herr U. Berthold, Berlin, August 2, 1831 (Prussian Secret State Archives).
[2] Letter of Herr Reimann to the chief office of police at Berlin, September 3, 1831 (*ibid.*).
[3] Proposal of the police official Falkenberg, September 3, 1831 (*ibid.*).

ignored. On September 9, 1831, the Commander of the Palace Guard in Berlin reported as follows :

> Sentinels and patrols report that the greater part of the male population appear in the streets this afternoon smoking. Moreover, here and there, there are crowds in the Königstrasse, where speeches are made to the effect that they mean to disobey any prohibition.

The police at last asked their own physicians, and the latter recommended the repeal of the ban on smoking. Consequently the Chief of Police, on September 11, 1831, resolved to propose to the Minister of the Interior, Baron von Brenn, the temporary suspension of the order. On September 16 the Minister ordered that while the cholera prevailed smoking should be overlooked. This measure was a bitter pill for the commander of the Berlin garrison, General von Tippelskirch ; but owing to the cholera he did not dare to oppose it outright, and agreed to the publishing of the notice permitting smoking, but with the intention of slipping in a clause providing for the future revival of the prohibition. He was successful on this point, and on September 23, 1831, the following order was published in Berlin :

> During the prevalence of Asiatic cholera smoking in the public streets and squares and in the Tiergarten has lately been permitted, so as not to deprive anyone of any possible protection against infection. It is understood that no one must smoke in places where there is danger of fire, or near any sentry on guard. When the cholera has ceased the previous regulations will remain in full force.

This ordinance caused a division of opinion among the population, according as they were smokers or non-

smokers. An amusing instance is the practical suggestion
made in an anonymous letter to the Chief of Police at
Berlin. The writer says that the permission to smoke
in the streets during the cholera had led to much abuse,
to the great annoyance of all sensible men, as boys, shoe-
makers' apprentices, and journeymen tailors strolled round
the streets "with flaming cigars or uncovered pipes."
After the cholera had ceased, however, smoking should
not be forbidden, but a tax should be laid on every one
who wished to smoke in the street, for the benefit of the
cholera hospitals and the poor-box. This tax could be
farmed out to no one fitter than the writer.

The cholera had hardly ceased when General von
Tippelskirch returned to the charge. "The cholera is
over," he wrote to a Privy Councillor at police headquarters, "and we must bring back the good old regulations to the capital."

In answer he received a hint that he must first come
to an understanding with the Minister of the Interior,
Baron von Brenn. Tippelskirch hastened to do so. "On
the cessation of the cholera in this city," he wrote to
Brenn,[1]

I at once approached the Chief of Police to stop the disgusting
habit of smoking in the streets and the Tiergarten, which is
against all decency. By far the greatest part of the public is
interested in this, and non-smokers have a clear right not to be
annoyed. I must earnestly request you to direct the police on this
point as soon as possible, for any further winking at smoking will
make it harder to restore the good old rule. . . . Smoking can
easily be stopped again now, but if we wait some days longer it

[1] General von Tippelskirch to Baron von Brenn, Berlin, February 12,
1832.

will be harder, and I cannot refrain from observing that I have been asked from the highest quarters to put a stop to it.

Tippelskirch's efforts were successful, largely on account of his very plain reference to the King in the letter just quoted. On February 13, after the cholera had disappeared, the prohibition of smoking in public was renewed in its former terms.

The King went still further. In a royal order of December 9, 1832, he declared that he gave all local police authorities the right to forbid smoking in certain spots, under penalty of a fine of from ten groschen to one thaler, to go to the poor-box, since "smoking, even when there is no danger of fire, may annoy the public." King Frederick William III did not smoke, and thus had no sympathy with the tastes of his subjects. Smoking in public was often regarded as a demonstration against the system of government. Just as anyone who wore a soft felt hat instead of the fashionable top-hat was suspected of holding revolutionary views, every one smoking in the streets was regarded as a dangerous democrat. Some of these democrats, on May 27, 1832, in the Kestenburg, near Hambach, dared to curse the princes of Germany as traitors, and to call for the sovereignty of the people. This *fête* has its importance in the history of what is now the smoker's indispensable companion, the match. At first there was only flint and steel, and then the tinderbox. This fell into disuse again. In 1680 Robert Boyle, the great English physicist, made a mixture of sulphur and phosphorus which ignited by slight friction. At the beginning of the nineteenth century chemical lighters were invented in several countries by different chemists,

almost simultaneously. First came a complicated arrangement in which chlorate of potash, sugar, and sulphuric
acid were combined to get a light; then there was a slip
of wood coated with sulphur which had to be dipped into
an asbestos phial of sulphuric acid.

I. F. Kammerer, of Ludwigsburg, a student of chemistry,
and an enthusiastic democrat, had been studying the
subject. For taking part in the *fête* at Hambach he was
sentenced to six months' imprisonment; but the governor
of the prison, an old colonel, allowed him to go on with
his chemical researches. He invented and perfected a
match which ignited merely by friction. As there was
no patent law in force then, not only was the invention
unprotected, but the inventor, who, on his release, was
manufacturing these matches on a large scale, was forbidden to make or sell such " dangerous contrivances."
When he tried to make his matches privately he was
discovered; his machinery was destroyed, he himself
was severely punished, and his property was confiscated.
Further, the Diet of the German Confederation at
Frankfort-on-Main issued an ordinance for all the German
states forbidding the manufacture and use of these most
dangerous friction matches. Meanwhile the same idea
had been taken on or rediscovered elsewhere, by Walker,
an English chemist of Stockton, and by others. Matches
started on their career, developing to their highest point,
the Swedish safety match, a necessity of life to modern
man. Kammerer, however, went mad, and died in 1857
in the asylum at Ludwigsburg.

Complaints against the prohibition of smoking in
Prussia went on without result. On October 25, 1832,

the worthy Schultze wrote in the name of his fellow-citizens a memorial which was duly pigeon-holed and forgotten. It ran thus:

> In exercising the right vested in every citizen by the common law, the right of petition against unjust laws, I say as follows, on behalf of my fellow-citizens:
>
> There is in existence a law, dating from the barbarous ages, forbidding smoking in the streets and public places, although this pleasure hurts or hinders no one; even the pretext that it is a breach of propriety is contradicted by the fact that it is not considered improper in many great cities of Germany or in highly civilized France that people who go for a walk should enjoy this gratification. . . . If our excellent police would withdraw this prohibition they would rise greatly in public esteem, and would be amply compensated for any fines they would lose, and the undersigned would be able to go again to the Tiergarten, which he has avoided, since he could not smoke his pipe there in peace.

It was a case of 'Love's Labour's Lost'—the letter was pigeon-holed, and the prohibition of smoking was annually reissued in the old terms, till 1837, when the cholera reappeared in Berlin. As long as Tippelskirch was Governor he saw that the edict was not forgotten, and when he rode out in the Tiergarten his chief occupation was hunting smokers and sending his gendarmes to hale them up before the police. Through his action the Bellevuestrasse and the Potsdamer Chaussee were reckoned as part of the Tiergarten, so that the law against smoking held good there too.

The police were somewhat influenced by the information they received from various quarters. The high police authorities were not so hostile to smoking as the Governor, and would have been glad to get rid of the burden of enforcing the regulations; but they were doubtful about the King's attitude, and were afraid of doing anything to call down the anger of 'the highest quarters.' According to the order of December 9, 1832, smoking was allowed in places where there was no danger of fire, except in Berlin and Potsdam, unless local authorities made special rules for special reasons. This regulation would seem to apply to Charlottenburg also, but as the King often stayed there, the question arose whether his residence there did not afford a reason for a special prohibition. Hitherto smoking had not been allowed in the streets of Charlottenburg; if it was now permitted, any change in the former condition might offend 'the highest quarters.' This consideration moved the Chief of Police on April 27, 1834, to ask the Minister of the Interior to find out what the King's views were.

" It may be," wrote the Chief of Police,

> that since his Majesty is so frequently in Charlottenburg, and resides there for part of the summer, the same reasons which have caused Berlin and Potsdam to be excepted from the general rule may hold good for Charlottenburg. On the other hand, his Majesty has for many years gone along the Berliner Strasse to Charlottenburg, and seen the guests at the inns smoking—as is allowed by exception—in the gardens outside the houses, without expressing any disapproval, and thus it may be that his Majesty would allow in the pleasure resort of the citizens of his capital a liberty which for other reasons is denied them in the capital itself.

On May 11 the police were informed that the King saw no reason for changing the former rule as to smoking at Charlottenburg. Everything remained as it was.

But when the cholera broke out again in September

1837 in Berlin the smokers triumphed. Tippelskirch had reluctantly to sign his name to another temporary suspension of the rule. In November the epidemic ceased, and there was a well-founded fear that Tippelskirch would hasten to put the ordinance in force again. A citizen of Berlin appealed to the Chief of Police, von Gerlach, begging him, if he would win the love and gratitude of the Berliners, to allow smoking in public at least during morning and evening twilight.

The request was too modest to hope for success. The petition was scrawled across with a big " To be filed for reference," and on December 11, 1837, at seven in the morning the prohibition was again put into force. Tippelskirch backed up the edict with an order to the garrison.

" Sentinels and patrols are to see that this ordinance, which prescribes to every one proper behaviour toward the non-smoking public, shall be generally observed."

No one was to go past a sentry, or stand near him, with a pipe alight, but only the police were allowed to take pipes away from the citizens. Tippelskirch was still unwearied in persecuting smokers, though their number was continually growing. On September 25, 1839, the Governor had to write to the Chief of Police that he had noticed for some time a great increase in smoking in the streets, and requested that this impropriety should be strictly visited with fines, according to his Majesty's order of December 9, 1832. He was indignant at finding that workmen employed in the Tiergarten had been allowed to smoke at their work, and he demanded that the prohibition of smoking should be posted up there. Until he resigned his governorship in 1842 he joined the Chief of Police in renewing the ordinance every year.

Now and then individual members of the public presented earnest petitions for freedom to smoke. A painter named Otto Gennerich wrote to the King on February 14, 1843:

> In filial reliance on the paternal ruler who has given us freedom of thought, and thereby let us know that he would like to see the barriers between sovereign and subjects removed, as rendered necessary by this age of progress, I venture to present a petition expressing the desire of many thousands in Berlin.
>
> In Italy smoking is allowed everywhere; we now ask Your Majesty that we Berlin smokers may claim a similar compliment to our loyalty from the Government. I now ask that Your Majesty, showing Your trust in Your loyal subjects, will graciously permit smoking, if not in the streets of Berlin, at least in the Tiergarten, as the only refuge for those who want to take a walk.

The only answer was that on February 15, 1844, the old decree forbidding smoking within the walls of Berlin and in the Tiergarten was issued by the new Governor, von Lützow, and the new Chief of Police, von Puttkammer, that the Lennéstrasse and the Schulgartenstrasse were now reckoned as belonging to the Tiergarten, and smoking was forbidden in the Potsdamerstrasse and on the Potsdamer Platz. Yet, in spite of all edicts, smoking grew steadily, to the great displeasure of the King, who repeatedly questioned his Minister of the Interior about it. The latter wrote in January 1846 to Puttkammer:

> The offence of smoking in the streets of the capital, which is forbidden under penalty by law, has, we are informed, so increased of late that it appears necessary to pay more strict attention to such breaches of the law.

The Minister therefore demanded that in order to stop "this defiance of police authority" proper measures should be taken to secure respect for the law. Every offender should be strictly prosecuted and punished. In a letter of March 30, 1846, the Minister, at the instance of the King, repeated his warning to the Chief of Police, and remarked that the most casual observer could see every day numerous instances of this offence.

" During last year," he wrote,

there were only 3712 prosecutions for this offence, although, in any street where there is a certain amount of traffic, more than ten instances of it may be noticed in one hour. This impairs respect for the authorities; we must tax this growing lawlessness heavily, so that the police may be free from the justified reproach that by their tolerance of offences they are accustoming the public to disobey the law. His Majesty has several times spoken to me on the subject with justified severity; and for this reason I expect your Excellency to find means to punish this abuse.

The people of Berlin could find no satisfaction. So long as everything remained as of old, and the system of government could not be changed by force, smokers had to give up the right to take their pleasure in public. They had to wait till the Revolution of 1848 for their deliverance.

Governments were far more liberal elsewhere. In Lombardy and Venetia, where the Austrian supremacy was regarded as a foreign oppression, everybody had long been allowed to smoke as he liked in the street. Even the order that soldiers in uniform were not to smoke in the streets, which had long been in force, was cancelled by Field-Marshal Count Radetzky in 1847. Smoking was general in Lombardy, and the so-called Virginia cigars of the Austrian *Regie* were very popular; but those who supplied the cigars, the masters of the country, were less liked. National feeling was rising in Italy, parcelled out as it was into many states. When Pius IX became Pope, in 1846, and won a reputation for liberalism and nationalism, he was looked on as the destined deliverer and unifier of Italy. The Italians had forgotten the benefits of Maria Theresa's time, the age when the Austrian Government had improved education and transport; they resented political persecution, the censorship, and especially the supremacy of a people of foreign speech and blood. The cry "Down with Austria!" was heard on the Cathedral Square at Milan, and Pius IX was publicly acclaimed. By 1848 this enmity had grown to a deadly hatred of the Austrians—or *Tedeschi*, as they were called. In the theatre every allusion to foreign dominion awakened applause. A ballet was once given with a theme taken from Afghan history,[1] and when an Afghan woman appeared in a red petticoat, a white blouse, and a green hat the audience went mad at the sight of the national colours. The Viceroy, Archduke Rainer, a man of no energy, did not venture to go to the theatre, nor did he dare to invite any member of the Italian aristocracy to dine, as the invitation was always declined on some pretext or other. All the influential families of Milan—the Borromei, the Littas, the Visconti, the Trivulzi, and others—headed the National party, in opposition to the Austrians. "They displayed their sentiments,"[2] it is stated in a report, "with almost incredible boldness."

[1] Count Ficquelmont to Metternich, Milan, November 9, 1847.
[2] Private letter from Ficquelmont to Metternich, December 3, 1847.

This attitude led to an event which affected smokers. Once in 1754 the Milanese had risen against those who farmed the tobacco monopoly, raised the price, and lowered the quality of the tobacco; they resolved to give up using tobacco and snuff so as to injure the monopolists and bring pressure to bear on them. Now they hit on the idea of ostentatiously stopping smoking, and thus injuring the Austrian monopoly. The first man who thought of this Smokers' Revolution was a Professor of Physics, Giovanni Cantoni, who explained his idea in the Café del Duomo, about the end of 1847, to his brother and others like-minded with himself. One of those present, Dr Gerli, undertook to circulate the plan. A manifesto was hastily drawn up, recalling the fact that Washington's fellow-citizens, oppressed by the English tyranny, had agreed, shortly before the War of Independence, to banish tea from their tables, so as not to pay the duty imposed by the English. This first revolt led finally to the freedom and independence of the North American colonies.

Franklin's fellow-citizens gave up their tea; do you imitate them and refuse Austrian tobacco. This is no vain attempt, but a duty, a master-stroke, and a sign of union and unity. We must make some sacrifice. Let every one who would be free begin by casting off foreign vices; tobacco smoke injures the body, and sorts ill with the sweet, inspiring scent of Italy's flowers. Who will dare to assert that this habit has become a necessity to Italians? A nation that wishes to rise must love its country and help her as best it can.[1]

This idea spread with lightning speed, not only through

[1] Vittore Ottolini, *La Rivoluzione lombarda del 1848 e 1849*, p. 25 et seq. (Milan, 1887).

Milan, but over the whole province. It was taken up with enthusiasm everywhere. The fashionable club Dei Leoni adopted the plan, and all its members obeyed the call of the manifesto. A report went abroad that many of the Austrian cigars were poisoned ; this was intended to deter even the unpatriotic from smoking. " *Chi fuma per la via è tedesco o è spia !* " [1] was the cry in the streets of Milan. The demonstration was fixed to begin on January 1, 1848, and on that day many smokers had their cigars and pipes knocked out of their mouths. The police had heard of the plan a fortnight before, but did not think it would take a really dangerous form. They were mistaken. On New Year's Day crowds of students gathered, and hunted stray smokers along the streets. On January 2 matters grew more serious. Nobody could appear in the street smoking without risk of being attacked and insulted. A proclamation by the Prefect of Police, Torresani, had no effect ; even soldiers smoking in the street were attacked, and drew their swords, and many men were wounded and hurt, and some killed. Some officers thought it their duty to promenade the streets with cigars in their mouths. On the square before the Scala Theatre Count Neipperg, a major of engineers, was walking up and down smoking, arm-in-arm with an Englishman named Castle, when in front of the Café Cova his cigar was knocked out of his mouth.

Field-Marshal Count Radetzky thought that the honour of the army demanded drastic measures, and reported to the wavering Archduke Rainer that he was forced to act, as many officers and soldiers who were smoking had been

[1] " He who smokes in the street is a German or a spy ! "

insulted and assaulted by the mob. Patrols of infantry and cavalry were sent out through the city streets, and the men who were not on duty were provided with cigars and allowed to go out and smoke if they liked; but they were advised not to venture out singly, and never to go through the streets fewer than three together. This was done, but soon these small groups of soldiers were met by increasing numbers of Italians who hooted them, insulted them, and tried to stop them from smoking. Faced with this opposition, the groups of soldiers gathered together into masses. Stones began to fly, and the soldiers fell on the unarmed crowd with sabre and bayonet; there were many casualties and some deaths. Matters were made no better by a difference of opinion at the Viceroy's Court. It was said that the soldiers should not have been allowed to go out without leaders, and officers' patrols would have been more suitable. It was wrong to leave the decision in the hands of mere privates. Radetzky answered that a soldier had a right to smoke, and nobody should dare to stop him from exercising his rights. As, on January 3, soldiers and civilians went on walking through the city smoking, the population considered this to be a deliberate defiance, and a rumour went about that the Viceroy had released convicts from prison on condition that they would smoke in the streets. This added to the fury of the Milanese. The soldiers, now warned beforehand, took the offensive in twenties and thirties on January 3, and pushed their way into the *cafés* and restaurants with cigars in their mouths, driving out the customers and threatening every one who showed hostility. This resulted in serious riots and affrays. On the night of January 3–4 the energetic Field-Marshal had the whole garrison put under arms and kept ready in their barracks.

This attitude imposed upon the population, and the next day was comparatively quiet; but the Viceroy, the Archduke Rainer, was alarmed and greatly depressed by the threatening attitude of the population. He and Ficquelmont tried to persuade the stern Field-Marshal to be more lenient. The diplomatist even ventured to suggest to Radetzky that he might revive the old order forbidding soldiers in uniform to smoke in the street. Soothing proclamations were issued by the Archduke Rainer.

But meanwhile the "Tobacco War" had spread beyond Milan. On January 8 there were serious fights between students and officers at Pavia, and two Austrian officers were killed. The Colonel - in - Command, von Benedek (afterward the general who lost the battle of Königgrätz), after consulting the Provincial Delegate, had forbidden the troops to smoke in the street, and sent Radetzky a report of what had happened. Thereupon the Field-Marshal reported to Archduke Rainer. "On receipt of his report about the events at Pavia," he wrote,

I charged Colonel Benedek to be most careful to avoid any collision between soldiers and students, but at the same time told him that I will not recognize or tolerate any secret society that insults and attacks peaceful smokers in the street, and exercises unlawful power. I must add that Colonel Benedek has expressly forbidden smoking in the street, and I consider that such an order, in the present circumstances, is unjustifiable weakness, and a submission to the revolutionary faction. As the murderous attacks on isolated soldiers still continue, I see no other means of avoiding further bloodshed than proclaiming martial law in Pavia, as your Imperial Highness has just done in Padua.[1]

In Padua, too, there had been fierce fights between officers and soldiers who were smoking, and the students of the university. The latter had called out to soldiers who were coming out of the *cafés*, "Drop your cigars, you Hungarian swine!" One of the soldiers asked, "Who said that?" and a student boldly came forward and answered, "I!" The soldier instantly drew his bayonet and cut the youth down. Similar affrays happened at the time.

From Padua the agitation spread to Venice, where, owing to the boycott of cigars, vast stores began to accumulate in the factory there. The Chancellor, Count Inzaghi, reported in his dispatch to the Emperor, January 29, 1848,

that the cigar disturbance seems to be spreading to Venice, and it is unfortunate that just when the cigar question is so severe the Virginia cigars made in the factory here are of the worst possible quality.

At Vienna, too, little importance was at first attached to these events ; now the authorities began to be anxious. Archduke Ludwig, who took the place of the incapable Emperor Ferdinand and helped Metternich to manage the business of the State, expressed his view of the case in a letter to Metternich :

This cigar business is in itself, as you rightly say, childish ; but it is an attempt of a faction to stir up the mob, and in that aspect

[1] Report of Field-Marshal Count Radetzky to the Viceroy, Archduke Rainer, Milan, February 12, 1848.

it is not so unimportant. It would be most unpleasant if we had to use force of arms, at a time when everything is represented in the most odious light in the newspapers.

Metternich himself was not pleased with the attitude of the Viceroy at Milan. On receiving the first reports of the troubles at Milan he wrote the Archduke a letter in his usual moralizing style, plainly showing his dissatisfaction, and declaring that at all costs the *Regno Lombardo-Veneto* must be held for the Crown. " Just now," he wrote,

> it is suffering from a disease which is both endemic and epidemic in character. The historic hatred against foreigners is endemic, and the epidemic part is the revolutionary spirit, which like other fashions has become a perfect craze.

Military help was not sufficient. Why had not action been taken against the club of the Leoni? "This club forbids smoking," he wrote.

> What right has it to do so? It does not trouble about that, for that is not its concern. What it is aiming at is to arouse an inevitable resistance among those who are not under its orders, those who feel they have a right to smoke, so as to lay the blame for the disturbances on them. If I, sir, had been in command, I would have closed the club at once, for a club has no business to order people about.

At the same time Metternich wrote to Ficquelmont to the same effect, but in much stronger language. The supreme authority in Lombardy, he said, did not need an Imperial order to close a club that dared to disturb the peace by forbidding people to smoke cigars. The Government of Lombardy had made a whole string of blunders.

However, the Archduke Rainer, who, being on the spot, could judge the state of affairs better, wrote that although, after what happened in the first days of January, quiet was apparently restored, the outlook was very gloomy. He told the Archduke Ludwig : " The feeling among the upper classes, except for a few right-thinking men, is very bad. Their watchword is hatred of the Government and the expulsion of the Austrians."

In fact, the " Cigar Revolution," that broke out in the first three days of 1848 in Milan, was the prelude to the far more serious events which came after Metternich's fall from power, and led to a general revolt in Lombardy and Venetia, and then to a war with Piedmont. At the start Radetzky, who was not in sufficient strength, was forced to evacuate Milan and surrender the city to the insurgents. Then smoking in the streets began again, for the people had looted the Austrian cigar-stores. This state of things did not last, and Radetzky's victory brought back the old *régime*. The revolted provinces and Piedmont learned the lesson, which they applied in 1859, that they could win their freedom only in alliance with one of the Great Powers.

The Revolution of February in Paris, and the rising in Vienna on March 13, 1848, found an echo in Berlin, where the inhabitants were still groaning under the prohibition of smoking in the street, strictly enforced by the police and the army. The cigar, as distinguished from the traditional Conservative, Philistine pipe, that might be smoked only at home, was still regarded as an unseemly novelty, a mark of Liberal audacity, the democratic badge of the agitator and stump orator ; it was therefore persistently persecuted. Now, when the Revolution broke out, in March 1848, and the people gathered before the royal palace, cries were raised for the repeal of the ban on smoking, as well as for more important concessions—such as lighter taxation, freedom of the Press, and so on.

The old rules were still in force, and on March 16, 1848, a gendarme stopped a French professor, J. Hutier, who was smoking a cigar in the street, and said:

"Don't you know, sir, that our King has expressly forbidden smoking?"

"No, I don't know that our King has himself forbidden it."

"You are French, but you have been living here, and you ought to know the law. Long live the King!" [1]

While the gendarme was taking Hutier's name and address the latter saw hundreds of people passing, all smoking. He was indignant, thinking that he had been stopped just because he was a Frenchman. The fact was that the police ventured to prosecute only in individual cases. There was a spirit of revolution abroad in the capital, which led to an outbreak a few days later.

Werner von Siemens tells us in his memoirs that he was present when, on March 19, 1848, the revolted townspeople brought the bodies of those who had been killed on the barricades to the Schlossplatz, to show them to the King and Queen. In the midst of the confusion, when some were wanting to storm the palace, now that the troops had been withdrawn from the city, young Prince Lichnowsky jumped on a table, and addressed the crowd in a loud voice. He said that his Majesty had graciously and kindly put an end to the fighting by withdrawing

[1] Professor J. Hutier's complaint to the Berlin Head Police Office, March 16, 1848.

all the troops and trusting himself to the citizens. All their demands were granted, and they had only to go home quietly. When people asked whether everything had really been granted he answered, "Yes, everything, gentlemen."

" Smoking too? " said another voice.

" Yes, smoking too," was the answer.

" In the Tiergarten too? " was asked again.

"Yes, gentlemen, you may smoke in the Tiergarten too."

That clinched the matter. "Well, then, we may go home," was heard on all sides, and in a few minutes the joyous crowd left the square.

Even if Siemens in his account has exaggerated the effect of the speech it was significant that such a demand should have been made at such a time. It is quite certain that nobody had given the required permission or authorized Prince Lichnowsky to make such an announcement. The permission to smoke in the streets and in the Tiergarten was due to the young Prince's presence of mind, and was made solely on his own responsibility.

So thought some 'peace-loving' citizens, who wanted to have matters settled by law and not in a revolutionary way. One who described himself as a lover of peace applied to the Chief of Police, von Minutoli, on March 23, 1848 :

Your Excellency cannot be ignorant that the dearest wish of the Berliners has long been the repeal of the order against smoking in the streets. For some days smoking has been free without leave of the police, but if you would withdraw this most oppressive rule you would earn the warmest gratitude on the part of the Berliners. If Your Excellency will consider that such a prohibition has long been repealed, not only in all other towns of the Kingdom of Prussia, but in all foreign capitals (even Vienna), and that we

Berliners are pitied and ridiculed by foreigners on account of the restraint on our smoking, you cannot possibly any longer disregard the prevailing desire of the Berliners for freedom of smoking.

This letter, joined with the triumph of the Revolution in Berlin, met with instant success. By order of the King, on March 25, 1848, the following notice appeared: " The prohibition of smoking, when there is no risk of fire, in the streets and suburbs of the capital is repealed." [1]

Thus was one of the daily pin-pricks of Berlin life removed; the guerrilla warfare with gendarmes and sentries arising from smoking out of doors was over, and henceforth all might smoke as they chose, limited only by fashion, habit, and care for personal safety, and not by official orders. Henceforth every one could walk out unchallenged with pipe or cigar alight, and the consumption of tobacco grew mightily. Snuff-taking declined, pipe-smoking was inconvenient in the street, and so the cigar triumphed in Germany, where it still holds its ground better against the cigarette than is the case in other countries.

Smoking was free; but this liberty did not appeal to all. Formerly the police headquarters were deluged with petitions for free smoking, now they received angry letters from non-smokers, asking to have the old rule restored. A certain C. Schartmann, " in the interests of public decency and morality and the common good," approached the Prussian Minister of the Interior on December 22, 1851, with the request

that he would check the consumption of tobacco, which has increased so enormously since 1848, and especially stop the

[1] Order by the Chief of Police, von Minutoli, Berlin, March 23, 1848.

cultivation of tobacco, or at least reduce it to its former limits, and restore the prohibition in Berlin, as it was in 1848.

It was monstrous that a bad habit should be allowed in public, and that those who had not been enslaved by it should have to tolerate it.

Toward the end the writer uses stronger terms. Every sense of decency, all modesty, is being destroyed and all morality undermined by smoking. The fertility of the ground is exhausted in the growing of tobacco, which serves only a vicious habit borrowed from savages. This wretched weed is now sown instead of corn, and puffed out in an idiotic and ridiculous fashion, into stinking smoke, tainting the pure air of heaven, the refreshing and invigorating gift of nature.

Another ' private person ' was of the same opinion, and declared that the unhappy Revolution of 1848, with all its sad consequences, disobedience, unbelief, and lawlessness, had also brought with it the " unfortunate " liberty of the smoking habit, which offended all decency.[1] " Non-smokers," so the writer ended his epistle,

hope that you, the Chief of Police, will restore the rule forbidding smoking, and the non-smoking public will give you their silent but heartfelt thanks for being able to breathe pure fresh air again.

Many non-smokers even now are heartily in agreement with this appeal. The history of smoking in Berlin only shows how hard—nay, impossible—it is for a man in authority to satisfy the contradictory demands of the populace.

[1] J. Pustan to the Head Police Office, Berlin, March 19, 1852.

CHAPTER X

WITH the revolutions of 1848 the last barriers to the progress of smoking may be said to have fallen. In spite of the continued popularity of the porcelain pipes, with their heads of famous politicians and prominent men of the time—such as Robert Blum, who was shot in the Vienna revolution, and Louis Napoleon, the new sensation of Paris—pipe-smoking and snuff-taking were steadily declining before the advance of the cigar. So far from opposing the habit, the governments which profited from the monopolies and taxes on tobacco did all they could to further its consumption. No more striking proof of the importance attached to its financial value could be found than the order issued in 1851 by Cardinal Giacomo Antonelli, Secretary to the Papal States, to the effect that for the future no one was to put any obstacle in the way of smoking, and that the dissemination of anti-tobacco literature would be punished by imprisonment. In fact, the leading statesmen of the time had completely changed their attitude, chiefly from financial considerations, but also to some extent owing to the discovery that smoking in moderation was not necessarily a danger to health. The number of cigars now consumed in all countries could be counted by millions, as the demand was still on the increase, although a rival had just appeared in the form of the cigarette.

According to the reports of missionaries and travellers, cigarettes were known to South America in the middle of the eighteenth century, especially in Brazil, where they were called *papelitos*. Spanish Americans had introduced the custom to their fatherland, where it was at once adopted by polite society. Casanova, the first ' foreigner ' to smoke cigarettes, mentions them in his memoirs; he describes a tavern-keeper of the Peninsula as follows :

> The good fellow was carelessly puffing at his cigarette of Brazilian tobacco wrapped in a little paper tube, from which he blew great clouds of smoke with evident enjoyment.

This new device found its way slowly into the neighbouring countries; we find it in France as early as 1844, and later in Italy, where also the Austrian *Regie* had put on the market an article called a ' paper cigar,' a sort of compromise between a cigar and a cigarette, which was filled with cut *canister*—*i.e.*, inferior tobacco.

But it was not till after the Crimean War (1856) that the cigarette was widely circulated in Europe; the various armies there assembled—Turkish, English, French, and Piedmontese—were not slow to appreciate the particular advantage of this new invention : to roll one's own cigarettes was much less expensive than to buy cigars all ready made, and officers and men alike continued to spread the habit on their return to their respective countries. Moreover, Louis Napoleon, who had lately made himself Emperor of France, became an enthusiastic devotee of the convenient novelty—indeed, we may truly say that in France the cigarette came to the throne at the same time

— PUFF, PUFF, PUFF. IT IS AN AGE OF PUFFING, PUFF, PUFF, PUFF.

Fig. 61. Caricature (1827): The New Fashion in Smoking

Fig. 62. One of the Earliest Pictures of Cigarette-smoking

as the Emperor. On the other hand, his bitter enemy, Victor Hugo, detested smoking in every shape as heartily as he hated the upstart of the house of Bonaparte.

When cigarettes were introduced into the London clubs by British officers they met at first with strong opposition, as is always the case with any novelty; those who smoked them were laughed at as dandies and 'snobs,' and the general public did not take kindly to the idea. But when, about the sixties, the manufacturers began to use good tobacco, and a finer sort of paper, the cigarette soon found favour in every part of Europe, and began to compete with the all-conquering cigar.

It was in Austria in 1865 that the first real cigarette— the ' double cigarette ' as it was called—was introduced by the *Regie*; it was about three times as long as those of to-day, with a mouthpiece at either end, and was cut into two before using. The demand for them increased so rapidly that in 1866 sixteen million were sold in Austria. Before long, however, they made way for the single cigarette of finer quality, while the cigar, especially the Virginian variety, continued to hold the first place well into the eighties; the Emperor Francis-Joseph, for instance, always preferred a cigar.

Germany was the country where the cigarette made the slowest progress, as the cigar appealed more to the German people than to any other. In England, on the contrary, they soon became the fashion and, as is generally the case, the common people made haste to follow it. The example set by London was imitated by North America, and very soon the manufacture and sale of cigarettes became one of the most important industries of the United

States. Thus the cigarette, which originated in South America, reached the northern half of that continent only after it had made the tour of Europe.

The War of Secession was responsible for the further spread of smoking in the United States, the cigar being the form most in favour. Of the two generals in command of the opposing armies, Grant, the Yankee leader, was a fervent devotee of the cigar, while Lee, in command of the Southerners, was a non-smoker. After the capture of Fort Donelson by Grant in 1862 all parts of the Union combined to present him with a gift of eleven thousand cigars,[1] since smoking, as the smokers jestingly remarked, was such a sharpener of the wits that it even helped a man to victory on the field of battle.

To meet the universal demand which now arose an enormous increase in output ensued, not only in Cuba, Havana, and the Antilles, the original home of the tobacco plant, but all over America, particularly in Virginia and Maryland; as soon as the war was over the country began to export tobacco to the value of many millions of dollars. The home consumption also showed an almost incredible increase, for which Napoleon III's disastrous project of establishing a Mexican Empire was in a measure responsible : not only were the Mexicans habitual smokers, but the adventure served also to extend the practice among the French soldiers. With Napoleon himself the cigarette habit had become almost a mania (at the battle of Solferino it was remarked how he lit one cigarette after another, while he muttered to himself : " Poor creatures, poor creatures ! What a terrible thing is war ! "); he is

[1] A. E. Hamilton, *This Smoking World*, p. 143 (New York and London).

said to have smoked as many as fifty a day, an enormous number for that time.[1]

His adversaries, Moltke and Bismarck, were also great smokers, but the preference of both was for cigars; the latter had smoked since the days of his youth, and in 1851, when acting as Prussian ambassador in Frankfort, he turned the habit to good account on a political occasion. The diplomatic reverse that Prussia had experienced at Olmütz rankled in his soul, and although there was no disputing the right of Austria to take formal precedence at Frankfort, Bismarck, as the jealous guardian of the interests of Prussia, refused to recognize it. Before the arrival of Bismarck, Count Thun, as the leading ambassador, presided over the meeting, and was the only one to smoke during the proceedings, the others refraining out of respect for his unique position. Bismarck, however, decided to ignore the unwritten law, and calmly lit a cigar.

Moritz Busch, in his *Tagebuchblätter* (Leipzig, 1899), gives Bismarck's own account of the affair:

> During the session of the Military Commission the Austrian ambassador was the only one who smoked; Rochow, who represented Prussia, would have liked to, but was afraid to venture. When I came on the scene I too was longing for a cigar, and as I saw no reason against it I asked the President, Count Thun, for a light, a request which seemed to come as an unpleasant surprise to his Excellency as well as to the others, who were obviously shocked. For some time the Austrian ambassador and myself were the only two who smoked; but the others apparently attached such significance to the matter that they wrote home for instructions. These, however, were long in coming, as the affair called

[1] See P. Guedalla, *The Second Empire*, p. 285 (London, 1927).

for mature consideration, and for the next six months only the two Great Powers, Austria and Germany, were represented by smokers. At last Schrenkh, the Bavarian ambassador, resolved to assert his dignity by joining us; Nostitz, the Saxon, would evidently have liked to do the same, but probably had not received permission from his chief. However, soon after, when he saw that Bothmer, of Hanover, was indulging in a cigar, he took one from his own case and began to smoke; he must have come to some agreement with Rechberg, for he was strongly Austrian in his sympathies, and even had sons in the Austrian army. There were now only Württemberg [1] and Darmstadt to be accounted for, and neither of them smoked. However, their own dignity, and the importance of the countries they represented, made it imperative that they should do so; accordingly, at the next session, the Württemberger took out a cigar—I can see it still, a long, thin, pale, straw-coloured thing—and smoked at least half of it, as a sort of burnt-offering for his country's sake. Only Hesse-Darmstadt held aloof, probably from a feeling that he was not big enough to compete with the others.

In times of great stress, such as the wars of 1866 and 1870–71, Bismarck would smoke more than ever, to steady his nerves; during the latter campaign his enthusiastic fellow-countrymen from every part of Germany used to send him cigars of the choicest brands. His adversary Napoleon likewise tried to quiet his nerves during a campaign by an enormous consumption of cigarettes; it was warmly disputed later between his enemies and adherents whether he really did smoke as much as he is said to have done at the battle of Sedan.

In the hour of Germany's triumph, when Jules Favre presented himself at the headquarters before Paris in order to discuss the terms of peace with Bismarck, the

[1] Their names were von Reinhard and von Münch-Bellinghausen respectively; both were strongly anti-Prussian.

great Chancellor delivered himself at some length on the question of smoking. When the French statesman entered the room, and the preliminary greetings had been exchanged, Bismarck offered his guest a cigar, with the inquiry whether he smoked. Favre thanked him, but replied in the negative. Bismarck replied: "Then you are wrong! When a man begins a discussion which may easily lead to heated argument, or even a show of temper, it is always better to smoke while one is talking. You see," he went on, lighting his Havana,

> a cigar held in the hand and nursed with care serves, in a measure, to keep our gestures under control. Besides, it acts as a mild sedative without in any way impairing our mental faculties. A cigar is a sort of diversion: as the blue smoke curls upward the eye involuntarily follows it; the effect is soothing, one feels better tempered, and more inclined to make concessions—and to be continually making mutual concessions is what we diplomats live on. It is true that you, as a non-smoker, have one advantage over me—you are more watchful and observant; on the other hand, you are more apt to be guided by the impulse of the moment.

In the discussion which followed it happened that Favre spoke warmly on behalf of Garibaldi, who had fought in the French army against the Germans; Bismarck at once grew excited, laid his cigar aside, thumped the table with his fist, and shouted: "No, no! He belongs to me! I will have him led through the streets of Berlin with a label on his back: 'This is Italy's gratitude.'"

At this moment Favre's adjutant, the Count d'Hérisson, with a deprecatory smile, handed Bismarck the cigar-box; the Chancellor, when he had recovered from his astonishment, understood the allusion, and said calmly, "You

[257]

are right, Monsieur le Comte ; it is no use getting angry —it does no good—quite the contrary."

With all his brilliant victories and successes Bismarck had known two crushing defeats in the course of his career : one was over the so-called *Kulturkampf* against Catholicism ; the other, of a more personal nature, was when he endeavoured to establish a tobacco monopoly in Germany, on the model of those in the neighbouring countries. To pass a measure like this would mean endangering the existence of a great many manufacturers and employees, and a sum of 257 million marks was proposed by way of compensation ; but this appeared to fall far short of the requirements, which others estimated at more than double that amount. Bismarck, however, backed the proposal with all the weight of his personality, and found a supporter in the well-known economist Adolf Wagner, who demonstrated to the Reichstag that the revenue to be derived from it would suffice to defray the cost of the sweeping social reforms which the Emperor William I had then in contemplation.[1] However, in 1882 the Reichstag refused to entertain the idea of a monopoly, on the ground that such an enormous interference with private industry was too risky an experiment. This, at least, was the ostensible reason, but it is probable that the members, who were nearly all smokers, were influenced still more by the clamour of the populace, who were afraid of a rise in the price of their favourite luxury ; in any case Germany remains to this day without a tobacco monopoly.

[1] For subsequent measures dealing with the taxation of tobacco in Germany see J. Wolf, *Der Tabak und die Tabakfabrikate* (Leipzig, 1912).

THE FINAL TRIUMPH OF SMOKING

The next stage in the progress of smoking was the decline of the cigar and the astonishing rise of the cigarette, which, owing to its combination of elegance with convenience, soon became the fashionable ' smoke,' with the result that the consumption increased by leaps and bounds, and, since the Great War, has reached quite fantastic heights. In the United States, for instance, the output for 1913 was 15 milliards, by 1927 it had risen to 60 milliards, and to-day the figure is something like 104 milliards; this means, for a population of 120 millions, about 800 cigarettes per head per annum.

In Europe, too, the sudden development, if not quite so enormous, does not fall far behind the figures just quoted; in Germany it works out to about 600 cigarettes per head per annum, while the annual consumption of cigars, though slightly on the decline, may be reckoned at about 100 per head.

The figures for the rest of the world would be found even more impressive, but those we have given will suffice to show how completely humanity has surrendered to the custom.[1]

Smoking, of course, has always had its opponents : with some of them the objection has been merely theoretical, while they themselves have indulged in the habit; others, like Goethe, have actually hated and loathed it. In the former category must be placed the great Kant,

[1] The number of cigarettes consumed in Germany between April 1, 1927, and March 31, 1928, was $32\frac{1}{2}$ milliards, in addition to $6\frac{1}{2}$ milliards of cigars and $3\frac{8}{10}$ kilogrammes of tobacco. In the little republic of Austria, with a population of $6\frac{1}{2}$ millions, the numbers were 4·6 milliards of cigarettes (as compared with 4·55 in 1927) and 201 million cigars (in 1927 the number was nearly 206), which works out at 719 cigarettes and 31 cigars, besides 731 grammes of tobacco and 19 grammes of snuff, per head per annum. (From the yearly *Report* of the Austrian tobacco *Regie* for 1928.)

who in his *Anthropology* has the following contemptuous comment: "Tobacco is one of the basest methods of exciting the sensual passions, whether taken as snuff, in a pipe, or in the form of a cigar, as the Spanish women do." Nevertheless Kant was a great snuff-taker, and would smoke a pipe now and then. Ludwig Anzengruber also belonged to the class of theoretical objectors. "Tobacco," he declares, "is a filthy and abominable vice; but the recognition of the fact does not stop me from thoroughly enjoying a cigar, especially in my leisure time, or when I am writing." [1] Heine, like Goethe, was a conscientious non-smoker.

In our own time there have not been wanting leaders of thought in the various professions who have said hard things about smoking. Haeckel, the famous philosopher, could write thus:

> I have had no experience of tobacco except in its botanical aspects; I have never smoked or even tried to do so, simply from principle (or obstinacy, if you like!). My father too was a rigid non-smoker. When we consider the enormous number of things which our modern civilization has taught us to regard as necessities it seems to me an advantage in the struggle for existence to know nothing of so tyrannous a ' necessity ' as tobacco.

Professor Theodore Billroth, the famous surgeon, in 1889 pronounced smoking to be a "disgusting vice" that ruins the health, and the passion for it to be the result of idleness and *ennui*. " Society," he said, "is becoming more and more neurotic, and this is due to alcohol and tobacco."

Tolstoy was not consistent in this matter; although a

[1] Dr Gustav Lewinstein, in *Für und Wider den Tabac* (Berlin, 1890).

heavy smoker himself, he denounced the habit as unhealthy and unnecessary—better plant barley than tobacco,
he said, and so help to feed the hungry. Accordingly he
resolved to give it up, but even his strong will was not
always strong enough to resist temptation. A governess
who lived for six years in the Tolstoys' house tells how,
when the others were smoking, the boy would bring
out the stump of a cigar and puff at it furtively now
and again, fearful lest he should be detected. In one
of his shorter essays, *L'Alcool et le tabac*, which in the
German edition appears as *Lasterhafte Genüsse* (*Sinful
Pleasures*), Tolstoy sought for an explanation of the
enormous popularity of smoking, and believed that he
had found it in man's desire to stifle the voice of conscience. " The brain," he wrote, " becomes numbed by
the nicotine," and the conscience expires. He goes on
to tell a gruesome story of a certain cook who attacked
his aged mistress with a knife and wounded her badly,
but at the last moment shrank from killing her outright.
He then retired to another room and smoked two cigars
to calm his nerves; instead of which his brain became
so dazed that he went back and completed the murder.
Tolstoy tells us further that whenever he had done wrong
he used to smoke in order to deaden his conscience.
"How is it," he asks,

> that men who have reached a higher stage of moral development
> are able to give up smoking altogether, while others fall back into
> the habit as soon as they find themselves in the sort of low company
> which is given to the vice? Verily man is at once a beast and a
> spiritual being! The stamping out of this fearful disease (the
> habitual use of strong drink and tobacco) would mean a new era
> in the history of mankind.

A HISTORY OF SMOKING

In order to estimate this verdict of Tolstoy's at its true value, it is only fair to quote his deliberate opinion on quite another subject, involving one of the most difficult problems of our nature. " A Christian," he says,

> can only regard all sexual relations as a departure from the law of Christ, and as actual sin; consequently, a sincere Christian will never desire the married state, but always avoid it.

Tolstoy fought all his life against smoking, just as he did against all other temptations by which we mortals are assailed. True, he fell away and for a time was false to his principles, but only occasionally, and it is said that after making his solemn resolution he never again became a regular smoker.

We will close this list of the opponents of smoking with an example from a very different class of society—Henry Ford, the great captain of industry. This gentleman, so well known as an enthusiastic advocate of work for its own sake, is almost a fanatic in his hatred of smoking; indeed, he would like to insist on all his workmen being non-smokers, did he not realize the impossibility of enforcing such a regulation.

In the opposite camp we see the vast army of those who are passionately addicted to the habit, who regard it as one of the greatest pleasures in life, and insist that it stimulates and increases the mental activities. Men and women, kings and poets, representative men of every calling and profession, are agreed in singing the praises of smoking. Physicians and scientists have written learned treatises on the effects of tobacco on the human intellect.[1]

Lenau, too, a confirmed devotee, has dedicated a song

[1] *E.g.*, M. V. O'Shea, *Tobacco and Mental Efficiency* (Chicago, 1923).

Fig. 63. Tobacco Plantation in the Tropics

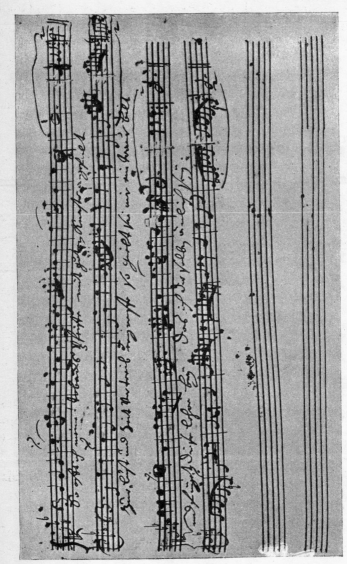

Fig. 64. Facsimile of the Manuscript of the Song "Die Tabakspfeife," by J. S. Bach

of admiration and gratitude to his pipe; and Thackeray wrote a stinging satire on "the silly social prejudice against smoking."

Many great musicians are to be found among its supporters—J. S. Bach, for instance, was a hardened pipe-smoker, and has left us a lasting memorial of the fact in the famous song *Die Tabakspfeife* (*The Tobacco-pipe*) (see Fig. 64).

Beethoven, too, according to his biographers Schindler and Holz, smoked occasionally, though only in the tavern and never at home or in the street; in his later years he would smoke a *cigarro* now and then. Snuff he seldom took, though at different periods of his life he owned several more or less valuable snuff-boxes; some of them had been given him, the others he had purchased for daily use.

In England Queen Victoria, who could not endure the smell of tobacco, was succeeded by Edward VII, a great smoker, who had doubtless long forgotten those trying days of his minority when the great Queen had detected him smoking in Buckingham Palace and punished him with some severity.

We may mention too the lovely and ill-fated Empress Elizabeth of Austria, who, always impatient of the cramping fetters of etiquette, openly rebelled when she found that they interfered with the enjoyment of her beloved cigarette; in the early years of her married life this highly strung woman would often smoke a Virginia cigar with her husband.

Edison, to whom we owe the electric light, is one of the many who acknowledge the help that smoking has been to them in their work.

[263]

A HISTORY OF SMOKING

There is one aspect, however, at which even its warmest supporters must look with suspicion; in every age since its first introduction any great war has invariably been followed by an enormous increase in the habit. The Thirty Years War was responsible for its rapid spread over the whole of Europe, which was followed by its universal adoption throughout the world. At a time when the habit of snuff-taking had relegated smoking to the background, for so long a period that many people pronounced it dead, the Napoleonic campaigns were the means of bringing it once more to the front in the form of the cigar.

Similarly, the Crimean War was largely responsible for the popularity of the cigarette, and there is no need to dwell on the unparalleled increase of smoking which followed the Great War of our own times: if there were any among all those millions of soldiers who were non-smokers when the War began there were none by the time it was over. The officers in command fully recognized the value of smoking as a means of deadening the men's susceptibilities to the fearful strain to which they were constantly exposed, as well as of mitigating the danger of periods of enforced idleness, and they used every possible effort to ensure a constant supply of the requisite materials. General Pershing, for instance, the commander-in-chief of the American troops in France, once cabled to Washington: "Tobacco is as indispensable as the daily ration; we must have thousands of tons of it without delay." [1]

On the return of these hosts of smokers to their native

---

[1] Hamilton, *This Smoking World*, p. 11.

lands the habit of smoking abnormally increased in all the combatant countries. The world's output of tobacco, which before the War was estimated at one and a half milliard kilogrammes, had risen in 1928, ten years after the conclusion of peace, to two and a half milliards.[1]

Although the fight between the smokers and non-smokers still drags on, with varying success, a glance at statistics proves convincingly that the latter are but a feeble and ever-dwindling minority. The hopeless nature of their struggle becomes plain when we remember that all countries, whatever their form of government, now encourage and facilitate the passion for smoking in every conceivable way, merely for the sake of the revenue which it produces. Those governments which possess a State monopoly are always keen on adding attractive novelties

[1] Average number per head, compiled from the official statistics for 1927 and (not complete) 1928 :

COUNTRY	CIGARS			CIGARETTES		
	Before the War	1927	1928	Before the War	1927	1928
Germany .	119	103	103	195	502	499
England * .	12	4	——	201	811	——
France . .	16	10	10	96	248	326
Holland . .	—	157	—	—	341	—
Italy . .	34	39	—	104	372	—
Sweden . .	38	33	33	115	233	—
United States †	90	62	——	143	798	840

* The steady decline of the cigar as compared with the cigarette is especially notable ; we must remember, however, that the short pipe is still very generally smoked.
† The total number of cigarettes smoked in the United States was 97 milliards in 1927, and 106 milliards in 1928. This table shows clearly the general triumph of the cigarette over the cigar ; only in Germany is the consumption of the latter still fairly high, though there too it has dwindled. Pipe-smoking has fallen far behind, while snuff-taking seems likely to die out, although a fair amount of snuff is still manufactured in every country.

For the above statistics I am indebted to Dr Flügler, the Syndic of the United German Cigarette Factories.

to the tobacconist's stock-in-trade, and where taxes take the place of a monopoly the private dealers vie with each other in a similar effort.

Here and there, but chiefly in America, where the prohibition of drink still maintains a precarious existence, a demand for the abolition of smoking crops up from time to time, and a few states have adopted the movement, which originated from the American "Women's Christian Temperance Union." There was a time when at every street corner in the United States one saw a poster depicting a mother with a baby in her arms and a cigarette in her mouth; there were no words—the mere presentment, it was hoped, would have a deterrent effect. But the anti-tobacco leagues, which are to be found in one form or another all over the world, have lived to see the very countries which tried to place difficulties in the way of smoking capitulate before the spread of the custom and the opposition of the populace. At one time, for instance, the sale of cigarettes was forbidden in no less than twelve states in North America, but in every case the prohibition has since been discontinued; the last to succumb was the state of Kansas, which withdrew the prohibition in 1927—since when the smuggler's occupation has finally disappeared. In certain states laws are still in force to prevent young people below a certain age injuring their health by smoking, and a certain amount of newspaper propaganda is still carried on.

In European countries no serious attempt to prohibit smoking has been made in recent times. Though it is still possible to enforce the drink laws in the United States, by means of a gigantic organization, any proposal to deal in the same way with smoking would call forth such a storm of disapproval as would instantly sweep any government out of office that attempted it, and the same may be confidently affirmed of every country in the world. If we consider how in the past the efforts of the most absolute despots the world has ever seen were powerless to stop the spread of smoking we may rest assured that any such attempts to-day, when the habit has grown to such gigantic dimensions, can result only in a miserable fiasco.

CHRONOLOGY

About 3000 B.C. The Egyptians burn sweet herbs and frankincense when sacrificing to their gods.

700–600 B.C. The Greeks begin to offer incense on their altars.

About the beginning of the Christian era the Romans offer incense and employ smoke for medicinal purposes.

In America in the early centuries of our era smoking, as a feature of religious ceremonial, is practised among the Mayas, probably in the district of Tabasco, in Mexico.

A.D. 470–620. Maya civilization at its height.

In the following centuries. Spread of smoking among the people in the Mexico region and the Antilles; dispersion of tribes northward by way of the Mississippi Valley and, by sea, as far as Brazil.

1492. Columbus discovers the Antilles; sees tobacco smoked for the first time.

1497. Romano Pane brings the first account of smoking to Europe.

1519. Cortez finds smoking practised among the Aztecs. Oviedo brings the first tobacco-leaves to Europe.

1526. Oviedo reports further on the custom of smoking.

1556. First tobacco seeds arrive in France from Brazil.

1559. Jean Nicot, French ambassador in Portugal, receives tobacco seeds from America, and sends some to the Court in Paris.

1560 (*about*). The tobacco plant introduced into Holland from France. England adopts the smoking habit.

1561 (*about*). The tobacco plant in Rome.

1565. Monardes praises the healing properties of tobacco.

1570 (*about*). The tobacco plant grown in Germany and Switzerland—also, as a medicinal herb, in Austria and Hungary.

1575. The use of tobacco forbidden in the churches of Spanish America.

1580 (*about*). The first arrival of tobacco in Turkey and Poland.

[269]

1585 (*about*). Sir Walter Raleigh and the colony of Virginia.

End of sixteenth century. Portuguese introduce smoking into India, Eastern Asia, and Japan.

1603. James I of England starts a campaign against smoking.

1605. James takes part in disputation at Oxford on the question of smoking.

1613–89. Prohibition in Russia under the early Romanoffs.

1616. Smoking in Switzerland.

1618–48. The Thirty Years War accounts for the extension of smoking.

1620 (*about*). Prohibition in Japan.

1622 *onward*. A great number of writers praise tobacco as a universal remedy.

1627. First tobacco monopoly granted to a *fermier* in Mantua.

1629. Richelieu puts a tax on smoking.

1630. Sweden learns to smoke.

1633. Savage repressive measures by Sultan Murad IV.

1636. The plague in Holland.

1642. Pope Urban VIII's Bull against smoking in the churches in Seville.

1648. Smoking generally prohibited. Writers now hostile to it.

1650. Spread of smoking in Austria. Pope Innocent X's Bull against smoking in St Peter's, Rome.

1657. Prohibition in Switzerland.

1659. First tobacco *appalto* in Venice.

1665. The plague of London.

1670. Count Khevenhiller's *appalto* in Austria.

1679. Abraham a Santa Clara and the plague in Vienna.

1689–1725. Peter the Great's advocacy of smoking.

1699. Louis XIV and his physician, Fagon, oppose smoking.

End of seventeenth century. Snuff-taking spreads.

1701–40. Tobacco councils of Frederick I and Frederick William I.

1706. Decline of prohibition in Switzerland.

1725. Edict of Pope Benedict XIII, allowing snuff-taking even in St Peter's.

CHRONOLOGY

1742. Frederick the Great's edict against the danger of fires resulting from smoking.

End of eighteenth century. Cigars take the place of snuff; the Napoleonic wars disseminate them throughout Europe.

1848. Abolition of the last restrictions in Berlin.

1856. Beginning of the popularity of the cigarette, as a result of the Crimean War.

BIBLIOGRAPHY

A VAST amount has been written about smoking and tobacco. Ever since the discovery of America scholars and men of letters, to say nothing of amateurs, have dealt with the subject from every conceivable aspect. The following bibliography will enable anyone to take a rapid but thorough survey of the whole field of such publications.

The first place must be given to the earlier bibliographies, with their valuable lists of books on special subjects. The most important are William Bragge's *Bibliotheca Nicotiana* (in English), 46 pages (privately printed, 1874), and O. Verlage's articles in the *Neuer Anzeiger für Bibliographie und Bibliothekwissenschaft* for 1875; see Part 4 (April), pp. 132–139, and Parts 8 and 9 (August, September), pp. 262–269; the references in the work, however, do not go beyond the year 1810.

The first-named, as might be expected, deals mainly with English publications, and there are many omissions in the lists of books in other languages. Both bibliographies are now out of date.

Quite recently an industrious Austrian writer, Eduard Maria Schranka, has compiled a very full work of a similar kind, the manuscript of which is now in the possession of the Austrian Tobacco *Regie* in the Porzellangasse, Vienna, where I was able to inspect it. This is the most complete bibliography in existence, but only a part of it is at present in print; a beginning was made in the official publication of the Austrian Tobacco Company for 1919–20 (Vienna, 1920), and the list of works given under the letters A to C occupies no fewer than fifty-four pages.

As Schranka goes carefully into the matter of Bragge's catalogue, containing 163 titles, as well as O. Verlage's collections (which are severely critical of Bragge), we need not insist on the importance of this work; it is simply indispensable for all who are interested in the subject, and it is to be hoped that the printing of the remainder will not be long delayed.

A HISTORY OF SMOKING

Wilfred Partington's book *Smoke Rings and Roundelays* has a very good modern English bibliography, which includes many titles that I have found nowhere else. Finally, for those who are specially interested in the medical aspect of tobacco, there is Pierre Schrumpf-Pierron's excellent *Tobacco and Physical Efficiency* (New York, 1927).

In the following pages only those works are included which supply dates for the history of tobacco in its relation to social progress. The first section contains works of a general nature drawn from the literature of every age; the other sections are arranged according to the different centuries.

GENERAL

ANTZ, C. C.: *Tabaci historia* (Berlin, 1836).

APPERSON: *The Social History of Smoking* (London, 1914).

BARBIER, C.: *Histoire du tabac. Les Persécutions* (Paris, 1861).

BIBRA: *Die narkotischen Genussmittel* (1855).

BLONDEL: *Le Livre des fumeurs* (1891).

CAPILUPI: *Noticie sul tobacco coltivato anticamente nell' alto Mantovano*, in *Boll. Com. Agr.* (Mantua, 1891).

CARDON, E.: *Le Musée du fumeur* (Paris, 1866).

COLUMBUS, J.: *Das Buch von Tabak* (Vienna, 1846).

COMES, O.: *Histoire, géographie, statistique du tabac* (Naples, 1900).

CREIZENACH: *Die französische Tabakregie* (Mainz, 1868).

CUDELL, R.: *Das Buch vom Tabak* (Verlag Neuerburg, 1927).

DEMOOR, V. P.: *Du Tabac : Description historique, etc.* (Paris and Brussels, 1858).

DENIS, FERD.: *Lettre sur l'introduction du tabac* (Paris, 1851).

DENIS, JULES: *Le Tabac : son histoire, sa production* (Geneva and Paris).

DEYACK, D. M.: *Geschichtliche Darstellung der ungarischen Tabakkultur* (Pest, 1822).

DIETZ, A.: *Frankfurter Handelsgeschichte* (Frankfort, 1910–25).

FAIRHOLT: *Tobacco* (London, 1859).

FEINHALS, JOSEF: *Der Tabak in Kunst und Kultur* (Cologne).

FERMOND: *Monographie du tabac* (1857).

FERRARIS: *Bibliotheca canonica*. See Moroni, *Dizionario*, vol. lxxii, fol. 176–179.

BIBLIOGRAPHY

GOFFARD: *Du Tabac, son histoire, ses propriétés* (Paris and Limoges, 1872).

GRAFE, VICTOR: *Handbuch der organischen Warenkunde. Narkotische Genussmittel*, vol. xiv (Stuttgart, 1930).

HAMILTON, A. E.: *This Smoking World* (New York and London).

HAMMER-PURGSTALL: *Geschichte des Osmanischen Reiches* (Pest, 1827–35).

HARTWICH, C.: *Die menschlichen Genussmittel* (Leipzig, 1911).

HELLWALD: *Naturgeschichte der Menschen* (Stuttgart, 1882).

HENRIECK, GA.: *Du Tabac, son histoire* (Paris, 1864).

HOFFMANN VON FALLERSLEBEN: *Der Tabak in der deutschen Literatur.*

HORNSTEIN, ANTON: *Der Tabak in historischer Beziehung* (Brünn, 1828).

HULL, CLARK: *The Influence of Tobacco-smoking on Mental and Motor Efficiency* (Princeton, 1924).

HUMBOLDT, A. v.: *Voyage aux régions équinoctiales* (Paris, 1814–25, 3 vols.).

HUTCHINSON, G. WILLIAM: *Lyra Nicotiana. Poems and Verses concerning Tobacco* (London).

IGER, ARTHUR: *Das Tabakskollegium*, in the *Deutsche Tabakzeitung* of November 17, 1904.

JAUCENT, HENRI: *Le Tabac, étude historique* (Paris, 1900).

JUCH, K. WILH.: *Über den Tabak und dessen Geschichte* (Augsburg, 1821).

LARBALÉTRIER, ALBERT: *Étude historique* (Paris, 1891).

LEFÈBVRE, J.: *Du Tabac* (Paris, 1866).

LEWINSTEIN, GUSTAV (editor of the *Deutsche Tabakzeitung*), in *Für und Wider den Tabak* (Berlin, 1890).

LIEBAUT, E.: *Recherches sur le tabac, son histoire* (Paris, 1851).

MACAULAY, LORD: *The History of England*, vol. i, Chapter III.

MAURO: *Monografia del tabacco* (1866).

MELLER, HENRY J.: *Nicotiana; or, The Smoker's and Snuff-taker's Comparison, containing the History of Tobacco, with an Essay in its Defence . . . Poetry and Anecdotes* (London, 1833).

MICHELER, JOSEF: *Das Tabakwesen in Bayern* (Stuttgart, 1887).

MILLIET, E. W., in *Schweizerische Zeitschrift für Gemeinnützigkeit*, 38th year (Zürich, 1899).

MÜLLER, JOH.: *Der Tabak in geschichtlicher usw. Hinsicht* (Emmerich, 1842).

MUNNOZ, JUAN BAPTISTA: *Historia del Nuovo Mundo* (Madrid, 1793).

Näche, P.: *Der Tabak in der Ätiologie der Psychosen*, in the *Kleine Rundschau* (Vienna, 1909, Nos. 48–50).

Nadaillac, Marquis de: *Les Pipes et le tabac* (Paris, 1886).

—— *Matériaux pour l'histoire primitive et naturelle de l'homme*, 15th year, 3rd series, vol. ii (1885).

Nitsche, Johann Ambros: *Geschichte des Tabaks und seiner Schicksale seit der Entdeckung Amerikas bis auf unsere Zeiten* (Prague, 1845).

Oppel, Alwin: *Der Tabak im Wirtschaftsleben und der Sittengeschichte der Völker* (Bremen, 1890).

Parbalétrier: *Le Tabac* (Paris, 1891).

Pezzolato: *Monografia delle Nicoziane* (1886).

Pilz, Hermann: *Der Tabak und das Rauchen. Ernstes und Heiteres aus der Kulturgeschichte* (Gustav Weigel, Leipzig, 1899).

Pritchett, T. R.: *Smokiana* (London, 1890).

Reichenbach, G. B.: *Der Tabak und seine Verbreitung. Kulturgeschichtliche und naturhistorische Beschaffenheit* (Berlin, 1866).

Rogers, J. S.: *An Essay on Tobacco, History of the Plant* (New York, 1836).

Rouillard, A.: *Effets du tabac sur l'intelligence* (Paris, 1886).

Salomon, Felix: *Englische Geschichte* (Leipzig, 1923).

Schosserer, Guido v.: *Das österreichische Tabakmonopol* (1908).

—— *Das Tabaktrinken*, in the *Deutsche Tabakzeitung* of October 6, 1876.

Schranka, E. M.: *Tabakanekdoten* (I. Feinhals, Cologne, 1914).

Schrumpf-Pierron, Pierre: *Tobacco and Physical Efficiency: a Digest of Clinical Data* (with annotated bibliography) (New York, 1927).

Schultz: *Das häusliche Leben der europäischen Kulturvölker vom Mittelalter bis zur zweiten Hälfte des 18. Jahrhunderts* (Munich, 1903).

Sebillot, P.: *Le Tabac dans les traditions, les superstitions, et les coutumes* (Paris, 1893).

Stein, Lorenz: *Lehrbuch der Finanzwissenschaft* (Leipzig, 1871).

Steinhausen, G.: *Geschichte der deutschen Kultur* (Leipzig, 1904).

Steinmetz, Andrew: *Tobacco: its History, etc.* (London, 1857).

Steinmetz, A.: *The Smokers' Guide* (London, 1878).

Stern, Alfred: *Geschichte Europas von 1830 bis 1848* (Stuttgart and Berlin, 1919–24).

Tidswell, H. H.: *The Tobacco Habit: its History and Pathology* (London, 1912).

BIBLIOGRAPHY

TIEDEMANN: *Geschichte des Tabaks* (Frankfort, 1854).

TOLSTOY, LEO: *Lasterhafte Genüsse* (*L'Alcool et le tabac*). From the Russian.

VEHSE: *Geschichte der deutschen Höfe*, vol. xxiii, section 4, Part I (1853).

WAGNER: *Tabakkultur, Tabak und Zigarrenfabriken* (Weimar, 1888).

WEBER, CARL JULIUS: *Demokritos*, Chapter VI, *Die Tabakslust* (Stuttgart).

WOLF, J.: *Der Tabak und die Tabakfabrikate* (Leipzig, 1912).

Alte Tabakzeichen (Berlin, 1924).

Code des tabacs: Sammlung aller französischen königlichen Verordnungen über den Tabak, 6 vols.

Manuscrits de la Bibliothèque Nationale. Table et règlements concernants le tabac (1629–91), several volumes.

Official History of the Tobacco Duty, in the Library of the Corporation of London at the Guildhall (Proceedings in the House of Commons, April 18, 1821).

Short Account of the Tobacco Monopoly in Japan (1905). *Historique de la loi concernant le monopole du tabac en Japon* (1902).

Tabaks Collegium des alten Schmauchers Muff, Das (Weimar and Berlin, 1842).

Tobacco Acts of Parliament 1670 to 1869. Act to prevent the planting of tobacco in England and for regulation of the plantation trade (1670).

Tobacco Talk and Smokers' Gossip: an Amusing Miscellany of Fact and Anecdote relating to the Great Plant in all its Forms and Uses, including a Selection from Nicotian Literature (London, 1884).

UP TO THE SIXTEENTH CENTURY

ASSALL: *Nachrichten über die frühesten Einwohner in Nord-Amerika und ihre Denkmäler*. Edited by Professor Mone (Heidelberg, 1827).

BECKER, LOTHAR: *Der Bauerntabak, eine Pflanze der alten Welt* (Breslau, 1875).

—— *Ein Rechenexempel für diejenigen, welche der alten Welt den Tabak vor 1492 nach Christi abstreiten*, in the *Deutsche Tabakszeitung* (No. 3, 1891).

BENZONI, GIROLAMO: *Storia del Nuovo Mundo* (Venice, 1565).

BONSTETTEN, G.: *Recueil d'antiquités* (Lausanne, 1864).

BRASSEUR DE BOURBOURG: *Monuments anciens du Mexique* (Paris, 1866).

Brasseur: *Manuscrit Troano, Étude sur le système graphique de la langue des Mayas* (Paris, 1869–70).

Bry, de: *Brevis narratio* (Frankfort, 1591).

Colombe: *Relations des 4 voyages entreprises par Colombe, traduites de l'Espagnol de Navarrete* (Paris, 1828).

Cooper, T. P.: *The Story of the Tobacco Pipe*, in the *Scientific American* (Supplement, No. 1693) of June 13, 1908.

Fellenberg: *Das Gräberfeld bei Elsried* (Zürich, 1866).

Fritze, Hans von: *Das Rauchopfer bei den Griechen* (1894).

Hariot: *A Brief and True Report of the New Found Land of Virginia* (1588).

Herodotus: *Historiæ* (*c.* 450 B.C.).

Huber, E.: *Hat man im Altertum Tabak geraucht?* in the *Umschau*, 33rd year, Part 56 (1929).

Las Casas, Bartolomé de: *Histoire des Indes*, 1520–59.

Löhr, Max: *Das Rauchesopfer im Alten Testament*.

McGuire, D.: *Pipes and Smoking Customs of the American Aborigines*, in the *Report of the U.S.A. National Museum for 1897*, pp. 351–645 (Washington, 1899).

Mela Pomponius: *De situ orbis*, Book II (*c.* A.D. 40).

Michelin et Ramé: *Relation originale du voyage de Jacques Cartier au Canada en 1534* (1867).

Oviedo y Valdes: *Historia general y natural de las Indias* (Toledo, 1526; Italian edition, Venice, 1556; new edition, Madrid, 1853).

Pane, Romano: *De insularium ritibus* (1497).

Pliny: *Naturalis historia*, Book XXVI (*c.* A.D. 79).

Plutarch: *Fragmenta et spuria*, III (3rd edition, Paris, 1855).

Quinquerez: *Les Forges primitives du Jure*, in *Mitteilungen der antiquarischen Gesellschaft* (Zürich, 1871).

Radin, Paul: *The Story of the American Indian* (London).

Reber, B.: *Les Pipes antiques de la Suisse*, in the *Anzeiger für Schweiz. Altertumskunde*, 1914, Part 4, and 1915, Part 1.

Thevet, André: *Cosmographie universelle* (1571).

—— *France antarctique* (Antwerp, 1558).

Report of the U.S.A. National Museum for 1897 (Washington, 1899).

Twelfth Annual Report of the Bureau of Ethnology of the United States, 1889–90.

BIBLIOGRAPHY

SIXTEENTH CENTURY

ACOSTA : *Historia natural y moral de las Indias* (Paris, 1616).

—— *Trattato della historia e virtù delle droghe medicinali* (Venice, 1585).

BLANCHARD : *Histoire des maîtres de requêtes* (article on Nicot).

BRY, DE : *Historia Brasiliana* (1590).

CANOTIUS, THIMOTEUS : *Tractatus de Tabacco indico.*

DODONÄUS, LAMBERT : *Cruydebock* (Antwerp, 1563, with illustrations of the tobacco-plant).

DRAKE : *The World encompassed* (London, 1628).

EVERARTUS, Ä. : *De herba panacea seu medicina tabaci universalis* (Antwerp, 1581).

—— *De panacea herba quam alii tabacum . . . vocant* (Antwerp, 1587).

FALGAIROLLE, EDMOND : *Jean Nicot, ambassadeur de France en Portugal au XVIième siècle* (Paris, 1897).

GESNER, CONRAD VON : *Hortus Germanicus* (1560).

—— *Epistolarum medicinalium, Libri Tres* (Zürich, 1577).

GOHORY, JACQUES : *Instruction sur l'herbe petum* (Paris, 1872).

HALL, JOSEF : *Satyres,* Book IV, Satire 4 ; Book V, Satire 2 (1597).

LIEBAULT, CHARLES-ÉTIENNE ET JEAN : *L'Agriculture et la maison rustique* (Paris, 1572).

LOBEL, MATHIA DE, AND PETRO PENA : *Nuova stirpium adversaria* (Antwerp, 1576).

MICHEL, E. : *Jean Nicot et sa famille* (Toulouse, 1897).

MONARDES, NICOLÒ : *Herba Tabacco d'India* (Genoa, 1578).

—— *Simplicium medicamentorum ex novo orbe delatorum, quorum in medicina usus est, historia* (Antwerp, 1579 ; French edition, Lyons, 1602).

PENA, PETRO—*see* LOBEL, MATHIA DE.

SCHMIDT AND SCHONN : *Geschichte des Tabakgefälls* (Vienna, 1818).

SCOT, REGINALD : *Discoverie of Witchcraft* (1584).

TYSLER : *The Life of Sir Walter Raleigh* (London, 1833).

Études économiques sur l'Amérique méridionale, vol. ii, *Lettres sur l'introduction du tabac en France par Ferdinand Denis* (Guillaumin, Paris, 1851).

Historia medicinal de las cosas que sirven al uso de medicina (Seville, 1565).

A HISTORY OF SMOKING

Introduction of Tobacco into Japan (illustrated) (Yokohama, 1878).
Life of Sir Walter Raleigh, The (London, 1868).

SEVENTEENTH CENTURY

ALBIN, BERNHARD : *Dissertatione de Tabaco* (1695).

ANDY, NICOLAS: *De la Génération des vers dans le corps de l'homme* (Amsterdam, 1701). The Appendix contains the speech of Fagon, physician to Louis XIV.

AUBREY, JOHN : *Letters written by Eminent Persons* (1669).

BACON, FRANCIS : *Historia vitæ et mortis* (London, 1623).

BAILLARD, EDMOND : *Histoire du tabac* (Paris, 1677).

BALDE, JAKOB : *Die truckene Trunkenheit . . . Satyra oder Straffrede wider den Missbrauch des Tabacks* (Nuremberg, 1658), being the German version of *Satyra contra abusum tabaci* (Monaco, 1657).

BARCLAY, WILLIAM : *Nepenthes ; or, The Vertues of Tobacco* (Edinburgh, 1614).

BAUMANN : *De tabaci virtute, usu et abusu* (Basle, 1629).

BEINTEMA VON PEIMA : *Panacea oder das allgemeine Hilfsmittel oder Lob des Tabaks* (Leipzig, 1691).

—— *Vernünftige Untersuchungen über die Frage, ob galanten und anderen Frauenzimmern nicht ebensowohl als denen Mannes Personen Taback zu rauchen erlaubt, und ihrer Gesundheit nützlich sey* (Frankfort and Leipzig, 1743).

—— *Tabacologia* (The Hague, 1690).

BOERNER, AUGUST : *Kölner Tabakhandel und Tabakgewerbe, 1628 bis 1910* (Essen on the Ruhr, 1912).

BONTEKOE, CORNELIUS : *Kurze Abhandlung über des Menschen Leben, Gesundheit, Krankheit und Tod* (The Hague, 1685).

BRATHWAIT, RICHARD : *The Smoking Age ; or, The Man in the Mist, with the Life and Death of Tobacco* (London, 1617).

BUSHELL : *A Work for Chimney-sweepers; or, A Warning to Tobacconists.*

CHARLES I : Proclamation, *De herba nicotiana* (1625).

CLAUDERUS, GABRIEL : *De herba nicotiana curiosa quædam* (1668). *Miscell. naturæ curiosor. germ.*, Dec. II., ann. 3.

DISRAELI : *Inquiry into the Literary and Political Character of James I* (London, 1816).

FAGON : *Ergo ex tabaci usu vita brevior* (Paris, 1699).

FRANKEN, JOHANN : *Dissertatio de præclaris herbæ nicotianæ virtutibus* (Uppsala, 1633).

BIBLIOGRAPHY

FRANKEN, JOHANN : *De præclaris herbæ nicotianæ sive tabaci virtutibus disputatio* (Uppsala, 1633).

GARDINER, EDMUND : *The Triall of Tobacco* (1610).

GRIMMELSHAUSEN, HANS JACOB CHRISTOFFEL VON : *Satyrischer Pilgram* (1667).

HAHN, ADAM : *Tabacologia sive de tabaco* (1667). In the edition of 1690 there is a special chapter on the question " Whether Tobacco turns the Brain Black ? "

HOHBERG : *Georgica curiosa* (1682).

JAMES I : *Misocapnus sive de abusu Tobacci lusus regius* (London, 1603).

LAUREMBERG : *Flugschrift, Bericht vom Tabak, woher er komme* (1678).

LEYRA Y AGUILAR, FRANCESCO DE : *Desengaño contra el maluso del Tabacco* (Cordova, 1633).

MAGNENUS, JOH. CHRYSOST. : *Exercitationes de tabaco* (Ticino, 1648).

—— *De tobaco* (Pavia, 1669).

MANDER, CARLOL : *Poema de pulvere tabaci* (Hahn, 1661).

MICHELER, JOSEF : *Das Tabakwesen in Bayern vor dem Bekanntwerden des Tabaks bis zur Einführung eines Herdstättengeldes, 1717* (Stuttgart, 1887).

MOSCHEROSCH, J.M. : *Wunderliche und wahrhaftige Gesichte Philanders von Sittewald* (1650).

MÜLLER, ERICH : *Peter der Grosse und sein Hof* (Munich, 1926).

NEANDER, JOHANNES : *Tabacologia . . .* (1622).

OLEARIUS, ADAM : *Beschreibung der moskowitischen und persienischen Reise* (Hamburg, 1696).

ORLÉANS, ELISABETH CHARLOTTE, DUCHESS OF : *Hof und Gesellschaft in Frankreich am Anfang des 18. Jahrhunderts.* Letters selected by Paul Volkmar.

—— *Briefe.* Edited by Hans Helmolt (Insel-Verlag, Leipzig, 1924).

OUDARD, GEORGES : *La Vie de Pierre le Grand* (Paris, 1929).

PEPYS, SAMUEL : *Diary.*

PRADE, DE : *Histoire du tabac* (Paris, 1677).

REDI, FRANCESCO : *Esperienze intorno a diverse cose naturali e particolarmente a quelle, che ci son portate dalle Indie* (Florence, 1686).

RETZER, JOSEF VON : *Die Tabakpachtungen in den österreichischen Ländern von 1670 bis 1783* (Vienna, 1784).

RUSDORFF, JOHANN JOACHIM VON : *Metamorphosis Europæ* (1627).

SANTORINI, ALESSANDRO : *Polvere schernito ovvero invettiva contro il tabacco* (Florence, 1654).

A HISTORY OF SMOKING

SATOW, E.: *The Introduction of Tobacco into Japan.* (*Cf.* the *Transactions* of the Asiatic Society of Japan, VI, i.)

SCRIVERIO, PIETRO: *Saturnalia seu de usu et abusu tabaci* (Harlem, 1628).

SIMON, PAULLUS: *Commentarius de abusu tabaci . . . Argentor* (1665).

SMITH, SAMUEL: *History of the Colony of Nova Cæsaria, or New Jersey* (Burlington, 1765).

STELLA, B.: *Il Tabacco, nella quale si tratta dell' origine, historia, etc.* (Rome, 1617).

SYLVESTER, JOSHUA: *Tobacco battered and the Pipes shattered by a Volley of Holy Shot, thundered from Mount Helicon* (London, 1615).

TAPPIUS: *Oratio de tabaco ejusque hodierno abusu* (Helmstedt, 1653).

THORIUS: *Hymnus tabaci* (Leyden, 1622).

TIECK, JOHANN LUDWIG: *Phantasus* (1816).

VAUGHAN, SIR WILLIAM: *Natural and Artificial Directions for Health,* section 11, Chapter VIII (1602).

VENNER: *A Brief and Accurate Treatise concerning the Taking of the Fume of Tobacco, which Very Many in these Days do too licenciously use* (London, 1637).

—— *Via recta ad vitam longam* (1650).

VITAGLIANI, ANTONIO: *De abusu tabaci* (Rome, 1650).

WIESER, FRANZ: *Über die Produktion, den Konsum und die Besteuerung des Tabaks im Kronlande Salzburg von 1657 bis zur Einführung des Tabakgefälles im Jahre 1817. Fachliche Mitteilungen der österreichischen Tabakregie,* 8th year, Part 1, March 1908.

—— *Zur Geschichte der Tabakproduktion in Tirol. Fachliche Mitteilungen der österreichischen Tabakregie,* 5th year, Part 3, October 1905.

ZAVORA, M.: *Abuso del tabacco dei nostri tempi* (Bologna, 1650).

ZIEGLER, JOHANN JACOB, *Tabak oder von dem gar heilsamen Wunderkraute Nicotiana* (Zürich, 1616).

Codex austriacus, vols. iii–vi, under " Tabak."

De tabaco: Epistolæ et judicia clarissimorum aliquot medicorum (Utrecht, 1644).

Mémoires complètes et authentiques du Duc de Saint-Simon sur le siècle de Louis XIV et la régence (Paris, 1829).

Ordinance of the Lords and Commons assembled in Parliament for the regulating of the rates on . . . tobacco (London, March 4, 1643).

—— (London, 1644).

Saturnalia seu de usu et abusu tabaci (Harlem, 1628).

BIBLIOGRAPHY

Taschenbuch für Tabakraucher (Regensburg, 1800).
Tryumph of Tobacco over Sack and Ale, in *Wit's Recreations* (1640).

Eighteenth Century

AMARANTHES: *Frauenzimmerlexikon* (1715). See under headings "Tabak" and "Schnupftabakdose."

ARNETH: *Geschichte Maria Theresias* (1863–79).

BARTHÉLEMY: *L'Art de fumer ou la pipe et le cigare* (Paris, 1844).

BARUFFALDI, GIROLAMO: *La Tabaccheide* (Ferrara, 1714).

BENEDIKT, HEINRICH: *Das Königreich Neapel unter Kaiser Karl VI* (Vienna, 1927).

BLEI, FRANZ: *Die Sitten des Rokoko.*

BUCHOZ: *Dissertation sur le tabac* (Paris, 1787).

CARLYLE: *Frederick the Great.*

CASANOVA: *Memoirs.*

CHARLES VI: *Erlass betreffs Besteuerung des Tabaks* (Vienna, 1714).

COHAUSEN, JOHANN HEINRICH: *Satyrische Gedancken, von der Pica Nasi; oder, Der Sehnsucht der lüsternen Nase, das ist von dem heutigen Missbrauch und schädlichen Effekt des Schnupftabacks* (Leipzig, 1720).

DREGER, MORITZ: *Baugeschichte der k. k. Hofburg in Wien* (Vienna, 1914).

FEISSLER, G.: *Deliciæ Historicæ, etc.* (Jena, 1707).

FLORINUS, FRANCISCUS PHILIPPUS: *Hausvatter* (Nuremberg, Frankfort, and Leipzig, 1750).

FÖRSTER, FRIEDRICH: *Friedrich Wilhelm I, König von Preussen* (Potsdam, 1834).

FRANZ, OTTO: *Aus dem Tabakskollegium und der Zopfzeit* (Leipzig, 1872).

GAVELLI, NICOLÒ: *Storia distinta del Tabaco* (Pesaro, 1758).

GUNDLING: *Leben und Taten des Freiherrn Jacob Paul von G., Hofnarr im Tabakskollegium* (Berlin, 1795).

HAINISCH, MICHAEL: *Das österreichische Tabakmonopol im 18. Jahrhundert* (Vienna).

HOFFINGER, JOH. GEORG: *Sendschreiben über den Gebrauch des Tobaks* (Schemnitz, 1790).

ISAMBERT: *Recueil général des anciennes lois françaises*, vol. xvi, No. 169 (Paris, 1829).

KLAR, MARTIN: *Die Tabatièren Friedrichs des Grossen* (Berlin).

[283]

KRÜGER: *Gedanken vom Café, Thee, Tabak* (1743).

LEUCORANDE: *Beweiss, dass ein honettes Frauenzimmer bei den Caffé Schmausgen erscheinen und eine Pfeife Toback dazu schmauchen könne* (Meissen, 1715).

MANARA, CAMILL: *De tabaci usu in Europeis* (Madrid, 1702).

MAURY, ABBÉ: *Opinion sur l'impôt du tabac, prononcée dans l'assemblée nationale* (Paris, 1790).

MIRABEAU THE ELDER: *Développement de l'opinion concernant le revenu public à établir sur la consommation du tabac* (Paris, 1790).

MYLIUS: *Corpus constitutionum marchicarum*, vol. v, section 2.

NATHANSEN, W.: *Aus Hamburgs alten Tagen* (Hamburg, 1893).

NICCOLICCHIA: *Del uso ed abuso de tabacco* (Palermo, 1712).

PASETTI, TOMMASO: *Il Monopolio del tabacco in Italia* (Portici, 1906).

PREUSS: *Lebensgeschichte Friedrich Wilhelms I* (Berlin, 1832).

PUISIEUX: *L'Impôt du tabac sous l'ancien régime* (Paris, 1906).

REIMANN, E. P.: *Das Tabaksmonopol Friedrichs des Grossen* (Munich and Leipzig, 1913).

SANDERSON, ROBERT: *Rymerifædera* (London, 1726).

WIESER, FRANZ: *Zur Geschichte des Tabakgefälles und der Tabakkultur in Dalmatien 1700–1884.*

Auserlesene Ergötzlichkeiten vom Tabak nebst Kestners " Recht des Tabaks " (Leipzig, 1715).

Collectio bullarum sacrosanctæ Basilicæ Vaticanæ, vol. iii, p. 265 (Rome, 1752).

Declaration des Edikts vom 28. April 1723 wider das unvorsichtige und gefährliche Tabakrauchen (Königsberg, 1742).

Déclaration du roy concernant la ferme du tabac, donnée à Paris le 17 octobre 1720 (Lille, 1720).

Déclaration du roy contre les fraudes des droits de la ferme du tabac, donnée le 18 sept. 1703 (Paris, 1703).

Déclaration du roy portant règlement général pour le tabac, donnée à Paris le 1 août (Paris, 1721).

Erneuerung und Verschärfung der Edicte wider das verbotene Feueranmachen und Tobakrauchen (Stettin, 1744).

Gründlicher und anmutiger Beweis, dass ein honettes Frauenzimmer ohne einige Verletzung ihres Renomee bissweilen by den Caffée-Schmäussgen erscheinen könne (Lindenstadt, 1715).

Historische, Politische, Juridische und Cameralische Reflexiones über die dermahlige Landes Verfassung des Königreiches Böheimb. (1718).

BIBLIOGRAPHY

Monopolgesetze und die Besteuerung des Tabakkonsums von 1683 bis 1783, Die. Fachliche Mitteilungen der österreichischen Tabakregie, 1912 annual, p. 86.

Nicotianische errauchte Polizeioder Tabaksordnung, etc. Fumarius, Schmauchbuch (Cologne, 1719).

Ordonnance du roy concernant la distribution du tabac de cantine aux troupes (Lille, June 12, 1748).

Rapport et discours à l'assemblée constituante, sur la prohibition de la culture du tabac et le privilège exclusif de la fabrication et du débit par P. L. Röderer (1791).

Rapport fait au nom du comité de l'imposition concernant le revenu public provenant de la vente exclusive du tabac (Paris, 1790).

Storia distinta e curiosa del tabacco (Ferrara, 1758).

Toback: Das geliebte und gelobte Kräutlein oder historische Merkwürdigkeiten vom Ursprung (Chemnitz, 1719).

Verbotsedikt, wodurch das unachtsame Rauchen in denen Scheunen, Ställen, Wäldern und auf denen Strassen verboten wird (Potsdam, October 14, 1753; Breslau, 1753).

NINETEENTH CENTURY

BLISMON, A.: *Manuel historique et anecdotique du fumeur et priseur* (Paris). The same book also under the *Tabacographia* (Paris, 1856).

BODE, WILHELM: *Stunden mit Goethe* (Leipzig, 1909).

BOEHN, MAX VON: *Biedermeier-Deutschland von 1815 bis 1847.*

CAILLOT: *Mémoires sur les mœurs et les usages des Français.*

CASATI, CARLO: *Nuove Rivelazioni sui fatti di Milano 1848,* 2 vols. (Milan, 1885).

—— *Storia dell Risorgimento Italiano* (Milan).

CATTANEO: *L'Insurrection de Milan.*

FERRARI, VITTORIO: *Carteggio Casati-Castagnetto* (Milan, 1909).

FLEURY, MAURICE: *Des effets du tabac sur la santé des gens de lettres, de son influence sur l'avenir de la littérature française* (1889). Awarded a prize by the Société contre l'Abus du Tabac.

GOETHE: *Aus meinem Leben, Dichtung und Wahrheit,* Part III, Book 14.

GOETHE, FRAU RATH: *Briefe.* 6th edition (Insel-Verlag, Leipzig 1923).

HELFERT, JOSEPH FREIHERR VON: *Geschichte der österreichischen Revolution* (Freiburg, 1907).

HÉRISSON, D', etc.: *Journal d'un officier d'ordonnance, du juillet 1870 au février 1871* (Paris).

LAS CASES: *Mémorial de Ste Hélène*, vol. ii.

MASSON, FRÉDÉRIQUE: *Napoléon chez soi* (Paris).

MEISTER, OSKAR: *Auch eine Goethehandschrift*, in *Der getreue Eckart* (Vienna, 2nd year, 1925, vol. ii, Parts 11 and 12).

OTTOLINI: *La Rivoluzione lombarda del 1848 e 1849* (Milan, 1887).

PASETTI, TOMMASO: *Monopolio del tabacco in Italia* (Portici, 1906).

RECHERT, EMIL: *Rauchringe*.

STEIN, A.: *Amor capnophilus* (Vienna, 1829).

WIESER, FRANZ: *Die Einrichtungen des französischen Tabakmonopols in den illyrischen Provinzen 1809 bis 1830. Fachliche Mitteilungen der österreichischen Tabakregie* of October 1910, Part 3.

Almanach des fumeurs et priseurs (Paris, 1858).

Almanach des fumeurs pour 1849 (Paris, 1849).

Jahresbericht der österreichischen Tabakregie für das Jahr 1928.

Mémoires de Bourrienne sur Napoléon, vol. iii.

Monopolio del tabacco in Italia: Cenni storico-statistici (Rome, 1900).

Rapport concernant la fabrication et la vente exclusives du tabac, suivi des comptes relatifs à cette branche de revenue pour l'année 1835 (Paris, 1835).

NEWSPAPERS, PERIODICALS, DICTIONARIES

COPE: *Cope's Tobacco Plant*, etc. (London, 1877–84).

Deutsche Tabakzeitung. The following articles (Berlin, since 1868): *Ausbreitung der Zigarre in Europa*, November 22, December 6, 1872, April 18 and 25, 1873; *Über den Ursprung des Wortes Tabak*, 7th year, 1874, Nos. 8a ff.; *Über den Namen Tabak*, 1876, Nos. 23 ff.; *Geschichtsschreibung und der Tabak vor 1492*, 10th year, 1877, Nos. 15 ff.; 12th year, 1879, Nos. 48 ff.; 14th year, 1881, Nos. 47 ff.; 15th year, 1882, Nos. 30 ff.; 16th year, 1883, Nos. 16, 17, 18; 17th year, 1884, No. 19; 24th year, 1891, Nos. 3 ff.

Dictionnaire des sciences médicales, 1819, vol. liv.

EBERTY: *Zur Geschichte des Tabaks und seine Besteuerung* (Berlin, No. 4, January 22 and March 24, 1891); Romagen, in the *D.T.Z.*, 1904, Nos. 14 and 15, of April 7, 14; *Nap. Tabakmonopol*, October 4, 1894.

Fachliche Mitteilungen der österreichischen Tabakregie, 1902, Part 1, pp. 20–24; 1908, Parts 1, 2, 3; 1911, Part 1; 1912, Parts 1 and 2.

BIBLIOGRAPHY

Figaro (Vienna, 1907, No. 52).

Frankfurter Zeitung, March 18, 1888.

Fremdenblatt, December 25, 1909; March 13, 1910; May 15, 1910.

GARTENLAUBE: *Zur Geschichte der Tabakspfeife*, 1894, Book VII, p. 208.

Globus, vol. xxix, pp. 251 *et seq.*, 266 *et seq.*, 284 *et seq.*, 644 *et seq.*

Guckkasten, Der, July 1912, No. 12.

Illustration française, July 23, 1892, the fourth centenary of the discovery of tobacco.

Internationale Sammlerzeitung (Vienna, 4th year, 1912, Nos. 10, 15, 16, 21, 22; 5th year, 1913, No. 2).

Kölnische Zeitung, July 1911.

LANDGRAF, J: *Zur Geschichte und Bedeutung der deutschen Cigarren-industrie*, "*Bürgerliches Industrie- und Handelsblatt*," 3rd year, 1897, No. 24.

Leipziger Tageblatt, February 21, 1888.

LEWINSTEIN, GUSTAV: *Die deutsche Tabakindustrie*, Nos. 142 and 143 of the *Heft der volkswirtschaftlichen Gesellschaft in Berlin* (1897).

MÉNAGE: *Dictionnaire étymologique de la langue française*, vol. ii, p. 247.

Moniteur, June 16, 1867. *Le Tabac en France*, by Marfoy.

Monopol, Unser Kaiser als Raucher, January 27, 1914; *Der Tabak im Dialekt*, February 21, 1914; *Der Tabak und Napoleon*, March 15 and May 1, 1914.

Natur, 1880, Halle, G. Schwetschke, vol. xxx, 1881, No. 38 (September 17), p. 459; No. 39 (September 24), p. 469.

Neue Freie Presse, No. 16754, April 13, 1911; No. 10129, November 4, 1892.

Nord und Süd, 1909–10, Dr Vlenten, *Ausserungen bedeutender Männer über den Zusammenhang von Tabakgenuss und geistiger Arbeit*.

Österreichische Enzyclopädie, vol. v (1836), pp. 267–280.

Österreichisches landwirtschaftliches Wochenblatt, 1879, September 13, p. 391, October 11, p. 431, November 15, p. 475, December 13, p. 507; 1880, January 31, pp. 35–36, March 20, p. 93, April 10, p. 117, May 8, p. 149, May 29, p. 173, September 25, p. 319. These articles have been published in book-form under the title *Csermelymenti, Gesammelte Aufsätze*.

Revue des tabacs, La (Paris, since 1925).

Revue internationale des tabacs, La (Paris, since 1924).

SCHRANKA, EDUARD MARIA : the following articles in periodicals—*Der Tabak und die Liebe, Deutsche Tabakzeitung,* July 2, 1881 ; *Der Tabak in der osmanischen Poesie, Deutsche Tabakzeitung,* February 17, March 8, 1881 ; *Der Tabak im Sprichwort, Stein der Weisen,* 23rd year, 1910, Part 13 ; *Der Tabak als heraldische Pflanze, Deutsche Tabakzeitung,* June 22, 1882 ; *Der Tabak im Bilde, Deutsche Tabakzeitung,* June 25, 1903 ; *Einführung des Tabaks in verschiedenen Ländern der Erde, Tabelle, Tabakzeitung* (Prague, July 15, 1903) ; *Zündhölzchen, Deutsche Tabakzeitung,* February 25, 1904 ; *Schiller und der Tabak, Deutsche Tabakzeitung,* November 9, 1905 ; *Bismarck und der Tabak, Ostdeutsche Rundschau,* April 23, 1910 ; *Der Tabak und die Religion, Fachliche Mitteilungen der österreichischen Tabakregie,* 11th year (1911), Part 11.

Socrates, 1918, supplement to vol. xliv, p. 47 *et seq.*

Tabacco, Il (Rome, since 1897).

Tabakpatenteverzeichnis, vol. xxiii of the sectional publications, 420–428.

Temesvárer Zeitung, pamphlet on Meerschaum, June 25, 1908.

Tobacco: a Weekly Trade Review (New York, since 1886).

Tobacco (London).

Veröffentlichungen der historischstatistischen Section Mährens, vol. xv, *Zur Kulturgeschichte Mährens und Schlesiens,* 1. T.; *Notizenblatt der historischen Section,* 1857, p. 91, Nos. 4 and 5 ; *Geschichte des Monopols in Mähren und Schlesien, Brünner Zeitung,* 1851, Nos. 106 and 110, vol. xv of the sectional publications, p. 593.

Westermanns Monatshefte, June 1913.

Woche, Die, 1913, No. 26.

Zedlers Universal-Lexikon, 1740, keyword " Nicotiana."

INDEX

INDEX

Deacon, —, 90
Dei Leoni, club, 241, 245
Demonology; or, Doctrines of Evil Spirits, by James I, 75
Denmark, smoking in, 143, 204
Diana, Father, 132
Diary, by Pepys, 167
Diaz, Bartholomew, 34
Diaz, Bernal, 46
Dichtung und Wahrheit, by Goethe, 215
Diemerbroek, Isbrand von, 99–100
Dietrichstein, Count, 221
Disease, smoking accredited as a cure for, 56–57, 58–59, 79–80, 88–90, 102–106, 166–167
Disraeli, Benjamin, 74
Don Juan, by Molière, 179
Donadoni, —, 157, 158 *n.*
Drake, Sir Francis, 68, 70–71

EDISON, THOMAS ALVA, 263
Edward VII, 263
Egmont, by Goethe, 98
Egypt, 22, 210
Elisabeth Charlotte, Duchess of Orléans, 180–181, 182
Elizabeth, Queen of England, 72, 73, 89
Elizabeth, Empress of Austria, 263
England, rise of smoking in, 67–96; cultivation of tobacco in, prohibited, 164–165; Peter the Great and smoking in, 176–178; introduction of snuff into, 187–188; introduction of cigars into, 222; introduction and popularity of cigarettes in, 253
Eugène, Prince, 192
Everartus, Ä., 61

FAGON, GUY, 184, 185–186
Falckenburgius, Hadrianus, 105, 173
Favre, Jules, 256–257
Feinhals, Josef, 203 *n.*
Ferdinand III, Emperor, 110
Ferdinand, Emperor of Austria, 244
Ferdinand, King of Aragon, 35
Ferdinand Karl, Archduke, 152–153
Ferdinand Maria, Elector of Bavaria, 113–114, 159
Ferraris, —, 107 *n.*

Festin de Pierre, Le, by Corneille, 179–180
Ficquelmont, Count, 239 *n.*, 245
Florinus, Franciscus Philippus, 201 *n.*
Flügler, Dr, 265 *n.*
Ford, Henry, 262
France, Thevet claims to have introduced tobacco into, 51–52; introduction of tobacco into, by Nicot, 54–60; snuff-taking in, 149, 187; Richelieu imposes duty on tobacco in, 149–150; tobacco trade farmed out in, 160–161; cigars in, 207, 222; cigarettes in, 252–253
Francis I, King of France, 57
Francis II, King of France, 57, 60
Francis-Joseph, Emperor of Austria, 253
Francis of Lorraine, Cardinal, 56, 57
Franken, Johann, 103, 143 *n.*
Frankfort, 211, 215, 255
Franklin, Benjamin, 205
Frederick I, King of Prussia, 188
Frederick II (the Great), King of Prussia, 200, 201, 203–205, 212, 220, 223; as Crown Prince, 191–192, 193, 194
Frederick III, Elector of Brandenburg —see Frederick I, King of Prussia
Frederick William I, King of Prussia, 188, 190, 191, 192, 193, 194
Frederick William II, King of Prussia, 220
Frederick William III, King of Prussia, 220, 223, 227, 229, 232, 235, 236, 237, 238
Frederick William, Elector of Brandenburg, 161
French Revolution, the, and tax on tobacco, 208–210
Frey, Father, 160
Friederike Sophie Wilhelmine, Princess, 191
Fritze, Hans von, 23 *n.*
Funk, Johann, 61–62

GALLIANI, COUNT, 151
Gardiner, Edmund, 88–89
Garibaldi, Giuseppe, 257
Gennerich, Otto, 237
Genoa, smoking in, 64, 127

[291]

INDEX

INDEX

A HISTORY OF SMOKING